THE
LIBERAL TRADITION

A Study of
The Social and Spiritual Conditions
of Freedom

WILLIAM AYLOTT ORTON

NEW HAVEN

YALE UNIVERSITY PRESS

LONDON · GEOFFREY CUMBERLEGE · OXFORD UNIVERSITY PRESS

To

EDWIN BORCHARD

Justus H. Hotchkiss Professor of Law

in Yale University

THE OLIVER BATY CUNNINGHAM
MEMORIAL PUBLICATION FUND

The present volume is the twenty-first work published by the Yale University Press on the Oliver Baty Cunningham Memorial Publication Fund. This Foundation was established May 8, 1920, by a gift from Frank S. Cunningham, Esq., of Chicago, to Yale University, in memory of his son, Captain Oliver Baty Cunningham, 15th United States Field Artillery, who was born in Chicago, September 17, 1894, and was graduated from Yale College in the Class of 1917. As an undergraduate he was distinguished alike for high scholarship and for proved capacity in leadership among his fellows, as evidenced by his selection as Gordon Brown Prize Man from his class. He received his commission as Second Lieutenant, United States Field Artillery, at the First Officers' Training Camp at Fort Sheridan, and in December, 1917, was detailed abroad for service, receiving subsequently the Distinguished Service Medal. He was killed while on active duty near Thiaucourt, France, on September 17, 1918, the twenty-fourth anniversary of his birth.

PREFACE

PREFACES should be written last, as this one is. They then reduce the writer to a seemly frame of mind, as he compares what he set out to do with the little he has been able to accomplish. This book is an attempt to restate in terms suited to our time the noblest of political philosophies. Against the temerity of the aim must be set the urgency of the occasion. No treatment would be adequate that depicted liberalism as a thing merely of today or yesterday; but the wealth of material made a brief presentation very difficult. The method finally chosen involves first, a fairly full account of the foundations; second, a survey of the historic obstacles and opposed positions; finally, a rough sketch of some leading contemporary applications.

While I am solely responsible for all opinions expressed, I am under many and deep obligations. Among these it is a pleasure, after many years, to acknowledge my debt to the Cambridge historians of my time, especially Z. N. Brooke of Caius, D. A. Winstanley of Trinity, and my former tutor C. R. Fay of Christ's. The obligation I share with all liberals to the work and teaching of L. T. Hobhouse will, I trust, be evident. Particular thanks are due to two of my present colleagues: to Professor F. H. Hankins for the generous tolerance with which, through twenty years, he has clarified the discussion of opposing viewpoints; to Professor V. M. Scramuzza for detailed and constructive criticism of a large part of the manuscript. I am further indebted for constant encouragement and counsel to that distinguished jurist and gallant liberal to whom this book is dedicated.

W. A. O.

Northampton, Mass.

ACKNOWLEDGMENTS

FOR permission to quote, acknowledgment is hereby made to the following authors and/or publishers: Harcourt, Brace & Co., Koffka, K., *Principles of Gestalt Psychology;* E. P. Dutton & Co., Sorokin, P. A., *The Crisis of Our Age; Fortune Magazine,* Niebuhr, R., *A Faith for History's Greatest Crisis;* Alfred A. Knopf, Inc., Hendrick, I., *Facts and Theories of Psychoanalysis;* J. B. Lippincott Company, Belloc, H., *Cranmer;* Charles Scribner's Sons, Niebuhr, R., *The Nature and Destiny of Man,* Berdyaev, N., *The Meaning of History,* and *Slavery and Freedom;* The Viking Press, Inc., Laski, H. J., *The State in Theory and Practice;* Penguin Books, Inc., Nicolson, H., *Why Britain Is at War.*

CONTENTS

THE LIBERAL TRADITION

Introduction

THE crying need of modern liberalism is for a clearer perception of principle. A great tradition—the oldest and richest in
political history—is all but lost in a fog of careless words
and empty phrases. Particularly in America, the term "liberal" is
being used to cover policies ranging from nineteenth-century
laissez faire to dictatorial collectivism; more, it is being deliberately misapplied by persons whose programs, whatever their merits, are in temper and outlook, as to means as well as ends, radically
alien to the liberal tradition. This has become possible because the
public and the popular press have almost forgotten the existence
of political principle in the sense in which Jefferson and Lincoln,
Acton and Gladstone understood it; nor have they found in recent
events, domestic or international, much to remind them.

The political life of our time has shown a passion for quick
returns. Since the century opened, popular attention in France,
Germany, England, America has been increasingly focused on
short-run tangible objectives. Measures to bring specific material
benefits to the nation, or to whatever groups or classes could secure
control, have engrossed the public interest, raising the political
temperature while they shortened the political perspective; so that
along with considerable achievement there developed a growing
instability. A new and dangerous temper pervaded public life as
the ability to envisage policy in the larger and more permanent
sense tended to disappear. The kangaroo beat both the donkey and
the elephant.

But the true life of a community is not a series of violent jumps
to particular objectives; it is a constant process demanding a
steady sense of direction, a continuous realization of principles not
exhausted in their application to a transitory set of circumstances.
The lapse of such a sense, the ignorance of such principles, have
disastrous consequences. The bewilderment and cynicism of our
younger citizens are due less to the complexity of the problems
they are called upon to face than to the failure of the older genera-

tion to transmit any thorough grasp of underlying principle and tradition. The youth of Victorian times was far more fortunate.

Now once again the familiar cycle of depression, militarism, war has further raised the temperature and shortened the perspective. In time of stress we naturally counteract our suffering with the thought of better days to come; and as the strain increases we advance the date. We draw spiritual as well as financial drafts upon the future, never doubting that they will be honored at maturity. In proportion as the means we must now employ are costly and terrible, so the more clear and close must be the vision of our ends. Thus readily we credit the assurances of politicians that the immediate sequel to a tornado of destruction will be a more abundant life for everybody, and mortgage our incomes, our property, and the blood of our children to a dream: lucky indeed we shall be if that dream does not again become a nightmare. For purposes of war it is enough that we will the supreme end, victory, leaving the means—the strategy and tactics—to our generals; but for purposes of peace free people must master means as well as ends. For the means will shape the ends—as the history of modern Germany reminds us.

In the battle of the faiths that is now actively involved, as it was three centuries ago, in the battle of the nations, those whose position is weak or ill defined will stand no chance at all. The faith of the liberal is the hardest to define because it is the boldest and the biggest. Rationalist utopias can exhibit (on paper) all the scientific neatness of the prison, the hospital, or the factory: liberalism does not propose to model the life of society on the prison or the hospital, and even looks askance at too many factories. Collectivists are fond of the argument "We did it in war, why can't we do it in peace?" Liberals do not propose to model the life of society on the army or the Wehrwirtschaft. In all the hard bright schemes that have crystallized out of modern materialism the ordinary human being is put in his place with a platonic knee, or something more urgent, at his back; the reason being that there is so much more to human nature than what the doctrinaires have any use for. But out of that more come both the folly and the wisdom, the passion and the insight, the virtue and the fun of human life; and the liberal will never sacrifice the full range of personal living to the symmetry of a mere political or economic system.

Liberalism therefore, with Aristotle for its godfather, stands firm rooted in the Christian ethos: the only one that takes the human being in all his concrete imperfection, and with everlasting forbearance seeks to make the best of him. It is significant that liberalism and Christianity (of which it is the political application) in modern times went down together; and now are coming up together. Liberalism, like Christianity, is a philosophy of means as well as ends; and with a modesty rare in these days, it prefers to talk about the means. It can never grant that the end justifies the means, as other creeds are doing—the ruthlessness and dissimulation of the political materialists are now notorious. And because of its particular concern with means, the liberal tradition is more clearly shown in action than in theory; that being the sphere in which principle becomes manifest. The historical approach is therefore the one we shall mainly follow, drawing from it certain specific lines of direction to the problems of today.

In thus surveying the record, however briefly or imperfectly, the reader will discover that the goal of liberalism has always been something more than the vague "liberty" that every demagogue appeals to: it is liberty-within-community, expanding liberty within expanding community. That, as Professor Toynbee has shown in his great study, is destiny's perennial challenge to civilization; and there is no assurance, not even a presumption, of success. Once already in this generation we have encountered it, and failed. No one can mistake the cost of that failure. Now again, perhaps for the last time, it rises to confront us with the ineluctable alternative, Succeed or perish. What are our resources?

I

Liberalism and Conservatism

1. Liberalism and its opponents. — 2. The nature of political principle: Burke. — 3. Acton on the same. — 4. Conservatism: Hearnshaw, Cecil. — 5. Liberalism: Muir. — 6. Liberalism the architect of community.

§ 1

THE words "liberal" and "liberalism" have, at least for English-speaking peoples, a vaguely favorable connotation, evoking the ideas of freedom, tolerance, and progress. In this sense, and to this extent, their meaning reflects a very common usage. A liberal person is one who is "free with his money." Liberal hospitality implies plenty of free entertainment. A liberal attitude is one that tolerates, within very broad limits, freedom of thought, speech, and behavior. A liberal education, whatever else it may be, stands in contrast to a dogmatic and restrictive training. About all that can be said of a liberal arts college is that it is one that awards a bachelor of arts degree: the arts are varied and surprising. Originally, however, the liberal arts were seven: grammar, logic, rhetoric, arithmetic, geometry, astronomy, and music. And why were they "liberal"? Because they represented the rising value set upon free enquiry: upon "broadening the mind"—which indeed they aimed at. Thus grammar included the forms of literature, rhetoric (to train rhaetors, pleaders in court or assembly) included law, geometry covered a wide and curious field of natural history; among the books were many encyclopaedias, some very diverting —one is reminded of the connection of modern liberalism with the French encyclopaedia of the eighteenth century. The scholastics, of course, intended that the liberal arts should find their consummation in the queen of the sciences; but the discipline is older than Christianity, with roots that even yet draw living water from the culture of Imperial Rome and the Athens of Pericles.

But of liberalism as a social or political philosophy it is far harder to frame a definition. By that name it is a bare hundred years old; and today there are many who would celebrate the centenary with a wake. The vigor of political liberalism is well attested by the fury of its enemies. It was the pet aversion of both Lenin and Trotsky. It has been dissected and denounced by Stalin, Hitler, Mussolini, Pius IX, and Professor Laski. Dogmatists and determinists of the red or the black, defenders of the tyranny of men or majorities, exponents of class war, racial war, or national war, have discovered beneath their differences a common determination to give political liberalism a premature burial. The prisoner of the Vatican saw it, in the 1860's, as a force that was not merely anticlerical but antireligious, undermining the foundations of faith, destroying authority in the name of a specious individualism, leading, in the end, to predatory materialism and social chaos. The disciples of the rival Church of Moscow inform us, in tones no less authoritative, that liberalism was the mere rationalization of the interests of the bourgeoisie. Professor Laski agrees with the Pope as to the connection between liberalism and individualism; but in his view, and that of the school of thought he represents, the whole complex was simply the self-assertion of the social class that is supposed to have shaken off its mediaeval shackles between the Reformation and the French Revolution. The new philosophy that thus arose was "directly related to freedom; for it came as the foe of privilege conferred upon any class in the community by virtue of birth or creed. But the freedom it sought had no title to universality, since its practice was limited to men who had property to defend. . . . The individual liberalism has sought to protect is always, so to say, free to purchase his freedom in the society it made; but the number of those with the means of purchase at their disposal has always been a minority of mankind." [1] It would seem to follow that the self-assertion of the more numerous class of nonowners will impose, as of right, yet another philosophy in which if there is any privilege, it will at least be based not on birth or creed but on interest; and we are tacitly invited, by the modern utilitarians, to assume that the greatest good of the greatest number is an adequate substitute, in both theory and practice, for the common good of all.

In similar vein, the political machinery of parliamentary representative government, so closely associated with the rise of

1. Laski, H. J., *The Rise of European Liberalism*, chap. i.

liberalism, has been under attack so general that it is hardly worth while to quote instances. Leaders of the totalitarian systems have without exception vied with one another in abuse of the parliamentary tradition, recognizing—quite rightly—in the peculiar quality of mind it demands and instils an inherent obstacle to the sort of ends they had in view. The necessary imperfections of the liberal method have been eagerly exploited by men whose purpose was not to reform but to destroy it, whose ideals were quite other than those which it proposes; and their assault has been aided from within, in states that were lately free and in those few that are free still, by demagogues who fail to grasp the nature of the ultimate issue. It would be difficult for that historical chimera, the impartial observer, to decide whether in modern Germany, Spain, and France, more harm had been wrought on the cause of freedom by the extreme left or the extreme right. In both England and America the battle between the power of numbers and the power of money is being fought over the prostrate body of liberalism, and the two sides actively compete to see which can kick it hardest.

Yet liberalism, in its essence, is a part of life; and where it is destroyed, the alternative is death. It represents the effort to formulate, as a principle of collective action, certain fundamental dispositions of human nature. As such, it inherits a tradition unmatched by any other political principle; yet it is not the only principle, the only tenable position, and nothing is gained by speaking as if it were. To describe liberalism, as many of its American exponents do, in terms so broad as to exclude the possibility of belief in its opposite is in fact to rob it of serviceable meaning. A distinguished Englishman speaking from the Tory standpoint in the United States in 1914 remarked that "the average American thinks that he understands the aims and views of the radical party. They are the aims and views of all sensible and enlightened men!" Such a frame of mind does not make for clarity. Along with modern liberalism, conservatism grew in strength and self-consciousness —its necessary foil and complement. Together these principles reflect the polarity of life itself, of all phenomenal existence. Force and inertia, action and reaction, change and stability, the dynamic and the static—without this universal dualism, meaning and reality, on the human plane at least, vanish into nothingness. No mechanical system of checks and balances, no reorganization of

collective life on the basis of mere interests or areas, can altogether supplant this deep polarity; nor, in the end, can any
tyranny destroy it. Without the centripetal check of conservatism,
liberalism flies off in tangents toward doctrinaire radicalism, academic utopianism, or philosophic anarchy. Without the centrifugal urge, conservatism becomes mere dead-centrism, ossification
of class or caste structure, Colonel Blimp with his what-we-have-
we-hold. The practical significance of either school is to be sought
in their constant interplay throughout the course of history, in
the record of events rather than in a priori definition; it is only
after such a study that any comprehensive statement of the issue
can be profitably attempted or any analysis of the basic assumptions made convincing. But from the liberal such deeper understanding is especially required inasmuch as he is more frequently
cast in the role of innovator, with all its risks and responsibilities:
the wrecks of ill-judged innovations are as much a peril to social
navigation as are the rocks of vested interest. Liberal thought in
particular therefore needs the keen edge of discrimination, the
trained and critical appreciation of possibility.

It is evidence of the political instinct of the English that out
of the struggles of Whig and Tory two strong parties finally
emerged frankly calling themselves Liberal and Conservative.
Each has developed in modern times its central core of philosophy
going well beyond matters of mere interest or expediency, and
each has had its great exemplars and spokesmen. It is unfortunate
that no such development has taken place in the United States.
The lack of any consistent political philosophy in the two American parties has become conspicuous in the past decade, and they
can now no longer be distinguished even along the line of special
interests. The confusion has deprived the electorate of the political
education which it is one of the functions of a well-founded party
system to supply; it has permitted all sorts of persons and pressure groups to call themselves "liberal" whose policies are far
from deserving the name; and it has impaired the authority of that
court of nine men which constitutes the ultimate sovereign of the
United States.

§ 2

THE need of clearly conceived political principles has increased
with the appalling array of issues on which the electorate and its

representatives are vainly supposed to be informed. The development of the popular press and the spread of political broadcasting have stimulated the interest and concern of the masses hardly less than the prod of taxation; but they have also engendered a sense of bewilderment and frustration. Walter Lippmann described it in his penetrating study, *The Phantom Public* (1925): "The facts far exceed our curiosity. . . . The man does not live who can read all the reports that drift across his doorstep or all the dispatches in his newspaper. And if by some development of the radio every man could see and hear all that was happening everywhere, if publicity, in other words, became absolute"—then, says Mr. Lippmann, the ordinary person would have to give up in despair. "General information for the informing of public opinion is altogether too general for intellectual decency. And life is too short for the pursuit of omniscience by counting all the leaves on all the trees."

In business it is well known that the more numerous the small stockholders of a corporation, the smaller, as a rule, will be the size of the group required to exercise voting control. Something of the sort, as Mr. Lippmann recognizes, obtains in politics: "normally people leave their proxies to a kind of professional public consisting of more or less eminent persons. Most issues are never carried beyond this ruling group: the lay publics catch only echoes of the debate." In what the eminence of the eminent persons consists, how it is acquired, we need not for the moment consider: ideally it vindicates Burke's theory of representative government—which, says Lord Acton, "laid down for ever the law of the relations between members and constituencies, which is the innermost barrier against the reign of democratic force." [2] The elected person, as all save those of the extreme left and right would now agree, represents not the interest of a particular section but that of the commonweal: "You choose a member, indeed, but when you have chosen him he is not a member of Bristol, but he is a member of Parliament." [3] What he owes his constituents is not obedience to their mandates—or, as it works in practice, the mandates of a mere majority of them—but the exercise of his independent industry and judgment in the interest of the whole nation. Logically and philosophically, that is the only answer. Actually, with the prevalence of "coupon candidates," instructed delegations, electoral

2. Acton, Lord, *Letters to Mary Gladstone* (1880), p. 97.
3. Burke, Edmund, Speech to the Electors of Bristol (3 Nov. 1774), *Works,* II, 96.

machines, organized pressure groups, and expensive publicity
agents, it remains an ideal—though an ideal more generally aimed
at, and more often approximated, than the cynics are willing to
admit. The really difficult objection is that which modern French
politics has vividly illustrated: what is to prevent these so independent legislators running off in a hundred different directions, so that the electorate behind them loses all sense of coördinated purpose, and eventually of common existence?

To that Burke had his answer—for he was well aware of the
danger—and the answer is what immediately concerns us. Organized groupings of opinion were in his day called "factions,"
and the word carried much of the opprobrium that the word "lob-
bies" bears for us. Burke lifted the idea of organization to a higher
level, gave it deeper foundations, stuck to it at a tragic price. Political principle, he held, was a valid and necessary basis for effective
action; and "party is a body of men united, for promoting by their
joint endeavours the national interest, upon some particular principle in which they are all agreed." [4] It was in that sense that the
party system became, in modern England, as good a solution for
the problem of freedom under law as the world had yet devised.

But its success depended upon certain imperative conditions.
The unity Burke had in mind must, if it were to bind honest and
intelligent men, be pretty deeply grounded; and their conception
of the national interest must transcend mere sectional or ephemeral ends. Moreover, since the system envisaged the possibility of
more than one such party, it tacitly assumed a still deeper unity
underlying all. Upon that supreme loyalty, that ultimate allegiance—never perhaps to be perfectly defined—both the stability
and the flexibility of the system would in fact depend. Whether,
or how far, these conditions obtain in contemporary politics it will
be one of our major tasks to enquire.

Burke described his ideal politician as the philosopher in action.
But it was no academic philosophy he had in mind. "All virtue
which is unpracticable is spurious," he said bluntly. His analysis
of the nature of public life is the more significant in that it arose
from strenuous practical experience, in a difficult and confused
era shot through with more than the usual amount of corruption.
The emphasis with which he states his conclusions has the note
of courage as well as conviction: "The greater part of the measures

4. Burke, Present Discontents, Select Works, I, 86 (Payne).

which arise in the course of public business are related to, or dependent on, some *great leading general principles in Government.*" [5] The italics are Burke's. Action taken without reference to such principles is likely to be, in the full sense, unprincipled; its criteria can hardly rise above mere expediency, which is seldom far from self-interest. Thus in advance Burke answered the economic determinists; and he may fairly be held to have shown that political action can be, in a real, not an illusory sense, disinterested, and that only when it is so does collective life become worthy of true human nature.

The current popularity of the doctrine that men are powerless to transcend whatever their biological heritage and material circumstances dictate is the natural product of an era in which collective greed has outrun collective intelligence. A feeling of bafflement and bedevilment, a mood of pessimism and despondency, results; materialism takes hold upon men's minds because it has so thoroughly informed their actions; and when it yields its invariable harvest of brute force and blind destruction, the pessimism and despondency are deepened and the vicious circle closes like a steel trap. Then force appears the only answer to force, and war the way to end war; and liberalism, which denounces such maxims as subhuman, is shouted down in the name of that identical pseudo-realism that created the bloody mess.

§ 3

A HUNDRED and ten years after Burke proclaimed his political postulates, a greater scholar gave them new meaning and confirmation. "The great object in trying to understand history," wrote Lord Acton in a much-quoted letter of 1880, "is to get behind men and grasp ideas. Ideas have a radiation and development, an ancestry and posterity of their own, in which men play the part of godfathers and godmothers rather than of legitimate parents." [6] "Party," he adds, echoing Burke, "is not only, not so much, a group of men as a set of ideas and ideal aims." [7] Acton did not mean that to be taken in a Platonic sense: he found too much reality in the world of human events to permit his soaring

5. *Ibid.*, p. 89.
6. Acton, *op. cit.*, p. 99.
7. *Ibid.*, p. 108.

off into the more ghostly type of idealism. What he meant was substantially what Burke meant, namely, that human purpose at its best, working through human coöperation, becomes explicit and effective on the level of pure intelligence: that the ideas, principles, concepts so formulated are the proper means of communication not only between individual men but between the generations. He speaks of "the impersonal forces, the ruling ideas" in history as having "grouped and propelled associations of men"; but he was too good a liberal—or perhaps too much an Englishman—to go all the way with Hegel. For him the interaction of general idea and particular circumstance is the very stuff of history, the plane on which the significance of the human struggle really lies; his genius consists in his being so uniquely at home on that plane. For example, he says of his predecessor at Cambridge, Sir John Seeley: "He discerns no Whiggism but only Whigs. And my great complaint is that he so much dislikes the intriguers of 1688 that he does not recognize the doctrine of 1688, which is one of the greatest forces, one of the three or four greatest forces, that have contributed to construct our civilization." [8] On the other hand, his verdict on the men of 1789 is that they sacrificed the actual human values of their cause to the tyranny of an abstract idea.

While Burke and Acton agree in their understanding of the nature of political action, the specific principles that inspired them were poles apart. It is precisely in such contrasts that the force of their fundamental agreement is revealed. The defense of liberty by the spokesman of the Whig oligarchy has its supplement in the analysis of authority by the great liberal who was also a peer of the realm and a Roman Catholic. From the argument of policy between parties of opposing political principle ultimate truth emerges, clear and acceptable to all men. Every element in what we may properly call civilization has been at one time the cause of a single group or party. Equality before the law, the supremacy of law over the executive, the abolition of slavery, the responsibility of government for the condition of the poor, the right of every child to fair opportunity, freedom of speech, religious toleration—all these have passed or are passing (one hopes) from the testing stage of partisan debate into the common heritage of civilization; and fresh aspirations ever advance new

8. *Ibid.*, p. 101.

issues in that continuous process through which intelligence arduously asserts its sovereign function.

Professor George Sabine, in his *History of Political Theory*—a fine work too little known to the reading public—aptly describes Burke as "the founder of self-conscious political conservatism." Burke's particular emphasis is on stability and continuity, on reverence for tradition and established institutions, including the religious establishment, on a rather hieratic view of the state as responsible to and for something more permanent than the popular will. While he was willing to credit "the species" with a sound moral instinct for the long run, Burke's distrust of what he understood by democracy was much more than horror at the violence of the French Revolution.

Acton—to point the contrast—struck the note of modern liberalism in his bold declaration that "Liberty is not a means to a higher political end. It is itself the highest political end." [9] Burke would hardly have accepted that, even with Acton's reiteration of the adjective; nor should anyone accept it unless he is prepared to master and live up to the philosophy of life which lies behind it. If that demand seems exigent, it is also evident that the rule is neither safe nor satisfying in any other case. And however encouraging that philosophy may turn out to be, it is noteworthy that Acton shared Burke's distrust of democracy. Both men discerned in the vague idea of "government by the people" a kinship not remote to what we now call "dictatorship of the proletariat"; and since each, in his own way, passionately cared for freedom, the tyranny of numbers was to them as dire a menace as the tyranny of cliques or individuals. Shall we say their fear was ill founded? This at least we must say: that there is no more urgent task for modern liberalism than to clarify the concepts of authority on the one hand and democracy on the other; for our wretched state is due in no small measure to the flagrant misunderstanding and practical abuse of both.

§ 4

CONSERVATISM is a very early and a very late characteristic of societies. Primitive peoples are conservative with the instinctive wisdom of women and animals. Mature societies find a more con-

9. Acton, *History of Freedom*, p. 22.

scious though not perhaps essentially different motive. A conservative philosophy will hardly become prevalent unless there is something satisfying to conserve—or something worse to fear. The motives mix; but governing classes are apt to be conservative for the one reason, the poor for the other. When the sense of security is disturbed, pride in past achievement unites with nascent apprehension to promote an explicit, sometimes an aggressive, conservatism. In Britain it is inspired by pride in the part Britons have played on the world stage, pride in the empire: no mean nor baseless sentiment, admirably embodied in the present leader of the conservative party, the scion of the house of Marlborough. In France conservatism has rested its pride not so much in the empire as in that living France which is older than the empire or the revolution: no mean nor baseless sentiment, tragically seeking now for a worthy voice. In America, since security is not threatened and pride so easily slips into arrogance, the roots of a true conservatism are difficult to detect. Can it be that the American people have been sedulously encouraged to take pride in the wrong things, while the right things are stealthily filched from them?

But beneath all the rationale of conservatism lies that fundamental polarity we spoke of; and in modern pronouncements it is very evident. Professor Hearnshaw, for instance, at the outset of his study of *Conservatism in England* (1933) distinguishes as basic social forces a "party of order" and a "party of progress": a distinction similar to that implied in the title of Bertrand Russell's *Freedom Versus Organization* (1934). Both parties, says Hearnshaw, are necessary to the working of a democratic state, and the distinction between them is mainly one of emphasis. Identifying the "progressive" and the "liberal," Hearnshaw admits that the "party of order"—the conservative party—originates in the fear of change: "civilization is a frail flower doubtfully struggling for existence amid a jungle of old luxuriant barbarism"; it can easily be destroyed, as it has been many times in the past; there is wisdom in the maxim "unless it is necessary to change, it is necessary not to change." Arising from this fundamental attitude, Hearnshaw enumerates twelve leading attributes of conservatism; they are: "(1) reverence for the past, (2) the organic conception of society, (3) communal unity, (4) constitutional continuity, (5) opposition to revolution, (6) cautious or evolutionary reform,

(7) the religious basis of the state, (8) the divine source of legitimate authority, (9) the priority of duties to rights, (10) the prime
importance of individual and communal character, (11) loyalty,
(12) common sense, realism, and practicality."

Not all conservatives would acknowledge all these tenets, and
liberalism is certainly not opposed to them *in toto;* the first six,
and the last, would command the assent of most liberals in some
degree, and some liberals would assent—in some degree—to the
whole series. But the liberal starting point is different. Fear of
change is certainly not a basic liberal attitude. Liberalism is much
more optimistic about the possibilities of beneficent change, and
the capacity of rational minds to achieve it; and, we must add,
liberalism is by no means convinced of the intrinsic value of much
that conservatism seeks to conserve. That a thing is old is for
liberalism no a priori evidence of its present usefulness—though
that fact is hardly enough to justify an optimistic view of destruction by violence.

Lord Hugh Cecil—whose title to speak on the subject is second
to none—states that "natural conservatism is a tendency of the
human mind. It is a disposition averse from change; and it springs
partly from a distrust of the unknown and a corresponding reliance on experience rather than on theoretic reasoning; partly
from a faculty in men to adapt themselves to their surroundings
so that what is familiar merely because of its familiarity becomes
more acceptable or more tolerable than what is unfamiliar. Distrust of the unknown, and preference for experience over theory,
are deeply seated in almost all minds." [10] Lord Hugh, however,
would never have claimed that this natural conservatism was a
dominant characteristic of "almost all minds"—not even, as his
definition might suggest, of all feminine minds. He well realized
that the tendency of men to adapt themselves to their surroundings was often overmatched by the tendency to adapt the surroundings to their ideals. Not for a moment would he have opposed slum clearance with such an argument. But his statement,
like his career, serves to remind us that both the conservative and
the liberal dispositions frequently coexist in the same mind, and
that the matter of political allegiance may demand a fine judgment
of circumstances as well as a rigorous self-examination.

10. Cecil, Lord Hugh, *Conservatism,* chap. i.

§ 5

IN EXPLICIT contrast to the foregoing statements stands a careful definition of liberalism by that eminent British liberal, the late Professor Ramsay Muir: "Liberalism is a belief in the value of human personality, and a conviction that the source of all progress lies in the free exercise of individual energy; it produces an eagerness to emancipate all individuals or groups so that they may freely exercise their powers, so far as this can be done without injury to others; and it therefore involves a readiness to use the power of the State for the purposes of creating the conditions within which individual energy can thrive, of preventing all abuses of power, of affording to every citizen the means of acquiring mastery of his own capacities, and of establishing a real equality of opportunity for all." [11]

While there are other significant definitions of liberalism, the foregoing statement by one who was very closely associated with the modern British movement serves to focus certain fundamental problems. Its optimism, in contrast to the tone of the conservative pronouncements, is obvious. As an element in that optimism, the notion of "progress" is taken for granted; and it is deliberately associated with the free activity of individuals. But the notion of progress has been under critical attack for more than a generation, and no student of recent social philosophy will consent to let it pass unchallenged. Again, the role of the individual in historical causation is a perennial problem; the currency of various deterministic theories, both popular and academic, sharpens that issue —especially in America, where "individualism" is still an effective slogan. The tacit assumption that the "emancipation" of "all individuals and groups" will tend, on the whole, toward a working social harmony, or will at least permit a tolerable *modus vivendi*, was surely never more hazardous than now: what if the "groups" represent economic vested interests? What if they are nations, or aspire to be called so?

§ 6

A PHILOSOPHY that upholds liberty as the highest political end, and collective intelligence as the specific means thereto, needs

11. Muir, R., "Liberal Party," *Encyclopaedia Britannica*, XIII (1940), 1,000.

nowadays to be very sure of its ground. The easy optimism on which it rested forty years ago has been completely dispelled, even in America: "When it was, precisely, that the blinds were drawn and the lights turned down on the morale of American liberalism, I should not undertake to say"—the speaker is Archibald MacLeish in New York, February 27, 1944— "It was long enough ago in any case to produce a funerary and unventilated atmosphere in which hope goes out like a miner's candle. Liberals meet in Washington these days, if they can endure to meet at all, to discuss the tragic outlook for all liberal proposals, the collapse of all liberal leadership, and the inevitable defeat of all liberal aims." [12] The whole position has to be rethought and reformulated; and the task has to be undertaken at a time when the destructive power of applied science has broken loose all over the planet, dominating not only the actions but the minds of men, to the discomfiture of every received faith. In such a situation it does no good for the liberal to stand amid the rain of bombs peddling pin-up pictures of the brave new world. We are all grown old: there are no customers now. And whatever the outcome of the war of states and the ensuing war of creeds, one has to remember that a victory won by force always confirms the conviction of the victors that their ideas were the right ones and that the outcome has proved it: a contention that is logically valid for either side, or for neither.

Where in this *dies irae* can the liberal find firm ground? In the light of the record, he can stand on one supreme historical fact, namely, that liberalism embodies the only known procedure by which the dynamic powers of man as a tool-making animal can be reconciled with his aspiration as a spiritual being to live in true human community. While conservatism may be the guardian, liberalism is the architect of community—of community ever widening in both physical and spiritual scope. The liberal method alone can transform the crude propinquity of force or necessity into the true community of mind and will. That is its perennial function.

The one thing certain about the whole human enterprise is that it will not stay still. There can be no such thing any more as a closed community: the American fleet disposed of that possibility ninety years ago. Every technical achievement of the contriving

12. Reported in *PM*, March 16, 1944.

animal widens the area of his effective impact on his fellow creatures—even when he tried to hoard his secrets; and much as he
would prefer that impact to become community, he finds that
like as not it turns to slaughter. It is hard for him to recognize that
all his contriving is ethically, axiologically neutral. Yet as fast as
he invents new weapons he discovers new enemies on which to
try them; and while he fashions new products for the health and
comfort of his kind, he fights for the plants and minerals from
which they come. There is nothing whatever in the nature of
human contriving to stop all this; yet if one suggests that its
outcome may well be general chaos or the extermination of the
species, something in the contriving creature protests that that
can not, must not, be. In some dim way the creature loves his
kind, even when he destroys it with all the efficiency his brain
affords him. He wishes, even as he kills, to know and dwell in
amity with these other people: not all the propaganda of all the
"experts" can quite eradicate that wish. He would, if only he knew
how, scatter life instead of death upon them: but for that he must
know more surely what life is. To ensure that man the contriver
is man the life bringer rather than man the destroyer is the specific
task of liberalism.

For a hundred and fifty years Western man has nursed the illusion that his increasing mastery of his physical environment, his
technical skill in adapting the material world to his animal comfort, and his ingenuity in organizing joint enterprise to that end
would of themselves somehow widen and strengthen the area of
human community. Even yet he is reluctant to admit that the case
is not so: despite the fact that the advance of material culture is
threatening to tear to pieces even such enclaves of true community as have slowly and painfully been brought into being.
The kind of intellect that has organized and achieved—to its great
credit—the triumph of technique is radically different from the
kind of intelligence that is required to create and foster a community of human living. Men have supposed that so long as they
were honest and efficient in the pursuit of their technical and economic ends, and willing to share the benefits on a fair bargaining
basis (with an occasional touch of charity), they would be sufficiently equipped to build the new Jerusalem. They are genuinely
pained and puzzled to find that they have let hell loose instead.

This of course is not to maintain that the sole cause of the twentieth-century turmoil is to be sought in the overvaluation of the contriving intellect as against the humane intelligence. That in itself may have been, as we shall see, a consequence of something prior; and there were plenty of wars before the industrial revolution. More recent contests, however, in so far (and it is very far) as they arise from a conscious and deliberate struggle for exclusive dominion over the valuable resources of the earth, have developed a rationale more sinister and a temper more abominable; in as much as the drive toward that sort of conflict contains within itself no germ of a unifying principle. In the mass adulation of the material culture and of the men who could control or manipulate it, other requirements of social health, and the most patent symptoms that all was not well, were recklessly disregarded; and certain urges were released, and others encouraged, that made the development of true human community progressively more difficult.

With such recognitions emerges the characteristic dilemma of the liberal. Such considerations seem to challenge him to a redefinition of human ends; and that is a game in which he is ill qualified to take part. Defined ends, in so large a sense, are apt to be either arbitrary or meaningless; and in any case, they make no satisfactory fusion with the patient empiricism which is the essence of the liberal method. All utopias and most blueprints, including that of the late League of Nations, have an intrinsic static quality, which necessarily increases as their authors attempt to provide for every conceivable contingency of an extremely contingent universe. For the forces that play upon the lives of men—from within as well as from without—are so much vaster than what the contriving intellect can catalogue that the schemers and planners, throughout all history, have been condemned to spend most of their time in futile explanation of the perversity with which the course of events has made fools of them. Should it be necessary at this time of day to point that out? Doctors, with many centuries of experience behind them, have learnt to be cautious in predicting what the body will do in given circumstances; but because they are cautious, and rely on experience, they are increasingly successful in their limited sphere. Global strategists and politicians might take a lesson from them, if humility were part of their equipment; for when it is said that the meek shall inherit the earth, the gospel word means really the teachable, those who are not so puffed up with their own omniscience as to be past learning. That, of course, is a spiritual and not merely an intellectual virtue.

Liberalism therefore offers no blueprint, no utopia; but its central principle becomes in practice a sufficient rule of direction. Liberty without community, community without liberty, each is subhuman. The core of the liberal creed (it was the supreme insight of the Greeks) is that in a true community the members are truly free. Community is a working consensus of free minds and free wills in which the individual lives spontaneously, taking and giving much or little, but of his own accord: as in a true family, a true friendship, a true coöperation. That does not preclude the making of rules by consent; but to proclaim it a visionary ideal is a counsel of despair; for it is abundantly on record, in both sacred and secular writing, that until it is attained men will go on killing one another in defense of their local and partial realizations of the common good.

The task of the liberal is to keep before men's minds the fact that such community, on the large as well as the small scale, is the only wholesome and durable mode of human association—however long it may take; to define in practical terms the conditions that make for it; while recognizing all the while that it will never be perfectly attainable, because the intention, as well as the extension, of community is capable of continuous enrichment. And one thing, in the historical perspective, strikes the liberal: communities of all types, as they become organized and self-conscious, have a tendency also to become closed. The "I belong" tends increasingly to imply "you don't." Consciousness of kind becomes increasingly consciousness of difference. And consciousness of difference tends, as among children, to be translated in terms of superior and inferior; and so put into action. This is true, and familiar if one thinks about it, of social groups and "classes," clubs and fraternities, schools and colleges, churches and religions, trade-unions and labor movements, nations and empires. Liberalism finds its immediate, specific, and unending task in preserving the open-endedness of human association, in combating this natural exclusiveness that appeals so powerfully to the conceit and insecurity of human nature. For it knows that peace among men depends on the open arms of the Christian cross—not on the twisted arms of another kind of cross; and it aspires to the vision of the great Christian poet who was also a keen politician, "that in this little plot of earth belonging to mortal men, life may pass in freedom and with peace." [13]

A paradox? Perhaps. But it is both man's ineluctable fate and his final consolation that he must hope for it, strive for it, and believe in it.

13. Dante, *De Monarchia*, XVI (Church).

II

The Classical Foundations

*1. The Greek ideal. — 2. Its relevance to a cramped cul-
ture. — 3. The danger from the doctrinaires. — 4. The
Greek foundations: supremacy of law. — 5. Government
by consent: qualifications.*

§ 1

SELDOM has the riddle of freedom versus organization, liberty versus stability, the party of progress versus the party of
order, been so dramatically presented as in the Greek republics. They failed to solve it, and their failure was their doom.
The freedom kept running off into anarchy, the order into tyranny,
and the whole process stalled on the notion of the city-state—
just as Western Europe stalled on the notion of the nation-state—
until sheer necessity, in the guise of superior force, cleared the
way for a fresh assault upon the problem: as it always does when
human intelligence fails to answer the demands of human destiny.
But in the course of that failure, and the reflections of the Greeks
themselves upon it, practically all the political problems of the
Western world received their first systematic exposition; and an
ideal was launched, a standard raised, to which men would still
rally twenty-four centuries later—as witness a curious incident of
recent Greek history.

The year 1937 saw yet another dictator ruling Athens; and the
Metaxas government, facing the same old riddle of liberty versus
stability, instructed the school teachers dealing with ancient
Greece to substitute a passage of Plato for the famous speech of
Pericles in Thucydides' history "because the praise of democratic
ideals given in the funeral speech is very exaggerated, and may be
misunderstood by pupils as an indirect criticism of the authoritarian system of government and of the general trends in the modern state." [1] More candid evidence of the vitality of ideas could
hardly be devised!

1. *New Statesman,* June 26, 1937.

What did Pericles say that was so dangerous? Here is the famous passage:

An Athenian citizen does not neglect the state because he takes care of his own household; and even those of us who are engaged in business have a very fair idea of politics. We alone regard a man who takes no interest in public affairs, not as a harmless, but as a useless character; and if few of us are originators, we are all sound judges of policy. . . . The great impediment to action is, in our opinion, not discussion, but the want of that knowledge which is gained by discussion preparatory to action. For we have a peculiar power of thinking before we act and of acting too, whereas other men are courageous from ignorance but hesitate upon reflection. . . . There is no exclusiveness in our public life, and in our private intercourse we are not suspicious of one another, nor angry with our neighbour if he does what he likes. . . . While we are thus unconstrained in our private intercourse, a spirit of reverence pervades our public acts; we are prevented from doing wrong by respect for the authorities and for the laws, having an especial regard to those which are ordained for the protection of the injured as well as to those unwritten laws which bring upon the transgressor of them the reprobation of the general sentiment.[2]

That was the gist of the panegyric, uttered at the beginning of a fratricidal war in which all the weaknesses of Greek democracy were to be fatally manifested. And the reason for its utterance, the motive of that proud and loving care with which the great historian defined the Greek ideal, was precisely that which in our own time has called forth so much writing about liberty and democracy.

Freedom, like health, is seldom discussed until it is disappearing; then suddenly it changes from a postulate to a problem. The man, be he ancient Greek or modern German, who is free to do what he likes without incurring the suspicion or the anger of his neighbors, does not go about discussing the fact; so long as he can find something satisfying to do, he does it, and talks about the job, the children, or the weather. He may not be making history, but he can at least make hay while the sun shines—which is a safer prescription for longevity. When men talk a lot about their freedom there is as surely something wrong as when ladies talk a lot about their virtue: a certain insecurity is to be inferred. The liberty of the

2. Thucydides, Book II, Year II (Jowett). Sequence slightly altered.

Greeks was never secure, externally or internally. Just as they were attaining political self-consciousness they had had to fight for their independence against the strongest of the Oriental despotisms. The war was a war of nerves and of ideas as well as a war of force; and since the Greeks were victorious, their ideas shared the glory of their courage. Any group, like any individual, that has succeeded in an arduous enterprise will read a little self-congratulation into the retrospect; and it was natural that the Greeks, like other people before and since, should adopt a racial explanation of their success. But they had the hardihood—as some others did not—to rise above it, and discern in that personal freedom they had defended so bravely, and were to enjoy for so pathetically short a time, a universal value; and the subsequent instability of their political life sharpened their sense of it. Thus in their time of troubles as well as in their golden age they were building the rational basis for the characteristic Western impulse to live one's life one's own way.

The tenacity of that impulse was never more evident than at the crisis of the world's most elaborately organized war. The outcry against "bureaucracy" in both Britain and America was almost comically at odds with the demands of the situation; but that did not still it. The London *Daily Mail* in May, 1944 (of all times!), was uttering this sort of plaint:

One of the biggest political issues of our time has still to be decided. . . . It is whether post-war Britain is to be a Democracy or a Bureaucracy. The British people will have to say whether they are to continue to control their own destinies or whether they are to be cosseted and straight-jacketed by ant-heaps of busy officials. . . . There is no vested interest so pertinacious or so perilous as that of the State official. We have seen minor officials becoming more numerous and more intolerant. They swarm everywhere from the home to the factory, and everywhere they are an unwelcome brake on enterprise. . . .

and so forth and so on. There is no recognition of the fact that total organization calls for an enormous increase in regulation and control. There is no reference to the fact that the purpose of the organization has overwhelming popular support, including that of the complainant. The editors know their public. They know that a periodic outcry against "government interference" is always sure of a welcome. They know that their millions of readers simply de-

test being ordered about in even the best of causes, and will submit to it only under the maximum emergency and for the minimum
time. Their objection is not to be interpreted as either for or against
any particular theory of society, nor is it confined to any particular
class or occupation. Little business as much as big business likes
to run its affairs its own way, farmers as well as wage earners re-
sent the state acting as schoolmaster even while they take its
subsidies, trade-unions castigate their own elaborate and expensive
bureaucracies. It is all an instinctive and irrepressible assertion of
the demand for a private sphere of activity: *laissez nous faire*—
the protest is both older and stronger than the theory; it goes back
to Pericles. And even when it is demonstrated, as it has been a
thousand times from Plato to Sidney Hook, that all sorts of collective desiderata could be encompassed if they would only be a
bit more submissive, the common people stolidly insist on elbowroom for their unimportant personal adventures, and are peren-
nially scolded by all the uncommon people who know better than
they do what is good for them. The impulse is the leitmotiv of
Hollywood, which has exploited it to the point of inculcating, quite
unwittingly, an ethos of sheer anarchy.

We have described it as a Western impulse (the term suggests
the innumerable "Westerns" of the screen) but the designation
needs a little scrutiny. In recent years the English-speaking peoples
have revived their ancient claim to a celestial patent on the idea
of personal liberty. Their popular spokesmen have formulated a
racial theory to match that of their military opponents, in which,
strangely enough, the Germans are credited with "an old strain
of endemic barbarism." "To the German," writes a Czech professor
in an American university, "National Socialist domination [*Herr-
schaft*] is both method and goal. It is a value in itself, the highest
value of all—an idea unacceptable to an Englishman or an American." [3] One could quote scores of learned theses to the same effect,
whether of this war or the last. Mr. Winston Churchill, whose interpretation of international events has never lacked color, informed the House of Commons on September 21, 1943, that they
—"the German people"—"combine in the most deadly manner
the qualities of the warrior and the slave. They do not value freedom themselves, and the spectacle of it in others is hateful to
them. Whenever they become strong they seek their prey, and

3. Munk, F., *The Legacy of Nazism*, p. 14.

they will follow with an iron discipline anyone who will lead them to it." Our gallant warriors of the cap-and-gown brigade, mistaking basic English for basic history, have generally followed that lead; but what may be more or less true of more or less Germans in the particular circumstances of a particular generation is not a safe basis for generalization on the policy-framing scale. The most elementary knowledge of European national histories shows up the fallacy of such a procedure.

German scholarship of the twentieth century has endeavored, with considerable success, to distinguish the German from the Roman contribution to Western culture; but what it has emphasized is the motive of free association, the growth of small communities at once less individualistic and less authoritarian than the seignorial development of the imperial system. Centuries later, the folk idea reached its best-known enunciation in Herder and the brothers Grimm; but it was suffused in that universalism which has so often characterized German idealism. It was a Latin Caesarism that started the Teutonic reaction. A great British archaeologist [4] once suggested that the tendency to follow a leader was a Celtic trait—and he was thinking neither of the Tudor despotism nor the Lloyd George government when he said so. Until very recent times the most conspicuous example of highly centralized authority was France. Germans have produced two of the most notorious rebels in history: Luther against the Church, and Nietzsche against the Lutherans. And who can forget how the French critics trounced those formless German romanticists—some of whom hailed from Berlin!

That there are, in a very broad sense, racial and even national differences of temperament no one would deny; though it is practically impossible in Europe to distinguish the two kinds. The former spring from slight biological variations, the latter from cultural causes that are often so recent as to be, in a historical sense, ephemeral. But to interpret the actual course of events in the light of either is simply to surrender to the popular preference for myth rather than history. So far as innate differences go, there is more variation between a Welshman, an Englishman, a Russian, and a Chinese than between the average Englishman and the average German; if the former are spontaneously united in the cause of freedom while their opponents are hell-bent for destruction, it is

4. Sayce, A. H., *Reminiscences*, pp. 475–476.

surely not due to any intrinsic qualities of their makeup. Few things are queerer in modern journalism than to find Jewish writers denouncing a racial theory of history on one page and endorsing a racial basis of peacemaking on the next. When Acton spoke of the impersonal forces in history that have "grouped and propelled associations of men" he did not mean biological forces, nor did he mean merely Englishmen. President Neilson of Smith, asked what he understood by liberal education, once answered, "It is that process which makes it profitable for an educated American to converse with an educated Chinese." There is such a process, and Neilson was one of its great exponents. It rests on our proven faith in the power of active intelligence to create human community out of the most diverse material—without, be it well noted, destroying the diversity.

We must therefore be skeptical of all exclusive claims to the love of freedom. It would be broadly true to say that whenever and wherever men have been so fortunate in their endowment and their circumstances as to attain personal freedom, they have loved it. Those occasions—Rousseau notwithstanding—have been brief and rare; still rarer the cases in which men have learnt so to use freedom as to make it the cement of community. That task is history's supreme challenge to human intelligence; and whether our generation can meet it more successfully than countless others have done is still an open question. It is the question that liberalism, alone among political philosophies, accepts as its chief concern.

§ 2

Aristotle, at the outset of his grand enquiry into human affairs, asks what is the object of the whole business. Characteristically, he wants that object stated in practical human terms, not hatched out of the inner consciousness of some philosopher; and to get at it that way, he says, one must know a good deal about human nature, though he need not be a professional psychologist. Following that line he enquires what it is that people generally aim at, what is the final intent of all their doings and strivings; and he answers quite simply, people want to be happy: "happiness is manifestly something final and self-sufficient, being the end of all things which are and may be done." [5] If a man is completely happy there

5. *Nicomachean Ethics*, I, vii (Chase). Everyman ed., p. 11.

is no need for further argument; whereas if a man is as good as Job, but also as miserable, there is obviously a lot more to be said.

But "to call happiness the chief good is a mere truism, and what is wanted is some clearer account of its real nature." There speaks the essential Aristotle; for what he means by "real nature" is not what abstract speculation may deduce but what careful observation may detect. The difference is fundamental. Once you start working backward from abstractly conceived ends to the policies and problems of actuality, there is no telling to what enormities your logic may drive you. Rationalism of the a priori type always ends by being inhumane and antidemocratic, because it can see nothing in the folkways and traditions of ordinary people except obscurantism. They get in the way of the ideal scheme, and that becomes a sufficient excuse for impersonal harshness and well-intentioned brutality. Plato is the classical illustration. Veneration for his poetic and literary genius has blinded generations of students to the practical tendency of his political approach. The Plato of the dialogues might today have been writing for *The New Yorker:* but the Plato of *The Laws* would have been chairman of the late Dies Committee. The plain fact is that *The Republic,* in its political and social implications, is one of the most horrible books ever written. Scholars apologize for this aspect of it by arguing that it was not meant to apply to any actual society (a somewhat doubtful plea); but even after he had tried his hand at an actual society, the rationalist in Plato was too strong for the human being. As Aristotle duly noted against him, his logic inevitably led to a government, not of laws, but of men (the wisest men, of course: they always are); and in the tenth book of *The Laws* Plato again endows those men with the most stringent censorship, with powers of ostracism and imprisonment for unorthodoxy, and finally with the death penalty for heresy. There is, one fears, something inherently attractive about this sort of thing to doctrinaire and academic minds; but both the liberal tradition and the Catholic Church have always been chary of too much Plato, preferring the more empirical, and therefore truly humane, approach of Aristotle. For the religious the antidote to Plato is St. Francis; for the atheist the antidote is Robespierre. There is no more dangerous fanatic known to history than the rationalist on a crusade.

Aristotle's primary observation about happiness is that it is not a passive but a very active condition. This is really characteristic of Greek thought until the final subjugation of the city-states; it was only when things seemed to be going so badly that no amount nor kind of activity could lead to happiness, that the notion of passivity gained much of a following—a phenomenon we can see paralleled today. Aristotle has far more to say about action than about feeling. Happiness, he insists, is a "working of the soul in the way of excellence"—and excellence is primarily a quality of action. Happiness springs from a full and complete life; and by complete he means not only a many-sided but a long life: "living well and doing well." He is therefore chary of all coercions, suppressions, and denials. When, for instance, he wants to show up the fallacy in mere economic success, the word he chooses is *constraint:* "As for the life of money-making, it is one of constraint, and wealth manifestly is not the good we are seeking, because it is for use, that is, for the sake of something further." [6] The prospect of an increase of wealth accompanied by an increase of "constraint" could never fool the true Aristotelian!

The warning that thus comes to us from over two thousand years ago needs today all the emphasis of which speech is capable. For the modern world has bought its material abundance at far too high a price, and it is beginning to find that out. Somehow— we shall presently discuss how—modern society has got itself into a condition which entails on ever-increasing masses of people the most appalling frustration of elemental impulses and functions; with the result that in millions of lives those impulses are perverted to ugly and cancerous forms, or are so atrophied that individuals can no longer rise above the level of mere mass existence. Healthful bodily exercise, fresh air and contact with nature, active play and good-fellowship, normal mating and maternity at a normal age, choice of occupation and a sense of creativity in work, with the measure of hope and confidence which that engenders, quiet affection and peace of mind in a natural human group—all these basic ingredients of the good life have become increasingly unattainable to increasing numbers, until they are hardly thought of or remembered. Instead, substitute gratifications are offered (for sale) that do not gratify, passive pleasures and pastimes that excite the nerves and benumb the mind, machine-made entertainment that rouses artificial emotions to no better outlet than a sticky

6. *Ibid.*, I, v. Rackham (Loeb ed., p. 73) gives "a hard kind of life"; literally "violent"—adjective denoting constrained as opposed to natural.

and diffuse eroticism not even strong enough to be downright sensual. Along with all this, and because of it, collective life shows a constant tendency toward herd action, with slogans and stereotypes passing for ideas, what Pareto would call "derivations" passing for realistic policies, and outbreaks of mass action that turn all the contriving instincts of the human animal to his bloody and hideous destruction.

Such results are often attributed to the spread of false ideas, to fallacious economic or political theories, or to the influence of evil-minded demagogues and dictators. But as Professor Sorokin has demonstrated, the power of such persons or ideas is a *consequence* of the condition of the masses; [7] and the ill in that condition consists primarily in the frustration it imposes on the normal life impulses of normal people. This is now almost a commonplace of modern psychiatry. Psychiatrists, starting from the problems of the individual mind, are being compelled to recognize that in innumerable cases the psychological cost of civilization has become unbearably high; with the result that an ever-increasing number of people, in the expressive phrase of the street, "go broke."

The will to live, the capacity to enjoy living, the strength to live well, are not the results of dialectic; they spring from the deepest biological roots, and rise with the active exercise of native impulse. It is an odd and wholly unintended effect of analytic psychology that the primary impulses should be generally regarded with abhorrence. Of no organism are the primary impulses such as to defeat its own existence. Growth obviously involves integration, and integration a principle of order and harmony: strange indeed that people who see that principle so successfully at work in plants and animals should fail to find any trace of it in human nature—and so failing, should conceive of human development solely in restrictive terms, as a process of repression, denial, and constraint. Granting that the demands made by his situation on the human being are of a complexity such as no other creature has to meet, the solution of the problem must always aim at preserving the maximum of personal and instinctual freedom; this for two reasons, both fundamental. One, the exercise of such freedom is a good in itself, a positive element in the joy of life. Two, the exercise of such freedom is a prequisite of strength and health, and its denial a danger to body and mind.

7. Sorokin, P. A., *Crisis of Our Age,* chap. i.

Bertrand Russell, writing for an American magazine some twenty years ago, said this: "For my part, I should judge a community to be in a good state if I found a great deal of instinctive happiness, a prevalence of feelings of friendship and affection rather than hatred and envy, a capacity for creating and enjoying beauty, and the intellectual curiosity which leads to the advancement and diffusion of knowledge." [8] Those criteria can never successfully be ignored; and failure to meet them cannot be made good by any other sort of achievement. To paraphrase a familiar text, material abundance cannot compensate for psychic starvation—which is perhaps the typical malady of industrial society. There is no need at this level of discussion to plumb the depths of any alleged "death instinct": causes enough lie right on the surface of the culture—the haunting loneliness of city life, for instance, to which millions of young people are ashamed even to confess, from which so much of their so-called free activity is only a desperate and aimless flight. An American psychiatrist, Dr. Karen Horney, has drawn attention to the conflict between the motivations inculcated by a competitive society, with its pattern of external economic success, and the spiritual needs of the normal individual.[9] Another, Dr. Karl Menninger, has vividly depicted some of the darker aspects of the situation, especially its relation to the war impulse.[10] With the deeper analysis we are not as yet concerned; our present point is simply that when the liberal, following Aristotle, says "freedom" he means freedom—an active, full-blooded personal liberty, experienced as such, and tenaciously held to as "the highest political end." It is now more than ever necessary to nail that intention firmly to the masthead. To do so does not solve any problems. On the contrary, it raises the most difficult problems human intelligence has to face, in practice as well as theory. But liberalism alone never has said, and never can say: Brothers, these problems are too many and too difficult for us; let us therefore turn aside and seek some other goal.

§ 3

THE difficulty of the problems was perhaps better realized by the Greeks than by the optimists of the eighteenth century, or certain

8. *The Dial*, August, 1923.
9. Horney, K., *The Neurotic Personality of Our Time*.
10. Menninger, K., *Man against Himself*.

old-fashioned individualists of the twentieth. The naïve notion of freedom—the opportunity to do what one likes, to exercise one's powers and follow one's impulses without let or hindrance—furnished Socrates and his disciples with the starting point of their ethical analysis. They had, as everyone knows, no difficulty in showing that this naïve notion by itself alone gives no sufficient foundation for lasting happiness or social peace. They therefore proceeded to construct a hierarchy of values—which in Plato became a hierarchy of men—and various definitions of the "good" life and the "good" society that became less and less serviceable as they became more and more complete. The freedom to which Pericles and the poets looked back was essentially a simple and immediate thing, the very air of the golden age; but by the time the philosophers had finished taking it to pieces no human power could put it together again. It does not detract from the merit of the analytic school to suggest that the opposition to it was also not without reason: though not the sort of reason that could be defined by the analytic method. The root of the trouble was, and is, that actual life and its aims as experienced can never be brought completely within the scope of a rational definition. The Socratic position that happiness is virtue, that virtue is knowledge, and that knowledge commands assent, did in fact leave something out; and that something, as Aristotle noted, was the breath of life.

So today academic philosophers, expounding the didactic legacy of Greece, render their exclusive homage to Apollo and Pallas Athene, leaving Dionysus and Aphrodite to the poets; but these are jealous gods, not always to be appeased with verses. It is far harder to impart the joy of life than the rules of living. The average layman, hearing the name of Hellas, thinks vaguely or vividly of theaters and temples, processions and festivals, painting and sculpture, wrestling and dancing, of lovely boys and girls under a Mediterranean sky; but so much a dream it is, the contrast with his own drab destiny escapes him. Yet as certain modern philosophers have insisted—Nietzsche, Spengler, Sorokin in particular—that Greek culture, like the high mediaeval culture, was all one. The banquet of Callias was no mere figure of speech: the Syracusan and his flute girl, Critobulus and the mimes, were as much a part of it as the wine and the wisdom. What the modern young are offered is little more than the bones of the feast.

Perhaps that is all that can survive in the dour and fretful era of ubiquitous mechanism. One can hardly imagine John Mill entertaining Autolicus, Lysis as much at ease with Mr. Gladstone as he was with Socrates, or Mrs. Carrie Chapman Catt at home with (or to) Sappho. But let us not therefore dismiss too brusquely the notion of naïve or animal freedom. To be able to do what one likes, to follow one's impulses without let or hindrance—the lack of just that may be one of our most fatal deprivations. A few years ago a charming and intelligent Englishwoman published a book called *The Right to Be Happy.* Is there no note of pathos in that title? And might it not fairly apply to innumerable novels and plays of our baffled and tortured generation?

Political theorists and social planners must take warning here; they are liable to what may almost be called an occupational disease—the disease of hyperabstraction. Criticizing the social order from the standpoint of ends that are the products of pure thinking, they set out to construct a better order based on a higher degree of rationality—and frequently achieve, from their point of view, considerable success. But somewhere along the way, the flesh-and-blood individual drops out of the process; only his ghost survives to walk the aseptic ways of a utopia in which even its inventors could hardly exercise their limited powers of existence. Reformers of society must take heed lest, in planning a better order, they increase rather than relax the severity of the demands made by the system upon ordinary individuals; not a few of them (Plato was one) when matters turned out so, have been willing to conduct surgical operations on the individuals for the sake of the superior system. In this respect radicalism and reaction have often come to terms, while liberalism, with its less obvious logic, stood embarrassed and aghast.

One of the wisest of modern liberals, L. T. Hobhouse, put his finger on this particular risk of social planning when he wrote: "Social and political institutions are not ends in themselves. . . . Any organised society may set before itself and may achieve ends which would be impracticable for its members if unorganised and perhaps would not appeal to them (e.g. national defence). But these must be ends which do appeal to the members of the community as members, and do further the fulfilment of their powers as men and women and the happiness of their lives." [11] Their powers as men and women—not as cogs in a machine nor as cells

11. Hobhouse, L. T., *Elements of Social Justice,* pp. 13, 28.

of some superorganism. The distinction is fundamental. Liberalism of whatever type or period has its hallmark in the fact that it takes the actual living person, the concrete human being, both as starting point and final criterion. To this extent an optimistic view of human nature is inherent in the liberal tradition; and while, so far, it does not commit one to the dogmas of either individualism or anarchism, it does distinguish liberalism from all mechanistic, deterministic, or transcendental systems. While of course liberalism does not reject a priori the notions of restraint or even coercion, it steadfastly insists that the latter be the exceptional remedy for the exceptional case, and always puts the burden of proof on the would-be restrainer. To the proponents of every collective end, be it national or imperial, be it cult or crusade, liberalism puts the question, Just what does this mean in the actual lives of these actual people? In what ways is the general good aimed at redeemable in the current coin of concrete experience? And here liberalism may claim discipleship of that great lover, not of mankind in the abstract, but of men and women and children in their concrete imperfection; whose every precept and example vindicates the apostolic statement of His mission: I am come that they might have life, and that they might have it more abundantly.

§ 4

IN OUR extremely voluble civilization, with its extraordinary number of people who make a living by gossiping, orating, lecturing, or writing about politics, there is a disposition to overrate the possibilities of political action: to assume that when once the right political formula (domestic or international) is discovered and applied, most of the difficulties of mankind will disappear. Aristotelian, as distinct from Platonic, thought supplies a corrective; for it sets out, not to create a perfect society of happy individuals by collective prescription, but to define the political conditions within which personal freedom and happiness are attainable: a very different matter. At the outset, the Greeks simplified their problem by deciding that the goal held good only for a certain section of their society. A good many people in the modern world are disposed to accept that limitation. We have only just (and perhaps only in theory) abandoned it in the case of women; and in many regions of Africa and America white people still endorse

Aristotle's dictum that "some are slaves by nature." But within the limits generally accepted in the ancient world, the Greeks succeeded in laying down for all time certain political conditions of freedom: two in particular.

First, they realized that no game is worth playing if the rules can be changed without notice; that was their main debating point against the Persians. From Herodotus on, Greek literature constantly emphasizes the disadvantages of despotism from the rational point of view. No man can be really free if there is no means of knowing what is going to happen next, if the rules of society may be unpredictably different next week from what they were last. Aristotle represents the general current of Greek thought when he argues against Plato "whether it is more advantageous to be ruled by the best man or the best laws," and decides every point in favor of constitutional government. To the Greek mind, the element of arbitrariness that is latent in even the most benevolent paternalism was abhorrent; and the concept of a deity who interfered with the world in that fashion, no matter with what good will, was quite unpalatable. There lay the difficulty in taking over, or making over, the Jewish concept of a father-god with its Oriental reference; whether the difficulty has ever been solved is perhaps open to question.

The fear of arbitrariness also underlay the Greek distrust of democracy, that is, in classical terms, the direct rule of the masses. It was the fickleness, the instability, of the mass mind that threatened the rule of law—in practice as well as theory. Classical thought of every school includes protective devices against it. Nowadays, when the financial support of so much political, journalistic, and broadcasting activity depends on mass patronage, there is a tendency to deny that necessity; but this is one of many points at which conservatism is an indispensable complement to liberalism. It is a good thing for any body politic to include a recognized group with a recognized philosophy that is prepared to challenge change. If shopkeeping millionaires subsidize radical propaganda then it is equally legitimate for property-holding millionaires to subsidize conservative propaganda. To flatter the masses by indiscriminate abuse of conservatism and all its exponents is no true service to liberalism.

But having said so much, we must recognize the special difficulties introduced by the economic factor—just as the Greeks had

to. As city life developed, the influence of private wealth became
more and more of a problem. The extremes of economic status,
said Aristotle, upset the rule of moderation, the principle of the
golden mean. The one class breeds "violent and great criminals,"
the other "rogues and petty rascals." "Those who have too much
of the goods of fortune . . . . are neither willing nor able to submit to authority. The evil begins at home: for when they are boys,
by reason of the luxury in which they are brought up, they never
learn even at school the habit of obedience. On the other hand,
the very poor, who are in the opposite extreme, are too degraded.
So that the one class cannot obey, and can only rule despotically;
the other knows not how to command, and must be ruled like
slaves. Thus arises a city, not of freemen, but of masters and slaves,
the one despising, the other envying; and nothing can be more
fatal to friendship and good fellowship in states than this." [12] The
action of both groups, seeking their own advantage, tends to upset the balance of public life; but "the practical difficulty of inducing those to forbear who can, if they like, encroach, is far
greater, for the weaker are always asking for equality and justice,
but the stronger care for none of these things." [13] Plato, pursuing
the same line of thought, follows it through to the ultimate stage
of the proletarian revolution. The whole argument forecasts the
inevitable breakdown of a party system at the point where the
parties come to represent distinct economic classes.

The ideal life for the citizen was in Greek thought the agrarian
life of the independent farmer: not because of its amenities, which
in Greece, as in most other parts of the world, were pathetically
meager, but because of the type of character it fostered. The
classical writers give a good deal of detailed consideration to the
problem of relieving agrarian life from the more extreme hazards
of economic insecurity. On this point Professor T. I. Cook has an
interesting comment: "Perhaps one might note that the agrarian-
ism of Jefferson, which was directed to the securing of this very
independence, has much in common with the theories of Aristotle,
and that the commitment of this country [United States] to the
industrial regime, which Jefferson so greatly distrusted, has in fact
produced a proletarian mass little capable of genuine citizenship.
Similarly, the growth of certain continental dictatorships with a

12. *Politics*, iv, 127 (Jowett).
13. *Ibid.*, vi, 192–193.

high degree of popular support at least raises the question whether the economically insecure are capable of reasoned political activity." [14] We shall subsequently have to consider whether the provision of financial security to an industrial population constitutes an answer to this question, or whether a more radical line of approach is indicated.

The Greek emphasis on the stability and impersonality of law as the necessary condition of freedom raised yet another question of urgency for our time. If the law—no matter how derived or defined—were merely the law of the tribe of the territory, what was to happen when tribes were mingled or territories disputed? Was there not, might there not be, a law absolute, universal, superior to all local claim or custom, binding by its very nature on all men? Again, since all enunciated law was to some degree imperfect and mutable, might there not lie, at least in certain cases, an appeal to something logically prior and morally more final? So at least thought Plato and Sophocles; Aristotle too in his very different way had hoped to find it. The question had an irresistible appeal to the Greek mind; and it has never been abandoned altogether. From time to time, as now, circumstances have forced thoughtful men to take it up again. The proponents and designers of current schemes for world peace, world government, world order are much concerned with it; but they have for the most part one lesson to learn from the Greek philosophers, which is simply that the second aspect of the problem as stated above is logically prior to the first. Current schemes are much engrossed in institutional matters, questions of form, mechanism, and procedure; but unless and until the philosophy of universal obligation is more clearly and compellingly stated, all such machinery will lack an adequate motive power. To this question also we shall return, since it is to liberalism, with its interest in the dynamics of community, that the challenge is most immediate.

§ 5

AT THIS point we come upon the second of the Greek foundation stones in the philosophy of freedom: the notion of consent. "What the Greek found wanting," says one of the foremost modern authorities, J. L. Myres, "when he came to know these so-

14. Cook, T. I., *History of Political Philosophy*, pp. 112–113.

cieties of the old East, compacted into their last and maturest superstructure, the Persian empire—was all trace of government by consent, all inward sanction of the commandment imposed from without; and it was just this inward sanction for which later Hebrew thought was ever searching, and never wholly finding, until it had been Hellenized through and through." [15]

The idea of government by consent has become so much a platitude of political thought that both its relative novelty and its difficulty are generally lost sight of. It is obvious enough that liberty can hardly be attributed to the condition of men who are governed without their consent; but exactly what is it that free people are supposed to consent to? Is it the specific collection of laws they are summoned to obey, or is it the general authority of the lawmakers? Push the former alternative too far and you get a manifestly impossible situation; push the latter too far and you may get a Hitler system. The technical and administrative resources at the disposal of any modern government, including control of the sources of information and the channels of communication, are so vast that the notion of consent can easily be made meaningless. Mussolini declared twenty years ago that he intended to govern with the consent of the majority: "but in order to obtain, to strengthen and to foster that consent I will use all the force at my disposal." Was he entitled to do that? If not, on what specific grounds do we base our emphatic and incorrigible dissent?

Greek thought failed to develop a full theory of consent because of the circumstances in which it arose. The Greeks were an invading race; and as usual in such cases, they cherished a strong sense of racial superiority which was reflected in a close restriction of political privilege. Both Sparta and Athens had large residual and alien populations by whom much of their economic life was carried on; but these people never became citizens, save in rare individual cases by special act of the assemblies. Conservative Athenians were inclined to argue that the residence basis had in fact been tried on a large scale by Cleisthenes, and that it had not worked out very well. In 507 B.C. Cleisthenes, in alliance with the populace against the old aristocracy, had enlarged the strict hereditary basis of citizenship by giving the franchise on a basis of residence and loyalty—the same qualifications as are now applied in Russian naturalization policy. He had organized

15. Myres, J. L., *The Political Ideas of the Greeks*, chap. i.

the voters in parishes or wards and regrouped these in such a manner that power speedily passed from the institutions dominated by the aristocrats to those operated by the democracy. At the same time he removed the ban on mixed marriages.

Fifty years later came the conservative reaction. The test of birth status was reimposed, applicants for citizenship being required to prove their descent from two generations of citizen forebears. Neither biologically nor politically, in the opinion of so acute an observer as Socrates, had the reforms proved beneficent. The "melting-pot policy" was especially condemned. "To the new shock of a general war, the 'second-cross' Athenians reacted quite otherwise than their grandfathers had done in the Persian crisis. Their tempers were uncertain, their judgement clouded by panic and prejudice, possibly even their physique upset in a way that made them easier victims to war-crowding and insanitary surroundings. . . . Above all, there was a notable lack of men of initiative and leadership, together with a superfluity of ill-balanced, temperamental enthusiasts, cranks and windbags." [16] Politically the democracy was beginning to show the characteristic vices of mob rule, and Sparta, which had preferred brutality to concessions, looked the stronger for its conservatism.

But it is not possible to saddle the democracy with all the blame. It was precisely those two crossed generations that raised Athens to the peak on which she stood at the outbreak of the Peloponnesian War; and if their conduct in that ordeal left much to be desired, it was lily white beside that of their opponents. The aristocratic or oligarchic parties throughout Greece, in their struggle to retain or regain control of their cities, showed themselves capable of the blackest treachery, plotting with whatever alien forces they could hire or cajole to the ruin of their fellow townsmen. If the democratic principle was corrupted, the aristocratic was infinitely more so, and with less excuse. The process was noted at the time, and as an almost universal trend in politics. A rule of birth may be all very well to begin with, may be strictly necessary in fact. But as time goes on, scions of the best families—even supposing they remain "best"—are likely to become relatively, and perhaps absolutely, fewer; and as they do so, an alliance almost inevitably arises with the oligarchy of wealth. The original holdings of the aristocracy in a growing community are likely, if they

16. *Ibid.*, chap. vi.

are not broken up, to increase in value; and other vested interests are naturally inclined to make common cause with them, in many ways, against the masses. Thus the royalists of descent find themselves aligned with, and even used by, those whom an American president has called the "economic royalists"; and a bloc arises which, unless it is very wisely led, may become a citadel of reaction and a possible objective of revolution.

The Greek practice of restricted citizenship involved however one principle of permanent validity, namely, that the possession of political power is not a universal right but a serious responsibility demanding special qualifications. To abolish all the qualifications does not do away with the reason that underlay them. This idea reappears in modern conservatism—in the thought of Disraeli, for example. As the notion of government by consent expanded into the theory of popular government, political power became a prize or a privilege rather than an obligation, and the necessity of any qualification for its safe or useful exercise dropped below the horizon. The necessity is still there, however; and the recurrent crises of this turbulent century remind us that it is not to be disposed of in any easy or half-hearted fashion.

But beneath the plane of politics lie more fundamental and decisive factors in the life of society. Political activity as such does not create community; it presupposes community. When a society shows signs of disintegration, the root of the trouble lies always on the deeper plane. This too the Greeks discovered, though the remedy was beyond them. Western society in our time has been beset by a plague of politics; there has been far too much of it for comprehension, let alone consideration; and a good deal of the affliction springs from the notion that when things do not run smoothly, the remedy is to pass more laws, make more rules, issue more orders. The prescription does not seem to have worked. The diagnosis must go deeper.

III

The Christian Synthesis

1. The idea of universal obligation. — 2. The "nature" of natural law. — 3. The Christian revolution. — 4. The "nature" of Christianity. — 5. The nature of man. — 6. The Christian foundations of democracy.

§ 1

ONE thing is certain about that state of perfect bliss of which men are prone to dream: it would be changeless. There would be no incentive to change; and the characteristic human skills and adaptive capacities would die out under disuse and disapproval. Adam in his bachelor days would have struck his descendants as an extremely uninteresting though highly tractable person, distinguished from all subsequent gardeners by a marked propensity to leave things as he found them. How the serpent entered the scene does not appear on the record; though the Lord set an example to all Christian gentlemen by accepting Mrs. Adam's account of what happened. That he had his reservations we may perhaps surmise from the fact that the serpent was allowed to continue his peregrinations; so he too probably has his place in the scheme of things—a view that Catholic theology inclines to support.

For without change humanity would not be human. Change is our destiny; and change means challenge—that is the theme of Professor Toynbee's great *Study of History.* Until quite recent times explorers could still find here and there isolated communities that had reached a sort of static equilibrium, both internally and externally; but such cases were very rare, and as a result of the current war there is probably not one left anywhere now. Development or retrogression is the rule.

In the successful cases the area of human coöperation grows intensively and extensively, and as it does so men become more fully aware of it and have to think more deeply about it. For the rules change too. Law, or whatever passes for law, has to be made more explicit, modified or added to. Interests conflict; and where genuine community exists—that is, where people really want to settle their differences without injuring one another—some criterion for the changing of the rules becomes necessary. The problem of the source or foundation of law emerges and gives rise to very significant thought. The concept of a law behind the law now finds expression: the notion of an authority in reserve as it were, something higher or deeper than explicit positive law, by which that law itself is to be evaluated, by which its development and alteration ought to be guided.

The primitive habit is to seek this authority in the words of some eponymous hero or tribal deity, remembered or engraved on tablets of stone or gold or inscribed in a magic book; or in mysterious communications to selected and awesomely environed devotees. All such things have of course to be interpreted in specific terms, and they generally give rise therefore to some sort of caste or hierarchy, usually tyrannical because there is no possible appeal from it. Nonetheless, a good deal of profound and disinterested thought might go into that sort of hieratic utterance, as it certainly did among the augurs and soothsayers of old, the priests and priestesses of the oracles, or the bibliolaters of Vedantic, Jewish, Mahommedan, or Puritan society. But in more advanced communities, where thought is free, we find a consistent and steadily developing line of approach to the problem of the law behind the law.

Consider the notion so familiar to every American in its formulation of the rights of man and the principles of the Declaration of Independence: the concept of rights prior to law—that is, both antecedent to, and superior to, all positive enactment. The notion was thoroughly familiar to the Greeks: we find it even in Homer. President Franklin D. Roosevelt, in a campaign speech of October 28, 1944, enlarged on the Declaration by enunciating the following "rights": "The right of a useful and remunerative job; the right to earn enough to provide adequate food, clothing and recreation; the right of every farmer to sell his products at a return which will give him and his family a decent living; the right of every family to a decent home; the right to adequate medical care and the opportunity to achieve and enjoy good health; the right to adequate protection from economic fears of old age, sickness, accident and unemployment; the right to a good education." No such "rights" are known to history, law, or jurisprudence. As desires, ideals, aims, these things are very familiar; but to call them "rights" is deliberately to mislead the electorate in a very dangerous direction. Innocent—and not so innocent—people may assert that they have an irrefragable claim on political authority for all these things, and that government is in duty bound to provide them. The check will bounce, or it will break the bank.

Rights properly so called are assertions as to the nature, and particularly the limits, of secular power, rooted in the deepest sense of human personality. Aristotle is very definite about the distinction between positive law, which is necessarily local and conventional, and something more binding and universal—more catholic, as we should now say. Most Greek philosophers thought that if you looked for it—as the greatest of them actually did— you would find everywhere a natural sense of right and wrong which was in fact as well as in theory the foundation of all particular systems: "a certain natural and universal right and wrong, which all men divine, even if they have no intercourse or covenant with each other"; [1] or in the words of Empedocles, whom Aristotle quotes, "a universal law stretching without break through the wide domain of the sky, and through the vast earth too." The idea was taken up by the Roman jurists, and underwent a tremendous development in Cicero and the Stoics.

The circumstances in which Roman law had to be applied gave it a powerful impetus. For as the Roman rule expanded, the old civil law—the law of the citizens—no longer sufficed to govern the relations of so many tribes and territories of noncitizens. The citizens, like those of any imperial power, were unwilling to have their private patrimony modified or diluted; and eventually their rulers, like those of Britain, embraced the liberal solution of the difficulty by extending full citizenship throughout the empire. But long before that policy was consummated, a complementary legal system had grown up: not so much in the theorizing of the law schools as in the actual workaday business of administration. For in the ports and markets of the empire, in the manifold business transactions of a world-wide commerce, in the drawing up of contracts and partnerships, the handling of foreign investment and foreign exchange, in marine insurance, ship chartering, the nego-

1. *Rhetoric*, I, xiii (Jebb).

tiation of letters of credit, the status of aliens and citizens in foreign parts—in all this practical life of an expanding community the administrators had to succeed in framing and developing a law that would work. They were elected officials, and they were elected on a "platform"—a program, reaffirmed in its main planks from year to year, that developed into nothing less than a universal law code: the law of the peoples, as it came to be called. And the Roman lecturers and advocates, quite logically, were inclined to see in it a law of people as such, and to identify it with, or derive it from, that natural and universal law about which Greek philosophy had so much to say.

The process is worth watching in Cicero. He selects, for example, as a problem in jurisprudence, Tarquin's rape of Lucretia. There was no written law against adultery; but "even then he had the light of reason deduced from the nature of things, that incites to good actions and dissuades from evil ones; and which does not begin for the first time to be law when it is drawn up in writing, but from the first moment that it exists. And this existence of moral obligation is coeternal with that of the divine mind." [2] He wants to establish mutuality as the basis of law; so he argues that "according to nature—that is, the law of the peoples—as well as by the statutes of particular communities, no man is allowed to injure his neighbour for the sake of his own advantage." Then he proceeds: "If nature ordains that one man shall desire to promote the interests of a fellow man, whoever he may be, just because he is a fellow man, then it follows, in accordance with that same nature, that there are interests that all men have in common. And if this is true, we are all subject to one and the same law of nature; and if this also is true, we are certainly forbidden by Nature's law to wrong our neighbour. Now the first assumption is true; therefore the conclusion is likewise true." [3]

But was the first assumption true? Perhaps it was in the sort of communities the cultured Cicero would be thinking about; but even then one might ask, Who is my neighbor? There were in his time, as in ours, plenty of communities in which a dual code of ethics persisted: the Germans were not the first to practice that— though many of them were torn in anguish between the persisting sense of human obligation and the order of a brutal government

2. *De Legibus*, II, 4 (Yonge).
3. *De Officiis*, III, 5, 6 (Miller).

to do it violence. The American Government has very recently shown that even the status of full native citizenship will not guarantee equality or humanity of treatment when racial passion is let loose. If universality were to be the criterion of fundamental law, the question of what specifically was universal would be a difficult one for the realist to answer. There was the question of slavery which the Aristotelians could settle only with an ipse dixit. There was the Spartan—and not only Spartan—practice of infanticide. There were the matrimonial customs of certain rulers of Egypt. There was the status of women, as to which Aristotle differed from Plato, who in turn would have differed emphatically from the Roman tradition. If it is to universal custom you are appealing, asked Ulpian, what about copulation? Is that part of the law of nature? In which connection it was not forgotten that most of the animals are less promiscuous than man. Lust, revenge, jealousy, greed are surely just as "natural" as the qualities the philosophers sought to inculcate. In fact, the more you press this appeal to universality as the foundation of law and morals the more difficulties you get into; until it becomes evident that whatever any theorist will pick out of Nature's cornucopia is a carefully selected sample of what he wishes to find there. Philosophers have a habit of salting their mines.

§ 2

WHAT the classical thinkers of the main tradition really meant by nature was not the phenomenal world as such, with its ceaseless flow and change, nor even those elements in it that appear to be most frequent or general. They meant the force behind it that makes for order and harmony, the regularity that makes understanding possible: that was the universal element they were looking for, alike in the material world and in the affairs of men. The quest gets under way with the attempt of the early scientists to understand the external world—that is, to perceive system or order in it—in contrast to the mythical or semimythical cosmogonies of their predecessors. Heraclitus and Anaximander are objective in their attitudes, to the extent, at least, of not shirking the dilemma with which their senses present them. The dicta of Heraclitus concerning universal substance, polarity, and flow belong to the realm of fact and hypothesis—formula—rather than law or principle.

But as his thought develops we trace the imputation of the value-judgment by which the transition from formula to principle is made. The idea of measure, for example, clearly foreshadows the conception of political justice in Plato. The notion of an "invisible harmony" in which all coexistent discords are resolved marks a further advance; and the idea of universal law existing from all time becomes clearly philosophical when we find the epithet "divine" imputed to it. The transition from formula to principle by means of the value-judgment is complete in such dicta as: "Wisdom is one thing. It is to know the thought by which all things are steered through all things." [4]

It is noteworthy that in the Platonic cosmogony the god or demiurge or prime mover is not the creator but the arranger, the imposer of order upon a chaos that he cannot wholly subdue. To discern this divine work is the true wisdom, to partake of it the true virtue; and the two, in Greek thought, are really one. For that very reason by which a man attains to understanding is what we also see at work out there, inspiring the universe itself with order and harmony. Thus in the *Republic* we have the idea of justice as consisting in adherence to true nature or function *because* thereby social harmony ensues; and in a noteworthy passage of the *Laws* the whole position is summed up: "How can there be the least shadow of wisdom where there is no harmony? There is none; but the noblest and greatest of harmonies may be truly said to be the greatest wisdom; and of this he is a partaker who lives according to reason; whereas he who is devoid of reason is the destroyer of his house and the very opposite of a savior of the state: he is utterly ignorant of political wisdom." [5] Or consider this passage from a Socratic dialogue, with its swift transition from a very hypothetical major premise to a very strong value affirmation:

But now, are you aware, Hippias, of certain unwritten laws?

Yes [he answered] those held in every part of the world, and in the same sense.

Can you then assert [asked Socrates] of these unwritten laws that men made them?

Nay, how [he answered] should that be, for how could they have all come together from the ends of the earth? And even if they had so done, men are not all of one speech.

4. Quoted in Burnet, John, *Early Greek Philosophy*, chap. iii.
5. *Laws*, iii, 689 (Jowett).

Whom then do you believe to have been the makers of these laws?

For my part I think that the gods must have made these laws for men.[6]

Why the gods and not the demons? Because it is well understood that the gods are concerned with order and harmony, and that these are the things which, as rational creatures, we too supremely value.

Professor Barker, in his masterly introduction to Gierke's work on natural law, distinguishes three phases of the Aristotelian conception of nature as applied to human affairs. It is something primordial or immanent in the constitution of man; it is a potentiality, developing with human coöperation; it is the "true nature of man" in the sense of final goal or purpose. Now it is apparent that when the idea of natural law is made the basis of political or ethical teaching, we are dealing mainly with this third aspect; and it is no less evident that the apprehension of "true nature" in this sense is rather a religious than a dialectical achievement. That is clearly the case, for example, in Antigone's famous appeal to the "unwritten and unfailing statutes of the gods," and in the choric hymn in *Oedipus Tyrannos*: "May I never break the sanctity of the unwritten laws. Heavenborn, they live and move on high and are not made by man, nor shall they ever sleep or be forgotten. In them is a divine power which grows not old." [7]

This essentially religious apprehension of "true" nature, in the sense of divine end or purpose, is evident in Plato and the neo-Platonic schools. It steadily deepened with the growing complexity of human affairs until it became the basis of the Stoic system. "To the Stoics," says Barker, "Nature was synonymous with Reason, and Reason was synonymous with God. They believed that the true city or polity of mankind was a single 'city of God' or cosmopolis (transcending the old historical and positive cities), and that all men were united, as reasonable creatures, in this city of God, which was also a city of Reason and of Nature." [8] Within this ideal city—whose ways Augustine was later to explore—ran the common law of all humanity as God had made it; and all men (and women, and slaves) were equal.

6. Xenophon, *Memorabilia*, iv, 4 (Dakyns).
7. *Oedipus Tyrannus*, 853 ff. (Campbell).
8. Gierke, O. F. von, *Natural Law and the Theory of Society*, Introduction. p. XXXV.

Obviously, we are far away, in this realm of discourse, from the conception of what is "natural" in the sense of what is actual, primordial, or universal. The most one can say is that such a program represents a potentiality, universal in that it is not confined to any chosen people, or class, or elite—which is of course precisely what St. Paul did say; but how to get it realized, bring it to earth, put the necessary power behind it—as to that, the classical tradition had in the end no answer. "The philosophers," says Reinhold Niebuhr, "were optimistic in their confidence that the wise man would be virtuous; but alas, they had no confidence that many would be wise. The Stoic Chrysippus could conceive happiness only for the wise and was certain that most men were fools. The Stoics tended on the one hand to include all men in the brotherhood of man on the ground that they all had the spark of divine reason; but on the other hand they pitied the multitude for having no obvious graces of rationality. Thus their equalitarianism rapidly degenerated into an aristocratic condescension not very different from the Aristotelian contempt for the slave as a 'living tool.' Seneca, despite his pious universalism, prays 'forgive the world: they are all fools.'" [9]

Perhaps we are: was that then to be the conclusion of the whole matter? Was the law behind the law so recondite that only the wise and prudent could get a glimpse of it? Had the wayfaring man really no choice but to err? By this time—the last two centuries of the pre-Christian era—wayfaring men throughout the disintegrating Hellenic world were desperately seeking some sort of solace. Pauperized, exiled, deracinated by the plague of "conquerors, wastrels and hangmen," this growing internal proletariat (to use Toynbee's phrase) could on occasion show its resentment with a savagery that exceeded even that of its oppressors; but within its suffering mass a new spiritual self-consciousness was gestating that no philosophy of the upper-class intellectuals could satisfy. Did the poor, the simple, and the weak count for nothing any more? Was their existence meaningless to whatever ruled the cosmos? Was it their everlasting fate merely to be pushed around the flinty world, told to kill or be killed, left to hunt or grovel for a living in the debris that power politics had made of their little communities? They flock to conjurors, astrologers, and sorcerers, they cry to every god they know—to Dionysus and Helios, to Isis and Baal and Cybele and Mithra—seeking not philosophy, but sal-

9. Niebuhr, R., *The Nature and Destiny of Man*, I, 9–10.

vation. And still above the clamor rise those grand clear voices of
the Jewish prophets, whose judgment of the nations will not condone the degradation of the peoples: the moral rot that every age
of confusion brings—the avarice of the rich, of the public contractors and the speculators, the venality of the lawyers, the extinction of pity, the sexual license rampant in high and low: be it
all never so universal, they will continue to denounce it with their
Thus saith the Lord—the Lord who is already being thought of
not as the god of the Jews but as the savior of the world. The man
he made, the man he loves, may not act so: one day Messiah will
come, and you will see . . .

§ 3

IT WAS at this moment of human time, this juncture of cultural
forces, that there occurred that catalytic event which Christians
call the Incarnation; and as if a larger life had suddenly entered
the human scene, it sent forth from Palestine a group of men girt
with power as of a rushing mighty wind: men who taught not a
doctrine but a fact, not a theory but a Person—the god-man newly
come into the world, bringing infinite love to vanquish infinite
evil, who opposed the way of gentleness to the way of violence,
whom the world crucified but could not kill, in whose nature every
man might see the meaning of his own. In that spontaneous recognition the human soul, drawn but not compelled, suddenly
achieved that contact with its own reality of which the philosophers had so long been talking; for being philosophers, they had
forgotten what common people know intuitively, namely, that
meaning is always concrete because it is a matter of living experience, not simply of thinking and theorizing. Thus the central
insight possible to man, the vision of what man is in relation to
what man is for, must be expressed in terms of total humanity because nothing less would suffice: no set of precepts, no body of
doctrine, could altogether contain it. And that is why the Church
has insisted through thick and thin, against all temptation to explain away its gospel in the contingent terms of philosophic abstraction or ethical idealism, on the entire and specific human
nature of Christ: entering our world from a human womb, manifest as a child among children, poor among the poor, hungry among
the hungry, a worker among workers, joyful in human gladness,

happy in the loveliness of nature, a man with very human friend-
ships, a sufferer in the midst of suffering, despised among the out-
casts, condemned among the criminals, unflinchingly human to
the uttermost—when, as if more evidence were needed, that awful
cry from the cross sets the seal on the completion of His human
nature. And precisely because it was complete, He became the
very voice of God on earth, the Word made flesh; and precisely
because it was concrete, the Church will tolerate no slick separation of the ideal from the actual, no canting connivance, in the
name of otherworldliness, at the perpetuation of a hell on earth.

The faith was not offered as a revolution, philosophical or political: it was offered as a fulfilment, as it had been foretold. And the
chosen instrument of its propagation—the records are emphatic
as to the special nature of the choice—was an ardent scholar of
the Jewish tradition, born and bred in a Greek metropolis uniquely
endowed with Roman citizenship: a man whose outstanding char-
asteristic, like that of the prophets before him, was his inability to
tolerate error. He too had believed in force and violence; to him
therefore the revelation came as a flash of lightning; through him
it changed the history of the world—bringing both a new possibility of redemption and, as its price, a new type of conflict.

Paul stood for liberation: and first, liberation from racial and
national exclusiveness. That was the bitterest struggle, for the past
was rich and strong. Then came liberation from the "bondage" of
the old moralistic law, which Paul compares to a censorious schoolmaster under whom we were "shut up," whom we have now outgrown; he contrasts it with the freedom that is "in Christ"—not
only in an esoteric but in a quite practical sense. Even as their master had scandalized the formalists of his day, so Christians are
to cease their concern about diet and circumcision and outward
observances. Popular asceticism is expressly and officially denounced; even on the question of sex, with which the disintegrating Hellenic world, like our own, was so obsessed, Paul is far more
tolerant than the puritans of either his time or ours. Certain sins,
censured by all the best pagan teaching, he too condemns; but for
the rest he is not anxious to lay down rules. Writing to the Greeks
of Corinth (where sex was big business) he is remarkably tentative: "I have no commandment of the Lord . . . I give my judgement . . . I think I have the spirit of God." The puritan heresies
would have found no sterner critic than Paul, unless perhaps it

were Peter—whom Calvin would never have recognized as one of the elect.

§ 4

IT WAS an essential part of the liberation that Christians were forbidden to think of, or treat, the world of nature as evil—as some of the Oriental cults were doing, and have continued to do. God looked upon the world that he had made and saw that it was good; and so did the Son of God, who shrank from nothing. "For every creature of God is good, and nothing to be refused, if it be received with thanksgiving; for it is sanctified by the word of God and prayer." Thus from the beginning the sacramental principle is the golden key to all creation: in particular, to the bodily life of man. Again in contrast to the Orient, Christians may neither despise nor abuse the body. Only the ignorance of modern times has supposed that there is a body-soul antithesis in Christianity. The temple of the spirit, as its instrument, may indeed be subject at times to onerous demands—as every creative worker knows—and in the nature of the case cannot be an end in itself; but its prestige is surely attested by the wondrous fertility of the Christian era in all the arts, including the art of bodily adornment. "The bible," says Niebuhr, "knows nothing of a good mind and an evil body"; and in an acute analysis he makes a fruitful comparison with Greek rationalism.[10] In their ascription of divinity to pure reason, conceived as something quite separate from the sensual and appetitive life, both Plato and Aristotle casually annihilate the individual human being; so that in their systems, as in all later rationalism of that type, "individuality is no significant concept, for it rests only upon the particularity of the body."

The Greek philosophers who adopted the Christian interpretation were well aware that the old doctrine of nature had worn thin; in fact, it had broken into two pieces. One piece, made out of the primordial element, was cynical and hedonistic, and has survived as an academic and aesthetic curiosity; the other piece, embodying the teleological emphasis, had the germ of a tremendous dynamism. For it was not to something more universal, but to something more perfect than any human ordinance that Antigone really appealed. It was no falling back on universal prac-

10. *Ibid.*, p. 7 *et seq.*

tice, no expression of a naïve naturalism, that made Socrates drink the hemlock or Christ carry the cross: on the contrary, it was the very uniqueness of those actions that established their sovereignty over the minds and hearts of men. Paul then, going consciously to the root of the matter, cleaves a bold dichotomy between the primordial and the teleological with his doctrine of the dual nature of man. Man as part of the natural order is but potentiality, earth bound, death doomed, sunk in the universal flux of things. But for man, and for man alone, to be no more than that is sin; because he is called—and he knows it and has always known it, as the earliest records testify—to a "rebirth," to "walk in newness of life," in "the law of the spirit of life": the words are so familiar, the meaning so remote to our generation.

Philosophy has never succeeded in defining the nature of man, and never will. Obviously, if my dog could define the nature of dog she would be more than dog to begin with; yet, being very elderly and wise, she not only knows a great deal about dog, she knows a good deal about me. This sort of knowing, of course, is the oldest and deepest kind: knowing in experience; it is what is referred to by that etymological root of immemorial antiquity, the k-n or g-n root that survives in words like cunning, connaître, king; it is what the English Bible means when it says "Adam knew Eve his wife," and again when it says, "Ye shall know the truth, and the truth shall make you free." This kind of knowing, which modern education systematically ignores, is not a matter of making sentences and syllogisms, it is all along a species of doing and experiencing; and what its exponents say (the Church is not the only one) is that by living according to a certain pattern, a man may attain practical wisdom and spiritual freedom. Of course, there are ways that lead to destruction via practical folly and spiritual bondage; and spiritual freedom is not the whole story; but it is surely the essential beginning, for men who are not spiritually free can hardly be relied on to create a free society.

We can reach the same conclusion by another tack. Scientists can define the nature of inert and much of organic life; when they do so, they talk in functional terms—they tell us what under a variety of circumstances things will do. They are not interested in the problem of what things are; that question, if it has any meaning (which is very doubtful), belongs to the province of metaphysics; the nearest the scientists come to it is in their amazing assemblage of *functional* equations. Similarly, when we try to say anything significant about human beings, we find ourselves talking in functional terms; even psychology, in its endless attempt to define its own subject matter, has hit on the functional basis. Without function no definition amounts to much. You can say, if you like, that a violin is a particular arrangement of wood, catgut, and horsehair, but nobody will accept that for a definition; you cannot define a violin without saying what a violin is for. Violins are made by men, so men can do that. Men do not appear, however, to have made themselves; so as soon as they try to define their nature, they find themselves using words that reach out beyond themselves, that are thrown forward, as it were, along certain observed lines of direction; which is what the Church does when she says, in her characteristic way, Man is made in the image of God, man is a child of God. That is not definition, it is open-ended description, which tallies with the open-ended experience of actual living—the infinite hoping and striving, the love, the sacrifice, the conviction of meaning and value, as known to common people and great poets: not in the laboratory, but in the home.

Contemporary culture suffers from a curious, and probably unique, illiteracy. Its vocabulary and stock of concepts are so exclusively quantitative that a large part of experience is never fully apprehended, because of the difficulty of formulation. Why this is so we shall enquire in Chapter XI; the fact puts an extraneous obstacle in the way of our understanding any different type of culture. The early Christians were certainly not bothered as we should have been by difficulties of formulation; though we flatter ourselves if we suppose that they could not think as clearly as we can. They had much less difficulty than we should now have in seizing a new apprehension of reality; and the problem of formulation became acute under external rather than internal necessity.

For many decades the Christian community got along with only the barest act of affirmation: the baptismal formula, to show who belonged and who did not belong. But as belonging or not belonging became the outstanding issue in a dissolving civilization, the Church found it necessary to sharpen up the formula. Nearly four centuries elapsed, for example, before the Trinitarian doctrine was officially defined; but, as Professor Bevan so justly says:

If Christians were going to come to the world with any affirmations about God, it was just intellectual sincerity for them to make up their minds what the words which they used meant. To-day, while the duty of being kindly and good-natured all round is very generally recognized, people often hardly regard it as a duty at all to think what their affirmations mean or what relation they bear to the facts of the Universe. If the essential thing about the Christian message was a new announcement of what God was, of what God had done and would do, the announcement could hardly be effective so long as Christians themselves had quite confused ideas of what the words which they used implied.[11]

Because Christianity is a school of life as well as a school of thought; and because its central message is that "the Word was made flesh and dwelt among us"; the terms of its affirmations are frankly, and rightly, anthropomorphic: any terms you may use about such matters are going to be anthropomorphic, no matter how long are the words you employ. Dogmatic affirmation does not preclude an ever-deepening understanding of the terms employed; but it ensures, and is maintained to ensure, that the essence of Christian truth shall not—as can so easily happen—be dissipated and lost in the philosophic mists of a world without clarity or coherence.

Cultural anthropologists have made a vast and fascinating collection of the forms assumed by the religious impulse in various societies, especially the more primitive; but the significance of this material has not increased in proportion to its quantity. Essentially, in its bearing on the development of Christianity, there is nothing new. Christians have always known that their cultus developed more by assimilation and transformation of older forms than by conscious innovation—as it still does, and always will. Religious forms are not invented or deliberately contrived; cranks have often attempted that, but the results have been singularly infertile. Just as some English words of richest meaning have Sanskrit or even pre-Sanskrit roots, so the elements of religious expression have primordial origins: for instance, the association of height with sublimity and divinity, of light with knowledge and illumination, of wind with inspiration and power.[12] Religious rites show something of the same catholicity, and the early Christians

11. Bevan, E., *Christianity*, pp. 83–84.
12. On the whole subject see Bevan, E., *Symbolism and Belief* and Hebert, A. G., *Liturgy and Society*.

were well aware of the fact. They were not acquainted with the Trobrian Islanders, but they had a first-hand knowledge of the cults of the Hellenistic and imperial eras, and their writings abound in it. "St. Paul's epistles are full of echoes of the pagan mystery-religions, and it became plain that the Christian Gospel was concerned with precisely those questions which the mystery-religions asked, about God and the soul, salvation and immortality. It was therefore natural and inevitable that the answer should be stated, more and more as time went on, in the terms in which the question was being asked, and that Christianity should appear before the world as one of the mystery-religions, and the ritual of its sacraments should follow the lines of the mystery rites." [13] But, as Fr. Hebert goes on to show, the new power that had entered the world was strongly at work not merely in molding the forms but in fulfilling the meaning. And precisely because this was an inward power, the Christian cult revealed its difference in a conspicuously outward matter, a life and death situation: it was the one cult that refused to worship the state. When the Church has recovered its courage, and will face the consequences as it did before, the future of Western man may begin to brighten.

§ 5

IT IS impossible not to sympathize with the bewilderment and exasperation of the Roman magistrates confronted with this seemingly perverse defiance. A formal courtesy, just a pinch of incense on the altar to *divus Augustus*—why make such a fuss about that? One is reminded of the refusal of a contemporary sect of Bible worshipers to salute the American flag: it is noteworthy that in both cases children stood firm under social and legal persecution; and in neither case did the refusal necessarily imply civil disobedience or even disrespect. The Christians were expressly taught not only to obey, but to honor, the powers that be; and the emperor cult could hardly in reason be regarded as just another piece of idolatry. The emperor had always been head of the state church; the barbarian recruits in particular came to see in him the very personification of order and majesty in the world; grateful subjects and cities often addressed him as "savior" and "redeemer"; the deification of living rulers was familiar to the whole East; and

13. Hebert, *op. cit.*, p. 55.

when the empire officially adopted the style it was in the interest of cultural as well as political unity—no unworthy aim. Probably the influence of the Christians was in some measure what would now be called subversive; but they certainly did not aspire to set up a rival authority. No: what they so quietly and so indomitably asserted was something far more fundamental: namely, the principle of limitation on all secular jurisdiction, the claim to reserve inviolate from its mandate the inner life of the individual. Between that claim and the pretensions of even the noblest secular absolutism there neither could nor can be any lasting compromise.

This involves much more than the conventional modern claim to "freedom of conscience," which in common parlance may not mean very much. For whatever constraint may lie upon a man's actions, his conscience cannot be anything but free so far as human agency is concerned (the contrary argument is deterministic and we shall examine it in due course). It means more too than the claim to act in conformity with conscience and not to be compelled to act against it; though that claim needs today very vigilant defenders. It means, in the final analysis, that state action is confined within a boundary that the state does not itself determine but which it may not transgress; and that on matters of right and wrong the state is denied the last word. The individual may say to the state in practical matters, I think you are wrong but for the sake of peace and expediency I will assent to your policy; but when the state says to the individual, I know I am right and I call upon you to testify to that fact—then comes the parting of the ways; one way may lead to tyranny while the other leads to the concentration camp and the firing squad.

§ 6

THE argument thus comes back to the question of rights, with which this chapter opened: one right in particular. The American Declaration of Independence states as the very first of its "truths" that "all men are created equal." The claim is made for "all," not merely—as the Greeks and Romans would have made it—for citizens; but the only support offered for the proposition is that it is "self-evident." Apart however from those Christian postulates which the founding fathers inherited, it is not evident at all, it is preposterous. To the natural eye men are certainly not created equal, neither in heredity, biological endowment, circumstance, opportunity, nor luck; and in fact no human ordinance can altogether counteract their inequality. The French declaration which followed (in both senses) the American one thirteen years later repeats the proposition, but adds "as regards their rights"; and in the preamble it claims "the auspices of the Supreme Being." But apart from such correspondence with him as the men of 1789 may have had, the statement remains a bare assertion; and the common man of today would be hard pressed to state the ground of it. If one were to ask him what he meant by saying that all men are equal, he would probably reply that "the other fellow has his rights the same as I have." But has he? How do you know? There are plenty of people in this modern world who deny that, in theory and practice, and they are not confined to Nazi Germany. And where, one might add, do you get yours? You are probably not the equal in wisdom, talent, energy, skill, of those who are set over you; in fact, you chose them—or you are supposed to have chosen them—because of their superior endowment: do you mean that nonetheless you are their equal, and that their rights are no greater than yours? Yes, emphatically: the average American does mean precisely that, and he means it with a depth of conviction that is unique among political societies. But if we still press him for proof, he will probably say—if he responds at all to a demand that seems obviously crazy— Well, we are all human beings, aren't we? And in some such statement as that we shall discover the core of a society which, as T. S. Eliot said, so far as it is civilized is still Christian.[14]

For it is only in the Christian doctrine of man that we can find a firm and reasoned ground for that American affirmation. There alone is it explicitly argued that in every human being is something which transcends the pragmatic valuations of the temporal order. There alone do we find the pattern of a community of spiritual beings among whom—on its own plane and in its own ethos— there is no higher and lower, no superior and inferior; by which every political society must be informed, to which every such society must continually aspire—or perish. And it is this doctrine, and none other, which sets limits to the presumption of every earthly power, and sees in each individual the embodiment of a purpose that goes beyond all secular objectives.

14. *The Idea of a Christian Society*, pp. 8–12.

Religion, says Christopher Dawson, "was the source of the moral standards and spiritual values which are essential to the liberal tradition, though liberals frequently ignored this and attempted to base them on abstract ideas. But the rational ideas of liberalism were abstracted from a historical religious tradition, and the liberal culture was strongest and most enduring precisely in those societies in which the Christian social and political consciousness was most alive." [15] The fact is that modern thought, which in so many directions has been struggling to get away from the logic of the Christian faith, has nonetheless been taking for granted the set of values which that faith, and nothing else, established; and the modern world has been coasting along in easy assurance that the values will survive the destruction of the system. The assumption is dangerous. Without the historical religious tradition, what becomes, in a secular analysis, of our customary regard for common people? Why, for instance, should we not set our experts to select the most promising among them, concentrate all our efforts upon that selection, and set the rest to labor in a general regimentation "for the good of society"? It has been done. Why should we let them continue to mate and proliferate spontaneously, instead of breeding the biologically fittest and sterilizing all the rest? It has been attempted. These, and many more of like tenor, are practical questions; and the liberal who does not know the answers is likely to find himself confronted by practical policies whose drift he profoundly distrusts or detests but to whose "expert" proponents he can make no consistent rejoinder. Much of what passes for liberalism in the United States today has already lost its democratic sympathies and is fast losing its humanity, for lack of opponents who really understand the ground of their own objections.

The fundamental values of the liberal tradition were in fact exemplified, formulated, and wrought into the texture of Western society by Christianity, not only as a school of thought but as a way of life and feeling: as religion, in short. It is not safe to assume that the Christian ethos will persist while the faith and doctrine that gave it birth are being deliberately abandoned. The logic of thought, the evidence of history, and the testimony of current events are all opposed to that assumption.

15. Dawson, C., *The Judgment of the Nations,* p. 123.

IV

The Breakdown of Universality

1. The vision of catholic unity. — 2. Two theories of the dissolution. — 3. Recurrent primitivism. — 4. Protestantism and the divine right of nations.

§ 1

THE transition from what we may roughly call a monistic to a dualistic view of human nature had tremendous practical effects. To identify the law behind the law with the will of God for man was not in itself a difficult step. "To man the eternal law says 'You ought'; to the rest of nature it says 'You must.'" That fact was evident even to thoughtful barbarians; and as Professor Robson points out, "it emphasized the distinction between man and the rest of the universe." [1] It remained for modern times to reverse the emphasis, in both theory and practice.

It seemed reasonable enough, too, that this supreme law in human affairs should call for continuous interpretation. That, as we have seen, was no new idea; and so long as the unity of the Roman world endured, it was natural for even barbarians to seek that center in *Roma Aeterna* (they were calling it that even in the second century). But with the disintegration of the Roman system a new problem arose. There was in human affairs also— there always had been—some sort of power that said "you must": said it with swords and grappling irons on occasion. Now that power was no longer centered in Rome; it was springing up in strange places, embodying itself in strange leaders, and frequently on the move. Was the supreme law for man to disintegrate likewise, was that to become local and migratory as the secular power was becoming? Few indeed were even the barbarians who thought so, or wished it so. Thus the secular disintegration strengthened, in both theory and practice, the spiritual supremacy of Rome.

1. Robson, W. A., *Civilization and the Growth of Law*, p. 220,

For while Goths, Franks, and Vandals might have power of the body, the Church had power of the mind. Not only did she hold the keys to life eternal; within her gates civilization itself had taken sanctuary—as it may do again—and under her banner letters and learning were to find safe conduct through the perilous terrain of a world in travail. While new centers of community arose and life in the cities and on the great estates acquired coherence, lore and custom were touched by the echoes of a larger order, and simple force sought once again its transmutation into authority.

For between power and authority there is the same sort of distinction as was later to be recognized between possession and property. While power may reside in persons or groups of persons, authority does not. Persons may temporarily be able, rightly or wrongly, to coerce other persons; but authority does not inhere in human beings. If in such a work as this we cite "an authority," it is not to the individual man as such that we appeal, but to the wider knowledge or deeper insight that has already been acclaimed in him; and if his scholarship is later shown to be in error or his judgment at fault, our authority is an authority no longer, and our appeal loses its compulsion. The appeal, moreover, is made in a limited field; and in every such case it is something transmitted or revealed through the individual that constitutes the real authority. If we learn through the eyes or ears of an artist to distinguish more surely the true from the false, it is the truth and falsehood of art itself that we experience, and the truth that compels our observance—literally compels; for once the recognition is achieved it is impossible, short of deliberate perversity, to get away from it. So it is with the pursuit of virtue: authority is as it were mediated through persons, never rests on a mere ipse dixit. So rulers and leaders of men, desiring a stable basis for social order, are impelled to seek the sanction of something that goes beyond the act of will, beyond local considerations of interest or expediency.

For a thousand years all Europe sought that sanction in the Catholic Church; and in those parts of the world which eventually rejected that authority, appeal was made to one of two—as it were, fragmentary—substitutes: either to state establishments that retained a church but dropped the catholicity, or to declarations of rights that retained the catholicity (in theory at least) but dropped the Church. Each had its limitations; and the two halves failed to make a whole.

In comparing our ideas and institutions with those of another age, a strenuous effort is needed to escape the folly of provincialism in time and space. We are beset by the temptation to seek only the "origins" of things we consider important—assuming that those origins lie mainly, or solely, in the temporal succession of events; to high light the picture so that all the rest remains obscure; and thus to produce the illusion that its entire meaning is exhausted in the satisfaction of our curiosity. In this way the nineteenth-century dogma of "progress" still controls our perspective. What we may profitably seek in history are the underlying truths of human nature, and the ways in which those truths have been implemented by other societies in other times. Among those ways some of great value—and some of little value—are still open to us; these we have in many cases paved and widened. But others are buried deep in the ever-encroaching jungle of human passion and perversity; and among them may be some that could lead us out of our present confusion. To search for these calls for intellectual and moral courage.

Particularly is this true in the neglected field of political philosophy. "It is very difficult for us to interpret the mediaeval temper: we are still in a large measure under the influence of a conception of sovereignty as representing some absolute and even arbitrary authority in the state or the church which was unknown to the Middle Ages. The only sovereignty they recognized was that of the law; and even that was subject to the law of God or nature." [2] It was evident—far more evident then than now—that the authority of the law could not, by its very nature, be merely local; and the conviction inspired the attempt to maintain a supreme authority in the secular sphere, whose title should be above that of all local lords and princes. Thus the cherished unity of the world was to be retained in the temporal no less than in the spiritual order.

It was a noble dream: perhaps more than a dream. But just as a traveler can see the distant summit more clearly than the broken ground between, so the vision of an earthly unity was lost in the actualities of the immediate struggle. The imperial title enhanced, but did not supersede, the nascent kingship. Its prestige enabled

2. Carlyle, A. J., *Mediaeval Political Thought*, IV, Part 3, chap. iii.

the latter to extend its scope and strengthen its authority; but it could not bind the newer groupings in a lasting unity. Under stress of necessity and in closer conformity with economic culture, the kingship was hardening in the rigidity of feudalism. A system of specific sovereignty was evolving which, despite its successive borrowings from the imperial ideas, resisted in the long run all attempts to perpetuate the imperial reality. As Bryce points out, the differences between *civitas, regnum,* and *imperium* became mere differences in size. The imperial crown became merely a prize in the struggle for power, with which even the Papacy, in its temporal aspect, frequently found itself in conflict. And with that, the ideal itself began to lose attraction. "As a matter of fact," says Gierke, "the principle of the Universal State was assailed while as yet the principle of the Universal Church was not in jeopardy. Especially in France, we hear the doctrine that the oneness of all mankind need not find expression in a one and only State, but that on the contrary a plurality of states best corresponds to the nature of man and of temporal power." [3] New solidarities absorbed the social consciousness as the new groupings stabilized. Monarchy, with its train of good and evil, partitioned the Western mind; Latin and Teuton carried their endless struggle into the forms and formulas of a new age; and the Holy Roman Empire, taking one prophetic glance at the nineteenth century, finally gave up the ghost in 1806—to be followed, from that day to this, by a succession of chimeras.

But the older vision of unity had more than a theory to sustain it. From the seventh to the seventeenth century the thought and culture of the civilized world had an actual unity that is hard for us even to imagine. Our ears are filled with the nauseating platitude that the world has become smaller; but in things more important than bombing planes and washing machines its distances are vaster than for a thousand years. The milder barbarism of the "Dark Ages" had the inestimable boon of a universal language as well as a universal tradition. The general pattern of education, and most of its resources, were in common to the whole mediaeval world. Scholars, students, and craftsmen traveled relatively more than those of the modern age; nor was their purpose merely to pick up a few exotic strands from foreign hedgerows that they could weave into a local homespun. They did not think of their

3. Gierke, O. F. von, *Political Theories of the Middle Ages,* sec. III, p. 20.

culture as territorial merely because their homes or workshops—
when they had any—happened to be in this place or that; nor do
we think of their great teachers and writers as belonging primarily
to one country or another. The monasteries and universities were
stubbornly defiant of local potentates, small or great; nor must
we forget the friars of the mendicant orders, who did in some
measure for the life of the spirit what the traveling merchant was
doing for the life of trade. Christendom was not a place but a
community. It could endure the incessant warring of the temporal
powers precisely because its basis was not territorial. It had its dissident movements, its sects and unorthodoxies, even its heresies;
but so long as these—even the last—had reference to a common
set of moral postulates, broadly based on a common faith, the life
of the community went on. And there was more in common between Pelagius and Augustine, or Anselm and Roscellinus, or
Thomas and John the Scot, even between Luther and Eck, than
there is between any two leading schools of modern thought.
Contemporary culture is riven from top to bottom by the lack of
agreement as to common postulates or common values, so that
its exponents seldom speak the same language even when they
use the same words; and because of that, it has become not only
departmentalized but localized. Thus even the idea of fundamental unity is lost—while politicians glibly proclaim that the
world is one—and American universities, following a German
style, sponsor schools of "American culture" with all the emphasis
on the adjective. It is the intellectual's version of the flag parade
with its uniformed coquettes cavorting round the big drum. For
while it is rightly held that every culture has its roots in the soil,
that is true only of the roots; and the soil does not provide the
seed. The difference between regionalism and fragmentation consists in the sense of a larger whole of which the particular field is
felt to be a part. And where there is no catholicity of values, the
amount of meaning any school of opinion may possess is necessarily limited in both breadth and depth; under all lies a common
aridity.

§ 2

NONETHELESS, that European synthesis did disintegrate. Is the
verb too strong? Not merely does its memory live in many minds;

the spiritual community on which it rested is not totally extinct. Most Christian people still acknowledge its postulates so far as they are aware of them; but even among the Christians, that sense is driven back into the fastnesses of the mind, whence it has little effect on the plane of action. And while other schemes of synthesis have so far catastrophically broken down—if indeed there was anything to break—it cannot be said that the old synthesis was dissolved in something larger: the fact, and the consequences, of disintegration are all too patent.

By many people who have not thought very deeply about the matter, the rise of modern liberalism is supposed to be intimately related to this disintegration, either as cause or consequence, or both. In particular, the role of Protestantism is often stressed in this connection; and since personal attitudes and value judgments are involved, a closer look at the transition is necessary.

To begin with, it was a much more gradual process than most histories make out; so gradual, in fact, that the more one studies it the more one feels one is studying not a particular event, nor even a particular movement, but an aspect of historical change itself. That is perhaps why it is tolerant of so many interpretations. Among these, two main types are of especial significance to the liberal tradition.

The first of these types is clearly indicated in Toynbee's statement that "a schism in the souls of human beings will be found at the heart of any schism that reveals itself on the surface of the society." [4] This is essentially the point of view of all idealist philosophers and historians (the adjective being taken here to indicate a simple antithesis to materialism) and it is the position to which liberalism naturally inclines. For liberalism of whatever type postulates a certain autonomy of the mental and spiritual life of man, and claims that developments may and do occur on that plane which act as efficient causes in human affairs. On this fundamental issue therefore Catholic historians—Acton, Dawson, Maritain, for example—are in agreement with those of other faiths, or of none. Dawson says bluntly: "the non-secular element in western culture has been the dynamic element in the whole process of change"; and speaking of the expansion of Western culture, he says "the fundamental causes of that process were spiritual and closely related to the whole spiritual development of western

4. Toynbee, A. J., A Study of History, V, 376.

man." [5] This is in striking concordance with the verdict of the Italian historian of liberalism, Ruggiero: "The revolt against an age-long religious tradition takes place not because of any need or impulse detached in some way from the personality of man, but from this personality itself. No yearning after external goods, but the love of that which is good in itself, drives the Protestants to their struggle against the Church and against her secular arm." [6]

The characteristic and all-too-familiar danger of the idealist approach lies of course in the overestimation of one set of values to a degree in which the full significance of the historical issue is lost. Among modern historians, J. B. Bury furnishes an outstanding example. Bury, true liberal though he was, really belongs to the school of nineteenth-century British rationalism. He could see nothing good in the Church, and little that was useful in any branch of what is now quaintly called "organized religion." To a chapter on the Middle Ages in one of his books he gives the title "Reason in Prison"; and of the adoption of Christianity by the Roman Empire he writes: "this momentous decision inaugurated a millennium in which reason was enchained, thought was enslaved, and knowledge made no progress." [7] Woe betide any undergraduate who submitted such a statement to the Regius professor! But Bury had a peculiar emotional persuasion of the truth of such a view; and the effect was both to curtail and to "date" the contribution of his great scholarship.

In lesser degree a somewhat similar qualification must apply to the work of a very recent Gifford lecturer. As a master—and exemplar—of radical Protestantism Reinhold Niebuhr has earned a unique position. The tireless erudition, and still more the profundity of insight embodied in his great work, render it a major event in the study of Western Protestant spirituality. But his insight, following his sympathy, stops short on the threshold of that against which Protestantism is supposed to be a protest; and we are struck by a curious inability, which seems almost a reluctance, to see the Church and its Christendom from the Church's point of view. Thus the corporate aspect of spiritual life is almost entirely absent from the perspective. Again, the full significance of the his-

5. Dawson, C., *The Judgment of the Nations*, p. 98.
6. Ruggiero, Guido de, *European Liberalism*, p. 14.
7. Bury, J. B., *History of Freedom of Thought*, p. 52.

torical struggle is dwarfed; and since Niebuhr is far too good a scholar to view the matter as a simple escape from bondage to liberty, a peculiarly difficult dilemma arises. It seems at times as if his sole solution lay in advancing from the priesthood of all believers to the principle of every man his own theologian—which in Cromwell's time led not so far as was hoped for.

The second type of interpretation is to most modern readers more familiar; it is that which emphasizes the interplay of secular impulse and material circumstance. In this view the expansion of trade, the rise of a money economy, the advance of science, and the discovery of the new world play the leading roles; to these and the derivative factors is ascribed the dominant influence in the development of the Protestant ethic. Contemporary materialism invokes the authority of Marx for this view in its extreme form; but as Tawney very justly observes,[8] Marx was a better sociologist than economist; and in his interpretation of history Marx was not a very good Marxist. He expressly denied that economic causes are the only ones, and expected them to become less and less important. Perhaps his modern exponents would consent to admit him as a "fellow traveler." The weight of his emphasis, however, as applied by Sombart, Weber, Tawney, and many others, has opened up a most valuable field of investigation; both our knowledge and our understanding have been immensely enriched—and the problem of historical interpretation given a fresh complexity.

Two major distinctions must be borne in mind in our approach to the mainsprings of the modern world. First is the distinction between the Renaissance and the Reformation which Niebuhr has recently developed with such fruitful care. Liberalism inherits far more from the former than it does from the latter. "The renaissance as a spiritual movement is best understood as a tremendous affirmation of the limitless possibilities of human existence, and as a rediscovery of the sense of a meaningful history." [9] To that impulse certainly belong the new interest in science and secular knowledge, the centrality of the individual, the growth of toleration, and the atmosphere of "this-worldliness" in which wealth—whatever might be its fate at the gates of heaven—was a prize that even the Church would not disdain on earth. Within that

8. Weber, M., *The Protestant Ethic*, Foreword, p. 4.
9. Niebuhr, R., *The Nature and Destiny of Man*, II, 160.

atmosphere the asceticism, the evangelistic poverty, of the Franciscan spirituals became ipso facto an offense to Rome; and Luther was the consequence.

To the Renaissance he contributed, as we shall see, only one thing, and that a very doubtful asset. With his great contemporaries, Copernicus and Machiavelli, he had little in common; and his spiritual forebears, Huss whom he commended, Wyclif who taught Huss, touch the Renaissance only accidentally. The accident lay in the use of printing. The printed Bible was—and in English was designed to be—a weapon against the Church. It was very effectively used, notwithstanding the rejoinder that since the Church had made the Bible there could lie no appeal against the living authority to the written letter. But since the Bible in the vernacular proved the greatest instrument of popular education the Western world had hit upon, in that respect the Protestant movement may be held to have furthered the Renaissance.

Niebuhr's comment, to which we shall presently revert, is that the flaw in Renaissance culture lay in its boundless optimism. From that characteristic sprang the idea of progress and the many types of secular utopianism that have colored all subsequent thought. Liberalism is deeply involved in this; for "the idea of progress is the underlying presupposition of what may be broadly defined as 'liberal' culture. If that assumption is challenged the whole structure of meaning in the liberal world is imperilled." [10] Yet who can deny today that it is challenged?

Niebuhr's favorite term for criticism, on the other hand, of the Reformation world outlook is an adjective derived, significantly enough, from the current war of ideologies: the term "defeatist." This brings us to the second of the distinctions mentioned above: the first was the basic distinction between Renaissance and Reformation; the second is the distinction between the original, and innate, impulses of Protestantism and their subsequent paradoxical development in the national Protestant societies.

§ 3

WHEN we think of the spiritual antecedents of Protestantism, we naturally recall the great revival of personal religion in the thir-

10. *Ibid.*, p. 240.

teenth century, and the trouble some of the Franciscans got into with their ecclesiastical superiors. But we cannot stop there. That was mainly a movement within, and radiating from, the orders; but in the twelfth century we find it among the people: among the poor men of Lyons, for example, and the women, and the lay Bible readers of northern France. And we are reminded of those Milanese "ragpickers" of yet a hundred years earlier, who stood up to the papal legates and made their case against the worldliness of the clergy and the corruption of the Church. Or we think of the homespun evangelism of Toulouse, Périgord, Languedoc, and Provence—some of it influenced, no doubt, by alien heresy, but most of it indigenous, with its farmer preachers and its tough antisacerdotal bent. Farther back still we could go: all the way back to those poor men of Galilee and their Master who remonstrated in vain with the ecclesiastics of His day. Or forward to His great disciple, Long Will of Langland, with his incomparable vision of the "fair field full of folk." And thinking of that, we recall the English mystics of the fourteenth century, who add their peculiar directness to the more famous work of the time; we catch a glimpse of the little people of London, apprentices and servingmen, tailors and smiths, bakers and wool dealers, secretly reading or hearing the Bible and other forbidden books. We remember the hedgerow preachers and their earnest auditors, we catch the echoes of the Lollard rhymes and the clatter of the mallets nailing up their libels, a hundred years before Luther, even on the doors of St. Paul's and the Abbey, in the name of "we, pore men, tresoreris of Cryst and His apostlis." History knows not how many, through all those centuries, gave up their humble lives for their simple truth.

The fact is, we are dealing here not with something sporadic and occasional but with something permanent in the life of society, something which is there all the time. For while we think of the social order as existing in historical time, changing its pattern, as a rule rather slowly, with the passing of the years, we must remember also that new life is flowing into it, and through it, every moment—intellectual and spiritual life as well as biological—in which respect, as Heraclitus saw, it probably resembles every other form that we perceive in the universe. This new life wells up from the mass of the people; and for the most part it assumes, naturally enough, the forms it itself has developed in the course of the generations, following the main lines of articulation of thought and conduct by a process which is more instinctive than reflective. But there is always a tension in the forms, always a certain stress in their perennial assumption; and while the great historians of culture, such as Spengler, Toynbee, Sorokin, trace out their major fluctuations, it is well for us to remember this quivering evanescence in the day-to-day life of society, and the factors on which normal stability depends.

For forms will be durable in proportion as they are true to the real *physis* of human nature; those which embody a more profound level of truth will persist while others change, and renew themselves if they are temporarily obscured. Thus certain religious forms have outlasted every other social type, and may in some degree be eternal. But we must not think of them too platonically, as existing *in vacuo*. Conscious intellect and curious experience affect the transmittal, so that both innovation and error may have more or less lasting effects. Truth is not a dead thing, not like a stone—even if the stone be a diamond: it is a living apprehension of reality, dwelling in the minds of living men; it can therefore be nurtured, and grow deeper, and it can be injured or neglected—with due consequences. The American stock market crash of 1929, for example, and the years of confusion that followed it, were directly related to the puerility of current American philosophy.

Historians of culture, especially Catholic ones, have shown how Christianity assimilated pagan forms and primitive faiths; we must now recognize that that process is not only a part of the past; it is going on all the time. For primitivism, with all its virtues and its limitations, is not merely a historical phenomenon; it is a normal element, a present condition of mind and culture, in every large society. It has its simple apprehensions of religious and political truth, which are not sharply distinguished—notions of the fatherhood of God and the brotherhood of man, an egalitarian sentiment arising straight out of the struggle to live, a tendency to search for a solution to the paradox of human destiny. And since it is never safe to assume the innate superiority of the upper classes, we shall find the primitive attitudes expressed, now and then, with power and originality among the unsophisticated. Innumerable sects have arisen in this way, and continue to arise: Universalism in the United States is a good example, or that indomitable society of bibliolaters calling themselves Jehovah's Witnesses. The leaders of such minor cults are usually people of passion and energy, and their powers of spiritual (and sometimes physical) healing are never quite illusory; for their followers have to support them without benefit of much organization. They range all the way from cranks and fanatics to the heights of a Joachim or a John the Baptist. But where a virile tradition is in existence, ubiquitous enough and sensitive enough, the greater part of this up-springing activity is colored by, and often assimilated by, the general system; so that even though complete unity neither can nor should obtain, tension does not reach the point of fragmentation. The fact is too frequently ignored that the power of the mediaeval papacy, though it could destroy monarchs, raise crusades, and move armies, was always a spiritual power, inasmuch as its ability to do these things rested on the widespread conviction of the mass of the folk that it stood for something valid, that its blessing and its cursing were well founded: without that wide consensus not all its organization could for long have produced results. The fact is patent in the contrast between the extent of papal authority over the lands of Henry IV or John of England and the remnant flung aside by Edward III. In the meantime, of course, many things had happened, including Wyclif and the Black Death.

But on this perennial primitivism other factors than that of a central tradition sometimes take hold. Its innate energy is apt to generate pathological foci when the life blood of the enveloping culture is thin or sluggish in its circulation. The rabble rouser is a phenomenon *an sich*, and never wholly absent. Oversentimental reformists are apt to assume that every *émeute* has its justification. That it has its causes no one would deny; but they are sometimes no better than an impulse to smash the furniture. The psychological adjustments demanded by marital or family life are trying, and result, as we all know, in occasional outbreaks of quite irrational action. The same thing happens in social life on a wider scale. It may be sheer boredom induced by the monotonous drudgery of labor with no end in sight; it may be a spell of bad weather or hard luck; it may be the irritation of a good system administered by stupid or arrogant men; it may be the strain of getting used to altered conditions, or the presence of strangers in the community —any one of a dozen accidental factors may foster an impulse to take it out on something or somebody; and there are always enough real grievances, enough real aspiration, and enough people with a personal itch and the "gift of the gab" to start something—if and when the integrative power of the central culture has grown weak. There is no doubt that this sort of motivation was strongly at work in the French *Jacquerie* of the fourteenth century, in John Ball and Wat Tyler, in the French Revolution and the Chartist movement. There can be little doubt that it underlies much of the labor and social unrest of the present day: the hair-trigger readiness to strike on trivial grounds, the race war in the United States, the latent violence that lies only just below the surface of that society—and all for the same reason: the decline of the integrative power of the central culture.

We may notice here a factor that will presently demand fuller examination. The humane toleration of varying opinions, with liberty to organize and propagate, solves one problem at the price of raising another. For insofar as the activity of a number of widely differing schools tends to weaken the central tradition, the more sects there are—political or religious—the more there are likely to be. The history of the Third French Republic illustrates this process rather vividly; and without attempting as yet any solution to the dilemma, we may remark that universal tolerance, by itself, is not the universal panacea it is popularly supposed to be.

Primitivism as we have described it constitutes the raw material for yet another kind of problem. The amount of sheer goodness in it, its latent energy and aspiration, make it the happy hunting ground of every kind of evangelism (or almost every kind: the pretentious effort of the so-called "Oxford Movement" to eschew it was as amusing as it was unsuccessful). Consequently there is no inherent limit to the eccentricity of the movements that may be fathered upon it when its grasp of the integrative culture is neither habitually nor intellectually strong. There was, for instance, in the early tenth century, a Slavic cult, coming originally from the Near East, that found its way across the Balkans, into north Italy and Central Europe, where it picked up a large number of doughty adherents. It had a corps of lay missionaries who taught that the world was evil and that the elect should avoid it. It denied the unique divinity of Christ and asserted that Christhood was the prerogative of every believer. It thus appealed to the native egalitarianism of Frank and Germanic lands, and it found a tangible and popular objective in the wealth of the clergy and the hierarchical organization of the Church. In that respect it became part of the growing agitation for reform; but unlike so much of that movement, it could not be absorbed or assimilated because its spirit was essentially hostile to the whole Catholic culture. Heresy is more a matter of intention than of doctrine; and this, by all accounts, was heresy. One is tempted to wonder whether the fate of those valiant Piedmont puritans—who clung so long like stepchildren to the skirts of Mother Church—might not have been less harsh, and their ultimate secession been avoided, but for the influence on them and on the hierarchy of this other group, with whom integration was radically impossible. Even an Innocent III must wonder, in that situation, how far he could safely go without letting the enemy into the citadel. As we now see, it was not the only time such a situation was to arise.

It was complicated, as such cases usually are, by the fact that both groups got mixed up in the play of power politics. So accustomed is the modern world to the complete separation of the temporal and spiritual powers that it can hardly envisage a different state of affairs. But that notion was slow in arising, and came as a novelty. And even after it had gained acceptance, with its famous metaphor of the two swords, the Church always had in reserve the superiority of the spiritual allegiance, so that it remained the right and the duty of the Vicar of Christ to admonish the temporal rulers. Nowadays the emphasis is all the other way, and modern potentates, in their broadcast praying, admonish the deity. But the separation of the two powers—"each divine in its origin, and each within its own sphere independent of the other" —was easier to define in theory than to work in practice; for there was the inevitable difficulty of getting agreement as to where one sphere ended and the other began. It was the undisputed duty of the Head of the Church to see that the work of the Church went on; and this involved, among other things, the maintenance of a vast organization with prelates and clergy possessed of extraterritorial rights and considerable economic privilege. Nor was the task, on the whole, simplified by the bishops, who, as territorial magnates, tended to be somewhat equivocal in the matter of allegiance. A tremendous amount of energy had to be devoted to keeping the emperors of Christendom on the rails; for those lords of the world, in their divinely grounded mission to make the Holy Roman Empire a going concern, fell foul not only of the ambitions of theoretically lesser magnates but of the interests of the papacy itself. In the rough-and-tumble of the early centuries the Popes had succeeded, by admirable skill and energy, in winning the homage of Normans and Lombards and other turbulent *arrivistes;* some of it they got as feudal overlords—feudalism being then the customary mode of human association. Thus the papacy found itself—not altogether by accident, nor altogether with regret—possessed of a very considerable stake in temporal affairs; just as the United States, in its disinterested endeavor to bring the four freedoms to every part of the world, finds itself possessed of an ever-widening chain of naval and air bases. There were people, then as now, who wished that the connection between the transcendental end and the temporal means could be a little more obvious. It is really striking to find, at the time of the tremendous victory of the papacy over the obstreperous Henry IV, writers—Catholic writers—who accused the Supreme Pontiff, the great Gregory himself, of bringing more strife into the world! With what unspeakable relief did the Church at last, on February 11, 1929, "viewing things from the standpoint of the blessed St. Francis," bid good-by to all claims of temporal dominion, renounce all offers of secular guarantees, and thus attain, after a thousand years of travail, the final liberation! [11]

We may so far disagree with that eminent historian, Mr. H. G. Wells, as to suggest that in the meantime its involvement in temporal affairs was, from the standpoint of the Church's mission, a necessity—subject as such to the ultimate destiny and interim tribulations of all such affairs. The manner of dealing with the nascent impulse toward Church reform, and the primitive piety that lay behind it, was inextricably involved therein. The Roman *patarini* of the twelfth century, for instance—who were probably heretical anyway—were being used by able people in their play against the temporal position of the papacy; and more important still, they became the focus of the really critical issue of the time, the demand for municipal autonomy. That gave them a positive position to rally about, such as, later on, territorial solidarity provided for Protestantism in general. And the clue to the success of

11. Speech of Pius XI to the Roman clergy, quoted in Williamson, B., *The Treaty of the Lateran,* pp. 34–38.

the radical cause is that, as the issue approached its climax, the authority of the Church had come to seem, in the minds of ordinary men, abstract, external, and arbitrary, in contrast to the claims of what was concrete, personal, and obvious. The papal schism at the end of the fourteenth century, when at one stage there were no less than four rival popes, was no very spiritual matter; and it is noteworthy that in the Council that settled it the compromise was argued on national lines—six bishops apiece brought in from England, France, Germany, Italy, Spain, to establish an early balance of power. The thing occurred at a critical time; for at that very moment the English, led (as they like to think) by Shakespeare's Henry V, were laying about them on the soil of France—only to run into the inexplicable opposition of a girl called Joan.

The significance of Joan's beatification, nearly five hundred years after they burned her vigorous young body, was rather lost on the English. Coming from Rome, it was, in a way, the *amende honorable*. She was now in bliss—though whether it was the faggots of the English, the prayers of the faithful, or the politics of the Action Française that had got her there is perhaps a moot point. Her voices, after all, had not been those of devils: in other words, the power of national sentiment now received, at last, the Church's blessing—which, it might be hoped in 1909, would turn out to be also a sanctification.

That was a handsome concession; for it was that power, far more than the heretical notions of a recusant German monk or an arrogant French lawyer, that had broken the temporal, and finally the spiritual, *imperium*. Those men were its instruments, not its progenitors. Luther was one of those many German souls in whom the mixture of much study and violent passion has produced not a synthesis but an explosion; but the explosion was merely that of a detonator. It was perhaps inevitable, as the new solidarities of city, estate, and finally nation cohered and intensified, that the claim of a supertemporal, extraterritorial allegiance should seem thin and extrinsic: had there been no Luther it would have been necessary to invent him. Henry VIII, seeking to consolidate his realm and satisfy his lust short of open apostasy, delivered himself and his subjects into worse hands than those of any honest heretic—the filthy hands of Thomas Cromwell, disciple of Machiavelli, whose stain four centuries have not been able to efface. It

is impossible not to see, in the breakup of the European comity—
turbulent as that had been—the introduction of a strain of sheer
brutality into affairs of state that was in time to make its full contribution to the glory of the British Empire.

§ 4

WESTERN historians, finding constant traces of the inherent Pe-
lagianism of the British, have strained their necks to see in the
Protestant movement a concern for individual liberty which is not
there. It was no part of Luther's intention, nor of Calvin's either,
that the doctrine of the autonomy of the individual conscience
should be construed, first in act and then in theory, to imply the
autonomy of the individual citizen; the note of desperation is
plain in their protests. The assertion of a divine institution of temporal authority, both general and specific, not merely survived but
was immensely strengthened by Luther and his immediate followers. If Luther "destroyed in fact the metaphor of the two
swords," [12] the one with which he equipped his "godly prince"
was double edged; and it was that fact alone which commended
it to the English Henry.

There is an inherent affinity between nationalism and absolutism. The tribal consciousness, which manifests its extremes of
good and evil in the former, tends to assert itself against all comers
in the latter; for consciousness of kind is really consciousness of
difference. The outstanding fact for Henry and his England was
that the pope was a foreigner. When the king transferred his suit
from the pope to Parliament, he was bringing it from an alien
to an English jurisdiction. The religious issue as such played a
very small part in the whole affair: that was to come later. The internationalism of the Church seemed by now to be almost wholly
political; and its spiritual authority, which neither the king nor
his subjects were at all eager to contest, was too weak to counteract the English swarming. When at last his majesty saw fit to endow the Church in England with his royal supremacy, his sole intention, as the preceding acts bear witness, was to make himself
master in his own house. Of course there were some very pretty
perquisites.

12. Figgis, J. N., *Divine Right of Kings*, p. 84.

To Cranmer and other German-trained ecclesiastics fell the task of refashioning the religion of England to fit the occasion; but however truly and earnestly they labored, and to whatever heights of spirituality their work might lead, certain peculiarities lay in the very nature of the task. They found themselves, at the outset, compelled to go farther than ever Luther would have gone; for Luther remained enough of a Catholic to see that the idea of a national church involves a contradiction in terms. They sought to keep the faith, but they could not keep the catholicity. Even so detached a critic as Niebuhr recognizes that "the Catholic version of the Christian faith is at least a bulwark against the idolatry of political and national absolutisms." [13] The Reformation writers, arguing against Rome and the Counter Reformation, were compelled to elevate earthly authority to a position from which there is no appeal; and leaders of the nation-states could now ignore the principle—for which Rome, at its best and worst, had stood —that a man may not be judge in his own cause: not even though he have a crown on his head or a ballot box to sit on, and all the science in the world for his scepter. The point has been made by Hilaire Belloc in a passage that deserves quoting *in extenso;* for when Belloc with his battleax hits a nail on the head, he drives it home. He is speaking of the coronation of Edward VI, by Cranmer, on February 20, 1547:

For the first time men had heard in England—loudly proclaimed—and in the seat of the English Kings, in Westminster Abbey—that strange new doctrine which was to be of such prodigious effect throughout the world, the Divine Right of Kings: the new Protestant doctrine, fruitful of many things. The doctrine fully born that day (it had been maturing ever since the beginning of the great revolt against Christian unity—ever since the leaders of change had pitted, each in his own State, the Prince against the universal Church) has never died. Though the word "King" be no longer used, though the word "Divine" has fallen out of fashion, the strength of the *thing* is as vigorous as ever. The lay state is sovereign; it has full power over the bodies and souls of Christian men; it admits no superior authority to represent the universality of Christendom or the Christian moral law; it stands equal and independent with other states, its like, round about it. The Christian Commonwealth of which each Christian state had been but a province and

13. Niebuhr, *op. cit.,* II, 241.

a part is wholly denied: for the Divine right had passed from the religion by which Europe once lived to governments which are but the heirs of the Kings. That Divine Right still rules. And against it the citizen has today no power at all.[14]

14. Belloc, H., *Cranmer*, pp. 239–240.

V

The Secular State

1. The hardening of the arteries. — 2. The Church of England. — 3. The Calvinist revolution. — 4. The triumph of money. — 5. The triumph of tolerance.

§ 1

THE process which culminated in the World Wars of the twentieth century may in one sense be regarded as an emancipation. Its basic characteristic was the revolt of ever-increasing numbers of men, in an ever-widening field, against the principle of external authority. Following the crisis in religion of the sixteenth century, the movement spread to politics in the seventeenth and economics in the eighteenth. It was not at first an affair of individuals but of groups, corporations, and estates —including those "great estates" that came to be called nations. But in the nineteenth century it came increasingly to permeate individual life in all three spheres; and with the triumph of "individualism" it became evident that the outward wave had reached its limits. It could go no farther. A confused backwash set in, with the emancipated individuals clashing against the emancipated states, and the emancipated groups and states clashing violently with one another. Significantly, politicians began to talk in "global" terms, with a cramping apprehension at the back of their minds that the planet was too small. Unfortunately, the moon is a dead world, traditionally associated with lunacy.

All this, we say, may in one sense be regarded as an emancipation—comparable to the growing up of children, as they emerge from the restraints of parental control (the idea will mean little to American parents, but still has relevance elsewhere) and become legally and socially autonomous. And it was natural that the movement should all along show itself first among city dwellers, who are mostly merchants, traders, and in general men of money. Just as money—genuine money—is the socializer of goods, so printing is the socializer of thought; and the two were necessarily related. Cities are the cells in which what has been called the cross-fertilization of cultures normally takes place; and though most hybrids are recessive or sterile, that does not affect the structure.

It was natural enough, therefore, that from earliest times the merchants and the men of money should act as the foci of the centrifugal impulse, while the country people acted, on the whole, the other way: which does not in the least mean that the city people were impelled merely by a self-interested materialism. It was they, times without number, who backed the adventurers in ideas as stoutly as they backed the merchant adventurers, and paid the price—often with their lives—of opposing an authority which, in its centripetal impulse, tended to seek its allies in the countryside.

But the dominance of the city is always dangerous; for its language, more abstract and purely rational than that of the land, has no words for the profound instincts of caution and continuity bred in the world of growing things; and its derivative activities constitute a sphere in which money, from being a good servant, easily becomes a bad master. The sixteenth-century looting of the Church, we must remember, was promptly followed by a ruthless enclosing of the common lands, often by the beneficiaries; and the fact that some good came of it does not compel us to agree that the market for wool was a better criterion of policy than the fate of a few thousand illiterate cottagers. "The growth of a money economy" is sometimes the polite historian's synonym for the spread of avarice; and the resources of the state for coping with it had, after all, been fatally impaired.

Not so much by the break itself perhaps, as by that of which the break was so largely a symptom. We must not press our growing-up analogy so far as to make the whole development seem involuntary, inevitable, and therefore—such is our prejudice —beneficent. That was the superstition which marred so much of nineteenth-century liberalism. For if the liberal likes—as he does —to preen himself on the triumphs of human intelligence and virtue, he must admit no less frankly the operation, and the cost, of human stupidity and vice. So only will he attain a realistic and robust philosophy which does justice both to the stature and the awful responsibility of man. If—to resume our analogy—the children as they become autonomous become also anarchical, caring only for themselves and not at all for one another or the community that nurtured them, we do not put all the blame upon the children. The Catholic system from which the Protestant economy broke loose in the sixteenth century had already lost much of its hold on the minds and hearts of men. It had come to rely on coercion rather than conversion, and to care more for its rights and revenues than the winning of souls. The iconoclasts for all their barbarism had struck a blow at superstition that should have been dealt before by cleaner hands; and when at last new blood began the great reform of the Church's mind and body, England was far away. Elizabeth could never look back. And when the pope proceeded not only to excommunicate but to depose her, and not only to depose her but to dispatch a foreign army against her, it was the voice of England that answered him. Thus the Virgin Queen supplanted the Blessed Virgin, and new litanies were sung to Gloriana.

But Elizabeth—partly because she was a woman, partly because she was a political genius—was quick to disclaim all spiritual authority for her official position, thereby easing the situation at the price of a new problem. For the principle of one realm, one religion, was generally accepted, despite the fact that both were now on a local basis. Men were still inclined to think that the "law behind the law" having one supreme source should have one supreme interpretation. But if the "Supreme Governor" of the Church relinquished all spiritual authority while retaining all power of appointment, what became of the old principle of the superiority of the spiritual allegiance? History knows the answer, but Hooker did not. The whole question of the relation between temporal and spiritual authority was reopened; and it has not since been settled. The continuous warfare of the secular states, with its fearful crescendo of mental, moral, and physical destruction, compels all thoughtful persons to wonder what are the limits, if any, on the exercise of temporal power; to what principles, if any, it should be subject; and how those principles are to be known. "Nought shall make us rue. If England to itself do rest but true," sang Shakespeare's Harry: a noble and popular sentiment—but was "itself" all that England was now required to be true to? Hooker answered in effect that it was. Church and state were not two separate societies, they were two aspects of one and the same; and the sameness, when one got right down to it, was not that of

Catholic truth but that of Englishmen—an idea that Mr. Middleton Murry has recently revived.[1]

§ 2

THE Church in England—the Anglican Church, as we may now call it—inherited a field that was largely fallow; but it also inherited a rich tradition of native piety. While the sixteenth-century settlement was getting under way, it was perhaps a good rule that everyone should be required to attend service. Most people went quite willingly. They liked singing the psalms in English rhyme—it was a very musical age: many of the psalters had the four-voice parts, and there would often be a few strings and wood winds in the back gallery. Nor were they as impatient of homilies and sermons as are modern newspaper readers. What Cranmer had done for English prose in that service was to be equaled only by the genius of the English Bible, in which Shakespeare himself may have taken a hand. As the difficult years passed into decades, and the decades into its first century, the Church of England, with its modest ritual and its unexacting doctrine, came to embody something as deeply English as the smell of the tide at Gravesend or the Crowhurst woods in April. The establishment, with all its subventions and endowments, gave to the life of England a not inadequate return. It brought to the countryside that unique institution, the village parson—and with him, take it all in all, the best of what English learning and gentility could provide. Little in the way of economic privilege or social status was ever the lot of these yeomen of the Kingdom. Many had entered the holy estate of matrimony under Edward, and paid more than the usual price for it under Mary. While there may be two opinions about the celibacy of the clergy, none can dispute the observation of Trevelyan that "a fine race of children were reared in the parsonages of England, for generations to come, filling all the professions and services with good men and true, and most of all the Church herself." [2] With all her limitations and her failures, the Anglican Church, looking back over these three centuries and considering the English temperament, may fairly claim that no

1. See Murry, J. M., *The Price of Leadership;* and comment by T. S. Eliot in *The Idea of a Christian Society.*
2. Trevelyan, G., *English Social History,* p. 176.

other communion could have done as much. If, as T. S. Eliot contends, "we have today a culture which is mainly negative, but which, so far as it is positive, is still Christian," the Church of England, for England, deserves most of the credit. In the sphere of authority her scholars could put up a case for as much apostolic succession as had the Bishop of Rome; but the historical argument is perhaps less cogent than the living witness. If the one communion has to admit the century ending about 1850, its senior cannot forget a similar spell three hundred years earlier. And if the younger may truly claim to stem from the old trunk, it will recall how trees similarly cleft remember in the crown their common footing.

But the limits on the spiritual power of a national Church were not slow in appearing. It was not merely because Archbishop Laud had taken the royal office too seriously that Charles I could not save him from the scaffold: he had taken his own office more seriously than men were now willing to permit. It is not within the competence of a state Church to be no respecter of persons; and though perhaps Wingfield-Stratford is too harsh in deciding that Laud's failure "involved the failure of the Church to stand for any intelligible religious principle," [3] the lesson of 1644 was never forgotten. There is exaggeration, but also bitter truth, in a recent comment of J. M. Murry: "The Church knows its place, which is that of a good wife to the state. Like a good wife, it never advises and never criticizes, and when there is a row it stands up for its husband." Much more to the same effect (one wonders just what effect) was said at the famous Malvern conference of January, 1941. All too well founded was the charge of Dorothy Sayers that the preoccupation of the official moralists with private and personal peccadilloes was a cheap and easy evasion of the more dangerous assault on avarice and corruption in public life. Seldom has an archbishop listened to harsher words than those of Sir Richard Acland: "For over a hundred and fifty years you have neglected your duty . . . because of sheer funk. The whole structure of society is, from the Christian point of view, rotten and must permanently frustrate your efforts to create for the individual the possibility of a Christian life. This has given Hitler the opportunity for saying 'To hell with the whole order.' . . . He said this, and from despairing humanity he wrung forth a tremendous

3. Wingfield-Stratford, E., *History of British Civilization*, p. 497.

and dynamic response. . . . You must be prepared to offend people who are determined to preserve the existing order."

But how far can a state Church afford to go in that direction? Laud's impeachment was the work of Parliament; and thereafter it was Parliament that had the final voice in determining the religious life of England. Churchmen had a sharp reminder of this when in 1927–28 the House of Commons vetoed the adoption of a revised service book agreed upon, after most searching debate, by both Convocation and the Church Assembly. The issue was sharpened by the fact that it was the votes of men some of whom professed no religion at all while others were actively hostile to all religion that decided the matter. Thereafter churchmen high and low—or to avoid ambiguity should one say lofty and humble—were compelled to ask themselves whether state patronage was not in fact, as many critics had maintained for generations, a comfortable prison? And what the conservative argument amounted to was that, even so, any establishment was better than none—a point on which practically all Americans would differ: which proves nothing, but suggests a good deal.

Just what was supposed to be the true relation between temporal and spiritual authority was not clear until after the doctrine of divine right had done its work. Indeed, it is not clear now; but that doctrine had a work to do. It was, as everyone knows, a Protestant doctrine; what is not generally recognized is that it had to defend society against a Protestant enemy.

Both Luther and Calvin had enjoined passive obedience to temporal rulers, including bad ones. They had been very emphatic about it. But the Calvinists promptly limited its application to rulers they approved of, and fought with rigor and vigor against Catholic courts in Europe and Scotland, and the Episcopal settlement in England. They would recognize no divine right in the Stuart monarchy, and they seized their opening in the struggles of the Scots versus the French, the English Parliament versus the king, and the American colonists versus London.

§ 3

THE system established by Calvin and his disciples was not, properly speaking, part of the Reformation; it was a revolution, as radical and as potent as the subsequent revolutions in France,

Russia, and Nazi Germany—with which it was not unconnected. While it utilized certain concepts of Catholic theology, and leaned for the letter of its law on the Bible—more especially on the non-Christian elements—it placed all its emphasis on tenets which the Church admitted only under the most stringent reservations, and thus fashioned a system that denied the cardinal basis of the Church itself. Luther neither did nor intended anything of the sort. The Calvinists preached and practiced a radically new religion—if religion is the name for it.

That is open to question. Religions grow, but this was invented; and if the essence of religion is the offering of a way of salvation, this one started from the assertion that there was none. Says the Westminster Confession of 1647: "By the decree of God, for the manifestation of His glory, some men and angels are predestinated unto everlasting life, and others foreordained to everlasting death. All those whom God hath predestinated into life, and those only, He is pleased in His appointed and accepted time effectually to call . . . the rest of mankind God was pleased, according to the unsearchable counsel of His own will . . . to pass by, and to ordain them to dishonour and wrath for their sin." And there was nothing they or anyone else—least of all the Church—could do about it. "There was no place for the very human Catholic cycle of sin, repentance, atonement, release, followed by renewed sin. Nor was there any balance of merit for a life as a whole which could be adjusted by temporal punishments or the Church's means of grace." [4]

Such conceptions of the nature and destiny of man were potent to stiffen the tempers of the revolutionaries—just as those of Marx and the Nazi doctrinaires were to be three centuries later. In all three systems the notion of an elect plays a cardinal role, both theoretical and practical. What is still more important is that membership in this elect has nothing to do with any existing or historical distinctions of rank, privilege, or function; nor can it be affected by any criteria or any policies originating outside its private organization—though the organization aspires to pass judgment (and execution) on all the rest of society. The believer is placed in an impregnable security: he has the truth, by faith and scripture; and it is a higher truth, whose service imposes a peculiar discipline and in return confers a peculiar emancipation.

4. Weber, M., *The Protestant Ethic*, p. 117.

The psychological gratification thus offered is immense; it constitutes the magnetic element in the evangelism of all closed systems; and it manifests itself by necessity in the sphere of ethics. For that is the sphere in which the profession of a restrictive (by definition, superior) code can most promptly confirm the self-evaluation of the individual. Thus the one element of human nature that the puritan—whatever else he might do about it—could never afford to forget was sex; because that was the commonest means for creating within himself the requisite state of tension, which he could then discharge (not sublimate) on the rest of society, and so attain that intoxication of the ego which so easily passes for the sense of sanctity. It was this psychological appeal of Calvinism, opposing and replacing the type of catharsis offered by Catholic religion, that made it popular. Its aristocratic and profoundly intellectual basis was dissolved, as the masses got hold of it, in an upsurge of primitivistic bibliolatry which countered the Counter Reformation with a new ultramontanism of the underprivileged. And between the two the English commonwealth was all but torn to pieces.

In that juncture the doctrine of the divine right of kings had, as we said, a work to do. Not only were the temporal interests of the papacy opposing the crown of England; not only were the scholars of the Counter Reformation pressing the traditional opposition of the Church to secular absolutism; but on the other flank a more dangerous enemy had arisen. Presbyterian democracy, based on the unprovable (but perennial) assumption that the electors would elect the elect, claimed the censorship not only of policy but of morals—a sphere which the elders defined; and their doctrine, opposing the establishment "root and branch," asserted the duty of the state to punish sin (papists were sinners ipso facto). Disfranchisement—as in Massachusetts—was to be added to excommunication. How near Britain came to it is evident in the wording of the ordinance imposing the discipline on England in 1648.[5] That was the year before the regicide; and Charles, facing a court whose jurisdiction he rightly denied, reflected from what it was he had sought—in vain, as it then seemed —to save the realm. The charges against the king were secular charges; but the issue—as he knew and maintained—was a spiritual issue. There was much truth in the saying that Jesuit and Cal-

5. See Figgis, J. N., *Divine Right of Kings*, p. 335.

vinist were two names for the same thing; for if the one system threatened to split the realm on the rock of Peter, the other would hack it to pieces with the sword of the spirit—which could now sever the necks of children as well as kings without remorse. Moreover, there was that to be said for the one system that could not be claimed for the other. "The Papacy, whatever might be said against it, was at least a standing witness to the need of international morality, and might be supposed to have the advantage of viewing political problems from a universal standpoint. . . . No such defence could be made for the Presbyterian system. It would have controlled the action of the state more completely than did the Papacy, while it would have strengthened instead of diminishing all the tendencies that made for a narrow patriotism, and that would lead men to regard local and provincial feeling as all-important." [6] That judgment of a great Anglican scholar, penned fifty years ago, was to be tragically confirmed when fate permitted a small-town Presbyterian from the southern United States to refashion the polity of Europe.

Ruggiero, who is far more friendly to the Calvinist tradition than other liberal historians, rightly emphasizes its role as "an education of the will and the character. It worked for conscientiousness and rectitude. It gave a systematic direction to the development of the individual's activities. As such, it was an immense expansive power in the modern world." [7] It certainly was. The doctrine of predestination provided a plausible pretext, when occasion demanded, for forgetting about the other world and concentrating on this; and to say so is not to impugn the good faith of the devotees. The pamphleteer of 1671 was no doubt quite sincere when he said: "There is a kind of natural unaptness in the Popish religion to business, whereas on the contrary among the Reformed, the greater their zeal, the greater their inclination to trade and industry, as holding idleness unlawful. . . . The domestic interest of England lieth in the advancement of trade by removing all obstructions both in city and country, and providing such laws as may help it, and make it most easy, especially in giving liberty of conscience to all Protestant Non-conformists, and denying it to Papists." [8]

6. *Ibid.*, pp. 187–188.
7. Ruggiero, Guido de, *History of European Liberalism*, p. 15.
8. Quoted in Tawney, R. H., *Religion and the Rise of Capitalism*, p. 180.

France, Spain, and Portugal might have been cited to show that Catholic states were no more indifferent than Protestant ones to the trading opportunities of the age of discovery; it was by the war against the Dutch that England was most frankly committed to a purely commercial basis of foreign policy. Commercial wars have certain advantages over dynastic or religious ones, in that they can be carried on more effectively in peacetime, and offer more tangible prizes. They entail, however, acceptance of the rule that the gain of one group is the loss of another—though no true patriot, of course, ever lost any sleep over that. The policy of aiming at a "favorable" balance of trade by keeping imports below exports is part of the same pattern: it becomes absurd unless each nation is considered, and considers itself, in isolation. To that frame of mind both the energy of the Calvinists and their propensity to think of themselves as a chosen people contributed handsomely.

§ 4

But the national states, with Britain in the lead, were now entering upon the truly modern period; which is characterized not so much by the use of physical force in collective competition as by the instrument of large-scale political debt; for without the latter the former could never have attained its current magnitude.

The wise restraint of English foreign policy under Elizabeth was not unconnected with the shortage of ready money. The trick of inflation, to which Henry VIII had resorted, can seldom be worked twice on the same generation; and Elizabeth had to clean up the mess. Thenceforward, as everyone knows, the provision of ways and means proved a valuable instrument for bringing the executive under control. In the course of the struggle to escape it, Charles I won a victory for absolutism that is still of some interest. He needed ships, and for a quite laudable purpose. In his effort to raise the wind he strained the executive power to a degree which eventually called for special measures of correction; but he was enabled for the time being to "get away with it" by an opinion of the judges—whom of course he appointed—that His Majesty was the "sole judge" of the question whether the realm was in danger. Even so, however, he had to demand cash on the barrel. Stuart credit was never good; and Charles II's repudiation of his debts came, at a critical time, as a reminder that financing monarchs was always a risky business.

It was, nonetheless, an old and well-established business—ever since trading for money created large accumulations in private hands. Christians as well as Jews went in for it when they got the chance; and the expulsion of the Jews from England in 1252 was forced on a reluctant king more by the jealousy of their rivals than by any other factor. For the Jews, confined by the laws of Christendom to city life, had on the whole sharper wits and more ready money; and they could enter into the usury contract with Gentiles when Christians could not.

What constitutes usury is the stipulation for the *unconditional* payment of interest on an unproductive loan; strictly speaking, it has nothing to do with the rate. The usury laws of several American states which proceed, as English law did up to 1854, by prohibiting or penalizing interest rates above certain legal maxima, are based on the assumption that higher rates are ipso facto extortionate, which does not always hold good. The idea behind them, however, is fundamentally the same as that which underlies the Catholic objection to usury. That objection is based theoretically on the Aristotelian tenet that money is barren, practically on the fact that a usurious contract places the claims of capital ahead of those of humanity. That is what evokes the curses of farmers on moneylenders to this day, from the American Midwest to Egypt and India. The problem of how to treat the defaulting debtor antedates even the laws of Solon.

There is solid substance in the Catholic contention that the Church's prohibition of usury, to use a Keynesian phrase, forced savings into investment. The would-be lender was compelled to share the risks, by some form of partnership or sale, as well as the profits—which could be very large. But by the sixteenth century Church authorities themselves were beginning to liberalize the traditional doctrine; and Calvin, in recognizing the usury contract, went only a little beyond current theory (beyond current practice he hardly went at all). But in the sequel there were attendant circumstances. For reasons which had to do rather with geography than with religion, there was more money in the Protestant states. Englishmen were making piles, not only in maritime adventure but out of the loot of the Church and the enclosure of the commons. Henry VIII saw the advantage of the Protestant position; and Cromwell reaped the benefit. What was a good risk had by now become the paramount question among those who were to supply the sinews of empire. The Fuggers had taken their licking on the Holy Roman Emperor. The probity of the puritans was proverbial. The Amsterdam money market opened its arms to the Lord Protector; and the Jews were readmitted to England.

From that day on the triumph of parliamentary government was assured. For in pledging the revenues of the realm as security for a loan, the advantages of a government of laws and not of men shone with refulgent glory. Men die; but parliaments do not—not if they can help it. What doomed the Jacobites after the Restoration was that they were a bad financial risk. What ensured the success of the Whigs was that a system of parliamentary rule offered better security.

Representative government has never succeeded—has never perhaps been very eager to succeed—in establishing responsible control over the borrowing power. It has been altogether too easy, and too tempting, for large deliberative assemblies to initiate, or endorse, large and popular programs, while leaving to small and secretive groups of officials and moneylenders the sordid business of finding the ways and means. Modern governments have gone ahead recklessly mortgaging the future earnings of their subjects in an endless series of transactions to which neither contemporaries nor historians have paid anything like adequate attention. Indeed, most of these transactions—like the Franco-Russian loans that paved the way for the first World War, or the deals that overthrew the British Government in 1931—have been deliberately enveloped in an air of mystery, as if there were something sacrosanct about them: as indeed, to the participants, there certainly was. The old principle of legitimacy was on its last legs in 1815; a new one had taken charge of international affairs. The question whether a government would acknowledge the debts of its predecessor, whatever the circumstances, and whether its signature would be good for a normal term of amortization has played, and is playing, a role in the shaping of international relations, not only in Europe, but in North Africa, South America, India, and China, of which the general public and its popular mentors have simply no idea. Compared to the powers that operate in that sphere, any popular assembly is like a youngster who has just got into long trousers and imagines he is a man about town.

Within two generations of Oliver Cromwell's death Englishmen were going crazy over the wildest stock market in history. Money was king, and it ruled without a constitution; a substantial slice of its domain lay in the profits of the slave trade, which in 1713 Bolingbroke took particular pains to ensure. The proletarian movement that had raised its loquacious head to bother the Lord Protector was safely silenced. Radical puritanism, with its deep piety and earnest probity that had always distrusted speculative capital, was reduced to the mere negations of "dissent" and "nonconformity." Marlborough, with the aid of a great deal of money as well as of genius, had restored British prestige abroad; and money was a major factor in the election of legislators and the tenure of ministers at home. The Protestant succession was solidly founded on the Bank of England. And Walpole—who had made a fortune on the South Sea Bubble, but was lucky enough to be out of office when he did it—now had the support of the people who really mattered in putting the ship of state on a solid business basis. "The balance of trade became as great a fetish as the balance of power, and demanded from its votaries as many sacrifices and as much blood." [9] To the men of the eighteenth century, it was worth what it cost. The cost was not great—at the time; cannon fodder was cheap, and foreign policy was almost as much a matter of subsidies as of armies. The gains were tremendous.

It is nonsense to say that Britain acquired the empire in a fit of absent-mindedness. The trading companies that laid its foundations; the investors who backed them; the politicians who helped to eliminate their rivals; the statesmen who decided when public war should succeed to private; the contractors who equipped the ships and the armies; the bankers who advanced the money; the diplomats who closed the deals—all these people knew quite well what they were doing and why they were doing it. If the eighteenth century is to be considered an age of rationalism, these were the true rationalists.

A lot of the proceeds, we must remember, went into the land; and as the enclosure of the fields followed on the enclosure of the commons, the returns on that investment were included among the proper criteria of policy. Thus the life of the countryside as well as the town was brought within the unity of the chrematistic states; and hungry peasants, as they trudged for hire, could enjoy the sight

9. *Cambridge Modern History*, VI, 50 (Temperley).

of the sheep on the hillside (before cotton killed them off) or the beauty of the parks (from over the wall) and reflect how much nicer the air was than in the coal mines or the busy factories. But perhaps the most significant thing about the eighteenth century is that it ended in revolution: a somewhat surprising climax to the "age of enlightenment."

§ 5

THE eighteenth century, so much beloved of modern rationalists, saw the development of two strains of policy that are at first sight hard to reconcile—though some of its admirers have managed to embrace both. Between the national states it let loose a naked struggle for power that finally dispelled the dream of community; while within some of them, particularly Prussia and England, it witnessed the development of toleration as part of the process of secular integration.

Toleration, of course, always has limits according to the gravity of the issues involved. If, for instance, all that the American colonists wanted was to work out their spiritual salvation, the English were glad enough to let them try; but business was a serious matter. Yet with all proper respect to the famous literary landmarks from Milton to Mill, the rise of English civil liberties probably owes as much to the expansion of business as it does to philosophical or political theory. In active economic life creedal and confessional distinctions are a nuisance; and after the Restoration no one was looking for trouble in that quarter. The press licensing law had lapsed before 1700, and the reign of the Whigs which began soon afterward, if not entirely liberal, was decidedly latitudinarian in temper. A fairly strict heresy law had indeed been passed as recently as 1698; but once the Tories were ousted the occasions on which it was used suggest that someone was deliberately raising an issue or hounding a victim. As the century went on the requirements of Anglican conformity were more and more easily satisfied, and the legal disabilities of nonconformists were relaxed in practice long before they were abolished in theory. The Corporation of London had a way of mulcting rich dissenters elected to office, and got a Mansion House for the mayor out of the proceeds; but it would hardly be correct to regard this grimly humorous procedure as religious persecution in the French sense. England had ceased witch burning quite early in the century; and the continued animus against Roman Catholics arose from the fact that they insisted on taking religion more seriously than the age had a mind to, and kept mixing it up with both domestic and foreign politics.

Toleration, which was hardly even an ideal at the Restoration, permeated the public mind during the three following generations; it was that fact which changed the attitude of public law; it was through that process that the joint work of the French and English liberals came at last to fruition. Very seldom does liberal thought attain an immediate result in policy; indeed its nature is such that it not only must work, but aims to work, through the general intelligence. It was the signal merit of Voltaire that he understood this so clearly: more clearly by far than Milton. The Platonic and Calvinistic streak in Milton held him back. Every student knows the famous challenge of *Areopagitica:* "Let truth and falsehood grapple; who ever knew truth put to the worse, in a free and open encounter?" But Milton was young when he wrote that; he was not so sure by 1660. The current of English life had passed him by, and left him bitter. Yet his own college, in times even more desperate than his, has recently demonstrated in the person of its Master the vitality of the tree he planted.[10]

As usual, however, it was in France rather than in England that the ultimate logic of tolerance was worked out. Tolerance came so easy, on the whole, to the English eighteenth century that the legatees have much too casually taken it for granted. In France that was not possible. Persecution, both ultramontane and Jansenist, continued through most of the period, and the attack on Christianity developed a cutting edge that even Gibbon shrank from. English thought more easily avoided extremes because there were so few extremes left to avoid. English deism disposed of the more troublesome aspects of the faith by arguing that after all Christianity was nothing but reason and common sense, that revelation and the supernatural were either incomprehensible or superfluous, or both; and as prosperity increased, few people cared very much. But in France things were different, and keen spirits

10. The present Master of Christ's College, elected in 1939, is the Reverend C. E. Raven, one of the outstanding exponents of the Christian opposition to war. His election, of course, does not commit the Fellows to his political position, but furnishes a suggestive contrast to the attitude of most American colleges. Milton is supposed to have planted the famous mulberry tree in the Fellows' garden.

cared a great deal. In Prussia Frederick the Great could reap the benefits of a consistent skepticism which both the English and the French, for quite different reasons, balked at; the French use skepticism as a weapon, but seldom as a philosophy.

England had caught a glimpse of the real issue in the debates of Cromwell's army: and did not like the look of it. "When I do hear men speak," said Colonel Ireton, "of laying aside all engagements to consider only that wild or vast notion of what in every man's conception is just or unjust, I am afraid and do tremble at the boundless and endless consequences of it. . . . If you do paramount to all constitutions hold up this law of nature, I would fain have any man show me where you will end." [11] Ireton had good reason to be afraid; for what he understood by "law of nature" was the Protestant theory of private inspiration; and as the history of the sects has demonstrated, anarchy is the mildest of the probable consequences. But the English, having glanced at the issue, wisely turned away from it. With an amazingly sure instinct they quietly lopped off all extremes that would distract them from their destined creation of national community; and in the end achieved a spirit so strong, and so impalpable, as to reconquer in the twentieth century the ruling class of America. The French faced the issue, and fought it out: to their cost.

So long as governments were expected, or allowed, to prescribe the religion of their subjects, it was inevitable that the agencies of religion—of which Rome was by no means the only one—should strive for the control of governments. Calvinism and ultramontanism must therefore always be viewed in relation to the growing absolutism of the period, which they supported when they could control it and attacked when they could not. In reply, the attack forced Louis XIV, as it had forced the Stuarts, to extend the absolutist position onto ground that was entirely untenable. The Gallican Church under Louis, like the English Church under Laud, had neither strength enough to persecute à outrance nor authority enough to prevail by other means. In the end, Charles was beaten by the left and Louis capitulated to the right; but in neither case did the victory settle anything. The English, with their instinct for compromise, hit on a solution that could serve, most of the time, as a via media; but in France the

11. Quoted in Ritchie, D. G., Natural Rights, p. 15.

battle of the Jesuit order and the Masonic order continues unabated to this day.

Yet it was in France—the France of Henry IV—that the true foundation of tolerance was laid; perhaps a time will come again when France will build upon it. The religious wars and persecutions of the sixteenth century had brought together a group of humane spirits, mostly but not exclusively Catholic, who came to be called the *Politiques*—the expression not being altogether complimentary. They stood for something new not only in the theory but in the spirit of government. It was not merely that they wanted to stop the killing and mitigate the hatred: in every war there is a small minority that wishes that, and it probably does not vary much in relative size. They saw that the scope and the pretensions of sovereignty itself must be curtailed if there was to be any chance of peace and freedom. Their unofficial spokesman was Jean Bodin: one of the precursors of modern liberalism. In their view sovereignty, the state, government, the prince, law itself, should be regarded in terms of function rather than authority. What function? Simply the function of creating and maintaining a political community. Bodin, avowedly following Aristotle, approached the matter from an empirical and realistic standpoint; and to him the outstanding fact was that there cannot be more than one source of coercive law, whatever the form of government. He is, so to speak, an Austinian in this respect; like Hobbes, he adopts a monistic theory of sovereignty. But what he clearly wants is to preserve the ordered life of a free community; and this was what Hobbes really wanted too, in spite of his sardonic way of putting things. Hobbes speaks of the function of sovereignty as "the procuration of the safety of the people" and immediately goes on to explain that "by safety here is not meant a bare preservation but also all other contentments of life" [12] Hobbes's bark was always worse than his bite. But Bodin saw much more clearly than Hobbes that this involves limitation, as well as confirmation, of sovereign power. He holds his sovereign subject to natural law, though to nothing else; but this holding was to prove highly significant, for, as Gierke says, "the natural-law theory of the State was Radical to the very core of its being. It was directed . . . not to the purpose of scientific explanation of the past, but

12. *Leviathan*, Part 2, chap. xxx.

to that of the exposition and justification of a new future which
was to be called into existence." [13] Bodin insists that the family is
prior to the state, so the state must keep hands off. He puts private property also beyond the reach of the state, and argues therefore that taxation may not be levied without consent. What was
still more important to the Politiques, and to the development of
the liberal tradition, was his emphasis on the exclusively political
nature of sovereignty, with the recognition that it does not and
should not try to constitute the sole basis of community. "He is
urging, in the manner of the Politiques, that the political bond
may be self-sufficient even though the political community be
divided by differences of religion and by the survival of local,
customary, and class immunities." [14] Preferring historical realism
to logical consistency, Bodin liked decentralization of government, and recognized the communal character of many types of
organization within the political unity; he envisaged even a variety
of languages.

The Politiques are the true precursors of modern liberalism.
They were attacked as skeptics and unbelievers (some of them
were) but they were the truer idealists for spurning the wild
horses of dogma and absolutism and keeping their feet on the
ground. They saw—and history has vindicated their insight—that
liberty in community depends on three great postulates:

First, there cannot be more than one source or kind of coercion
in a community. Secular power must in this respect be monistic.
That involved the rejection of the Dantesque principle of the
two swords, in the conscious hope that they might be beaten into
plowshares before too many generations had been impaled on
them. For purely practical reasons, the power to coerce must inhere solely in the political sovereign. It is noteworthy that where,
as in modern Germany, Italy, Russia, a party has succeeded in in-
troducing a second system of coercion, the result was the breakup
of the political community in revolution and despotism. Liberalism
can never allow any group or party, any church, corporation, or
trade-union, to violate this first postulate of order.

Second, the system of coercive law is itself subject to moral
principles which it does not itself determine, no matter who or

13. Gierke, O. F. von, *Natural Law*, I, v, 15, pp. 64–67.
14. Sabine, *op. cit.*, p. 405. Cf. the excellent study of Damville in Palm, F. C.,
Politics and Religion in Sixteenth-Century France.

what may be called sovereign. Even the pope, said Suárez, cannot change natural law; it is a part, said St. Thomas, of the divine order, the part that particularly concerns secular power. It was only a few Protestant extremists who ever affected to believe that if there is a law above the king, only the king can declare it. The lasting significance of natural-law theory is that it puts true authority beyond the reach of the tyrant, and says to the state, Thus far and no farther. Natural-law philosophy does not hold—perhaps it never did—that political society rests on an actual, historical, or implicit contract: even though such great scholars as Maine and Jhering thought that "all jurisdiction if we could trace it far back enough would be found to be in its origin not compulsory, but voluntary." [15] What this school through its modern exponents—Krabbe and Stammler, for example—does assert is that law derives its claim to obedience from something that informs the minds and wills of living persons dwelling in community, and from no other source whatever. As Krabbe puts it: "The fact is once for all that no one can exercise any control over the working of men's sense of right. The legislator or any other alleged possessor of power is as powerless as a private person to silence the sense of right of any individual whatever . . . It lies in no man's power to decide what shall have the force of law. For nothing is really *law* except what proceeds from the single source which alone can give a rule the quality of law, the ultimate sense of right. What does not come from this source may be enforced by the power of the state or it may be applied in the decisions of the bench, but it is not and never can be law." [16]

Professor Roscoe Pound and other modern jurists have criticized the natural-law basis of sovereignty on the same ground as the critics of the pre-Christian era: namely, that it does not furnish a specific consensus of ethical judgment. It boils down, says Pound, to what the individual conscience dictates; and consciences differ. "An eighteenth-century jurist laying down natural law and Bentham's man who claimed to be one of the elect are in the same position. Each is giving us his personal views and is assuming that those views must be binding upon everyone else." [17] The point is well taken as regards eighteenth and much of nineteenth-century

15. Maine, H. J. S., *Ancient Law*, Introduction by Sir Frederick Pollock, p. xvii.
16. Krabbe, Hugo, *Modern Idea of the State*, p. 110.
17. Pound, Roscoe, *Law and Morals*, chap. iii.

thought, under which there is no longer a common ethos. For lack of it, as Pound points out, jurists have fallen back on interest as the basis of law, and have conceived the problem of jurisprudence as the evaluation or harmonization of interests—as indeed, on the practical plane, it largely (though never wholly) is. But the problem is insoluble without criteria. The evaluation of anything is impossible without a standard. The assumption that out of the clash of group interests *as such* an harmonious synthesis can be devised or discovered is simply a return to natural law by the back window because the key of the door has been lost. As Woodrow Wilson said in 1918, "interest does not bind men together: interest separates men . . . There is only one thing that can bind people together, and that is common devotion to right." [18] The emphasis is on the word common. Only where there exists a fundamental agreement, not perhaps of explicit belief, but of outlook, feeling, and value, is true toleration possible. It was this that both Burke and Acton had in mind; it was to this that Catholic scholars referred —as they still do—when they made the secular state subject to natural law; it was this that made political freedom possible. Destroy that foundation and everything else falls to pieces.

The third of the liberal postulates is the logical consequence of the other two. First, it was held, political authority as such must be monistic, for reasons of sheer practical expediency. Second, it is limited by the natural law—the sense of right and reason that informs the minds of Christian men. Third, its exercise must be held to a minimum, both extensively and intensively, to preserve the peace and freedom of community which is the sole reason for its existence. This was the principle the Politiques drew from the wars of religion; and their work was not in vain. It was the ground on which Mirabeau, Paine, Madison, and Jefferson took their historic stand. Said Mirabeau: "The most unlimited liberty of religion is in my eyes a right so sacred that to express it by the word toleration seems to me a sort of tyranny, since the authority which tolerates might also not tolerate." [19] His point was that the state had no such authority one way or the other; and the American Constitution expressly implements that contention. Its framers realized that the secular state is a creature different from,

18. Speech at Manchester, December 30, 1918, in Baker, R. S., *Woodrow Wilson and World Settlement,* I, 300.
19. Quoted in Bury, J. B., *History of Freedom of Thought,* p. 111.

and inferior to, the soul of a man; and whenever it says to a man, You are impeding the exercise of my authority, the man may stand up and reply, Well, what are you trying to do? Its function is essentially, in Kant's phrase, "to keep conscious free-willing beings from interference with each other." The life of society is in them, not in it—all the variety of occupation and experience, of local and corporate community, of religious belief and practice, which Bodin with his historical sense valued so highly. As he rightly saw, social life can be pluralistic only where political authority is monistic; but the state is only a means to liberty, and whenever it claims to be autonomous in the definition of ends, then let liberals beware.

It is almost a platitude that eternal vigilance is the price of liberty; and the essence of vigilance is to discern from what quarter danger threatens. What those early liberals laid down as to the necessary limitation of political power holds true of any kind of a state, whatever its constitution. A democracy is just as apt to become tyrannical as any divine-right monarch. There is no more divinity attaching to numerical majorities than there was to human heads with crowns on them: perhaps less, in as much as the personal rates higher than the mechanical. If we all assent to majority rule, it is solely for the same good reason of expediency, and within the same limits. The mere fact that a state may rest its decisions on a majority vote, actual or retrospective, gives it no more right to invade the personal and spiritual liberty of its or anyone else's subjects, than has any other form of government; nor may it arbitrarily enlarge its scope or magnify its purpose in order to do so.

The term "conscientious objector" means for the contemporary reader the conscientious objector to war, who is prepared to carry his objection to the point of disobeying the relevant orders of the government. That is the one class of case for which special legal provision is made in free countries; and they should proudly cherish that provision as a very talisman of liberty. It is made because even today people are not quite easy in their minds about compulsion to kill, and because of the total nature of the disposal of persons which modern states claim for that purpose. But war is not the only possible sphere of conscientious objection. Religion of all kinds has produced it; and we may wonder how freedom would have fared if it had not. Educational policy in both France and Britain has proved, and may again prove, a critical issue; and in the United States the sphere of race relations is now very dangerous ground. The reason that there have not been more such issues is that on the whole, in the states of the English tradition, governments have learned to keep their hands off matters as to which the conscience or the deep conviction of any considerable number of people may be affronted; and the people in turn have learned that while a man may differ profoundly from his government as to the advisability of particular ends or the expediency of the means adopted, he may nonetheless be a good citizen. One wonders whether both lessons are not in some danger of being forgotten as the total compulsion of recurrent war engenders a disposition to extend it, on the grounds of "preparedness" or "security," through the diminishing intervals.

But even in the case of the objector to war, it is against specific acts or policies of the government that he usually protests. Very few of such protestants dispute the general authority of the government itself. In the United States for the past eighty years, in Britain for twice that span, the number of people who opposed the fundamental basis of the state has been negligible. That number, however, is now conspicuously increasing, both in Europe and in America. The doctrine that the state always represents the interests of an economic class is essentially an attack on the state itself, comparable in both tactics and dogma to the ultramontane and Calvinist attacks. It strikes not only at the policies but at the authority of government, and releases its adherents from all inner obligations of obedience and loyalty. The results are already evident, and are likely to be more so. For as the theory of communism influences more and more wandering minds, the principles and conditions of freedom under law are increasingly obscured. To take a critical instance: the practice of American courts and legislatures in regard to allegations of seditious utterance has on the whole, until very recently, followed Justice Holmes's criterion of "clear and present danger" directly and demonstrably resulting therefrom. It was an erstwhile liberal, now a prisoner of the left —Mr. Max Lerner—who was one of the first to urge the abandonment of that criterion. Mr. Lerner pleaded the national emergency, forgetting how stoutly the British House of Commons, in circumstances far more desperate, has resisted precisely that plea. The United States has developed a habit of emergencies; it will probably have one in the backwash of the European war, and will certainly have another if or when Mr. Lerner's political associates get within sight of office. The fact that the state has—or should have —the monopoly of coercive power makes it a valuable prize to any class that sets its own interest above justice or the common good. It is entirely possible for the state to be captured by such a group —it has happened several times in our generation—and successfully perverted. Marx realized that possibility, and made it the central object of communist strategy. That is a manoeuvre that liberals must resist from the outset; they betray their own cause when they give it countenance or encouragement.

The difficulty of keeping political authority within bounds is increased as constitutional representative government degenerates into popular democracy, and politicians turn propagandists. The idea of disinterested deliberation on which the American form of government is explicitly based is undermined by the adoption of mechanical and psychological techniques for manipulating mass opinion. The sphere of effective objection to state action is automatically curtailed, and made more perilous, by mass appeals, over the heads of the representatives, beyond the range of the actual speaking voice, in circumstances where oratory is inaccessible to prompt rejoinder. A self-denying ordinance is needed if the parliamentary way of shaping policy is to be preserved. Moreover, the struggle of the national states to acquire or retain territory, which is well understood and fought as such in Europe, has been endowed in America with the character of a moral crusade; and in that aspect it seems to warrant an enlargement of state prerogative that would be tolerated on no other pretext. Such a combination of interrelated circumstances has all the makings of a serious crisis for American liberalism.

In this juncture some of Acton's observations are worth recalling. "The most certain test by which we judge whether a country is really free is the amount of security enjoyed by minorities . . . It is bad to be oppressed by a minority, it is worse to be oppressed by a majority." He traced the decadence of Athenian democracy to "the possession of unlimited power, which corrodes the conscience, hardens the heart, and confounds the understanding of monarchs." In the decline of the Roman principate he noted "the dogma that absolute power may, by the hypothesis of a popular origin, be as legitimate as constitutional freedom." And with respect to the need for principle in affairs of state he said: "A government entirely dependent on opinion looks for some security what that opinion shall be, strives for the control of the forces that shape it, and is fearful of suffering the people to be educated in sentiments hostile to its institutions."

It is worth while also to recall Acton's constant praise of the American Constitution for its self-limiting qualities: "Whilst England was admired for the safeguards with which, in the course of many centuries, it had fortified liberty against the power of the Crown, America appeared still more worthy of admiration for the safeguards which, in the deliberations of a single memorable year, it had set up against the power of its own sovereign people." [20]

Yes: what was said and done that year has still its message for the American people—in more respects than one.

20. Acton, Lord, *History of Freedom*, pp. 4, 11, 78, 64–65, 83.

VI

Sovereignty versus Community

1. Responsibility for the people. — 2. Contract theories. — 3. Nature from Hobbes to Bentham. — 4. Locke and Laski on property. — 5. Adam Smith and the liberal tradition.

§ 1

ALFRED, philosopher and king of the West Saxons in the ninth century, took his responsibilities very seriously; and in his translation of Boethius he inserted some of his reflections on "the work which I was commanded to perform." He saw it as a kind of craft of which his people were the instruments. He must therefore cherish and provide for them. "This then is their provision: land to inhabit, and gifts, and weapons, and meat, and ale, and clothes, and whatsoever is necessary." He was insistent and careful that they should learn to read and have some good books, including their own history and legends; and he thought of the poor as his particular charge, since "the poor have no friend but the king." "For every craft and every power soon becomes old, and is passed over in silence, if it be without wisdom. . . . This is now especially to be said: that I wished to live honourably whilst I lived, and after my life to leave to the men who were after me my memory in good works." [1]

The sense of a responsibility that was upward, not downward, a responsibility not to but *for* the people, never quite faded out of English polity, even after the kings had ceased to acknowledge any earthly mentor; and the alliance of crown and people against privilege was, on the whole, in the Christian era, more than a matter of expediency. Responsibility for the people is a much more onerous burden than responsibility to the people, and no amount of theorizing about a "general will" can turn it into the same thing.

1. Cunningham, William, *The Growth of English Industry and Commerce*, I, 132–133.

It is an essentially aristocratic principle, indicating the necessity of aristocracy to all good government, whatever the constitution. It demands from those to whom power is entrusted standards of honor and foresight that it would be unreasonable to expect of average men; and the negative safeguards of "a system of checks and balances" are not sufficient to ensure the positive virtues. Says Hilaire Belloc, in his cheerful downright fashion: "All representative assemblies, if they are not aristocratic, are corrupt. That may be postulated as a general truth in political science. . . . Give power of the purse to a number of random individuals inspired by no special class code of honor, and they will as a matter of course pick the public pocket. . . . Corruption is as universally attached to our non-aristocratic European parliaments as fleas are to dogs. We expect it, and our expectation is not disappointed." [2] With due allowance for the subtler forms of corruption, the charge need hardly be confined to Europe.

When Englishmen wish to illustrate the failure of a due sense of responsibility, they point to the progress of French absolutism in the eighteenth century; but when one looks below the theory to the facts, it appears that parliamentary absolutism was no adequate alternative. One remembers, of course, that the mass of the people, like the American colonists, had no votes to sell; but the outstanding fact—so outstanding that it is generally ignored—is that as the century wore on, the mass of the people came to appear more and more as mere suppliants at the bar of the House, with anything done for them mere charity or concession, until in 1814 they are reduced to the status of sheer beggars—even though all they ask is that the laws be enforced. It was not so in Plantagenet or Tudor times, not so under Elizabeth and Burleigh. Liberals are too apt to assume that their main task was accomplished in this year or that, with the establishment of parliamentary rule and the successive measures of religious toleration—and so to become conservative, or even reactionary. But their current task was created for them in this great change, not in the structure but in the conception of government; and much of the theory that accompanied and masked it merely added to the difficulty of a problem yet unsolved.

Maine's famous description of government as developing "from status to contract" has been much overworked, and made to bear

2. Belloc, H., *The Contrast,* chap. iv.

interpretations that he would never have sanctioned. In particular, it will not sustain, and was not meant to sustain, a unilateral view of society as "evolving" from a static condition of servitude without liberty to a system of authority based simply on the conscious consent of free-willing individuals. The essence of a contract is mutuality; and the idea that government rests on some sort of compact or contract is a very old one. It goes back to Saxon times, and is still embodied in the British coronation service, where we have the dual ideas of consecration and assent. Preservation of the "customs and ancient liberties" of the realm has been for over a thousand years part of the bargain. The feudal system was essentially a structure of mutual rights and obligations; that was what gave it its strength and tenacity, and that was why it took so long to get the modern notion of sovereignty out of it: the counterclaims of the subjects were so strictly defined and so stoutly defended. Nor did the establishment of the political kingship do away with the traditional mutuality. "The king did not lose his representative character; but the coronation oath on the one side, the undertaking to be faithful on the other, made up the terms of a contract in which the fidelity of the subject was the consideration for a promise of good government by the king." [3] Absolute sovereignty, under whatever form, is and has always been foreign in both fact and idea to the Anglo-Saxon tradition. The rights and liberties of Englishmen rest on something far older and stronger than the theories of the "glorious revolution."

The theories were not at all new in substance; their prominence came from the newness of the occasion. Poor James II, who could do nothing right, who could not even manage to run away without assistance, had left a situation that only a short cut could solve. An *ad hoc* "convention," into whose authority it was best not to enquire, declared that he had abdicated, using the selfsame plea that the American colonists were to use against George III: he had "broken the original contract between King and People." That was not the first time anybody had heard of it, but it was the first time it had been put to such use—in England (the Dutch had invoked the idea against Philip II a hundred years earlier). But, as Gneist points out, what distinguished the English affair was not merely that the convention conferred the crown, but that William was required to sign the Bill of Rights before he got it.

3. Anson, W. R., *Law and Custom of the Constitution*, II, 9.

It was in that turning away, so to speak, from the historical to the argumentative that the revolution, so far as it was one, really consisted.

§ 2

THE full force of the contract idea was first let loose not by the Protestants but by the Jesuits, in their case against divine-right monarchy. Bellarmine, Mariana, and Suárez, developing the thought of St. Thomas, all emphasize the conditional character of secular rule. It is, says Thomas, divinely ordained; but for that very reason, say his later exponents, it cannot be absolute. They give it a "natural" origin very much resembling that of Locke and Rousseau; but they add that when the exercise of secular authority traverses the conditions of its ordination (which include of course due respect for spiritual authority) it is ipso facto void and must be cleared out of the way—if necessary, says Mariana, with an ax. The Calvinists, in effect, agreed with them, practically as well as theoretically; and the instinct of the English rejected both.

What later contract theorists are doing is to discuss sovereignty in terms of power when what they really want to talk about is function (their successors have very generally perpetuated the confusion). And in order to discuss the proper function of sovereignty in human affairs, one must have some theory or conspectus of human nature to begin with. That is why Hobbes, Locke, Hume, Smith, Rousseau, Bentham, the Mills, and many lesser lights have to set up as psychologists before they can be political philosophers. And that is why the living impact of their work lies so largely in theories and declarations of "natural rights." They are saying, This is the true nature of man, and *therefore* . . . If one does not agree with them the sentence will have a different conclusion.

It has been well said that the net value of the various contract theories lies in the implication that all authority has a voluntary basis. That is their great and lasting contribution to the philosophy of liberalism. It holds good even of Hobbes, whose "social contract" hardly comes within the category. His "natural" men agree with one another to surrender their "natural" freedom to an absolute ruler for the sake (there is the function) of security and protection from one another; and having once surrendered it they may by no means get it back. The reason for this peculiar transaction is that Hobbes's natural men are what Wingfield-Stratford calls "murderous anarchs"; and in the war of all against all, desires and passions reign supreme, without sin. "In nature every man has a right to every thing. . . . The notions of right and wrong, justice and injustice, have there no place. Where there is no common power, there is no law; where no law, no injustice. Force and fraud are in war the two cardinal virtues. Justice and injustice are none of the faculties neither of the body nor mind." They, together with other desiderata "as delivered in the word of God, that by right commandeth all things" (Hobbes could be very sardonic) are the creations of sovereign power—*"dictating peace, for a means of the conservation of men in multitudes."* [4]

§ 3

How Hobbes came so to envisage human nature we shall not stop to enquire—though the enquiry would be instructive. But perhaps he was right. Perhaps, as the material and the immaterial works of civilization together go down in ruin, that is what we shall find. Hobbes was no fool. His view was based on no mere misanthropy. And it is important to observe that if liberalism is supposed to revolve on a core of individualism, then it is in Hobbes, not Locke, that we find the theory of individualism first categorically stated. His society consists solely of self-interested individuals—which is precisely why it issues in a tyranny. The logic of that process was to be demonstrated on a colossal scale a hundred and fifty years later.

If Hobbes overworked his "mortal god" of a sovereign, it was because his state of nature was the very devil; and the difficulty of his more optimistic opponents was to get the play going without the introduction of the traditional villain. Nature, therefore, gets a little coaching before she is allowed to appear; and perhaps it is Richard Cumberland (1632–1718), with his "social instinct," who formulates the happy solution (and incidentally fathers a popular brand of American sociology). Cumberland was an Anglican bishop, a good man and an acute, though not a catholic, thinker; he was concerned to defend religion against the materialism of Hobbes, and his work illustrates very neatly the risks involved in

4. *Leviathan,* Part 1, chaps. xiii, xiv, xv.

individual apologetic uncorrected by an active catholic tradition. "Our own happiness cannot be separated from a studious concern for the happiness of all . . . The soul is naturally adapted to enter into society and unless it does submit to enter into a social state, it neglects its principal use and employment, and lets go the best advantage of its own natural disposition." It is a somewhat abstract proposition, but very comforting to a class that prized comfort. It made available on very generous terms what theologians called "grace." It eased up the old insistence on the necessity for moral effort. It paved the way for the latitudinarian tendency of the eighteenth century. It opened the door to Locke, the nonconformists, the deists, the unitarians, and the atheists. It nearly put the Church out of business. And so far as it went, it was both true and important.

Certain effects of the optimistic view of human nature are directly traceable to the circumstances of the elite. "In the early and middle years of the eighteenth century," says Professor Willey, "the wealthy and the educated of Europe must have enjoyed almost the nearest approach to earthly felicity ever known to man"; [5] and very aptly he quotes Thomson's lines, in *The Seasons*:

> —While thus laborious hinds
> Ply the tough oar, Philosophy directs
> The ruling helm . . .

In such circumstances, the helmsmen could safely plan a return to the monistic "nature" of the Epicureans, and fashion a Christianity without Christ such as "natural philosophers" could discreetly endorse. Under their soothing inspiration, religion was quietly having its teeth pulled: it would not need them any more. For if man was turning out to be only a link in a chain, it was a very grand chain, and unstinted applause could be tendered to the celestial designer. His work was done, and very well done (whatever Wesley might say); Carlyle's subsequent complaint that he did nothing was one of his virtues: he was not required to do anything. So for the time being God was allowed to retain his throne, on the understanding that, like a Whig sovereign, he reigned without governing. An American scholar, cited by Professor Willey, "has recently distinguished sixty different senses of the term"

5. Willey, Basil, *The Eighteenth-Century Background*, pp. 44–45.

nature—which should be enough to rival the attributes of deity. It was to "nature" that both Hobbes and Locke appealed—but not to the same thing; for since what nature disclosed to Hobbes was out of fashion, there had to be a revolution there too. It was a non-conformist revolution, not much concerned with what ten centuries of Catholic thought had learned about nature. Hartley's God "associated with all our pleasures" soon becomes the pleasant "nature" of the English countryside (with the laborious hinds out of the way) that could give such refreshing sensations to tired poets. And three generations after Cumberland we have Adam Smith developing a *Theory of Moral Sentiments* in which God is dismissed with a ceremonial bow to the "Author of our Being" and nature gets the capital N. Man's conduct is mainly determined by his *natural* desire to evoke friendly and sympathetic responses from his fellow beings.

But it is not, as yet, wholly so determined. Honest Adam, in this as in his larger work more sensible than systematic, admits that some factor other than mere sociability is at least occasionally operative; for there are times when men sacrifice their self-interest —however sociably you define self-interest—to some ideal that he clearly thinks superior. "It is not the soft power of humanity, it is not that feeble spark of benevolence which Nature has lighted up in the human heart, that is thus capable of counter-acting the strongest impulses of self-love. It is a stronger power, a more forcible motive, which exerts itself upon such occasions. . . . It is reason, principle, conscience, the inhabitant of the breast, the man within." But the man within—"the demigod within the breast" as Smith elsewhere calls him—stood on rather shaky metaphysical ground; he tumbled sadly when the next generation tramped over it. And for the most part Smith was well content to let Cumberland's "social instinct" carry on: "When we consider such actions, as making a part of a system of behavior which tends to promote the happiness either of the individual or of the society, they appear to derive a beauty from this utility, not unlike that which we ascribe to any well-contrived machine." [6] Exactly!

Succeeding generations produced an abundance of well-contrived machines, both mechanical and otherwise; and philosophy, by a natural contagion, took on more and more of their admirable

6. Smith, Adam, *Theory of Moral Sentiments* (11th ed., 1808), Part 3, chap. iii and Part 7, sec. 3, chap. iii.

character. The element of will, either external or internal, became increasingly redundant. The highly abstract "Author of our Being" was quietly dethroned in favor of the equally abstract "economic man," the author of our doing; and the pleasure-pain principle of conduct furnished an infallible ethic to philosophers whose circumstances, by a natural dispensation, offered them more pleasure than pain. Thus Jeremy Bentham—the Sidney Webb of his era —could solemnly announce that "Nature has placed mankind under the governance of two sovereign masters, pain and pleasure. It is for them alone to point out what we ought to do, as well as to determine what we shall do." [7] Note the "alone": the theological, as well as the ethical, problem is solved.

§ 4

LOCKE stands apart. Almost every element in his theoretical structure has been refuted. He had neither the persuasiveness of Hooker, the power of Hobbes, nor the sagacity of Hume. Yet so much alive is he that the valuation of Locke provides even today a good criterion for the classification of political thought. If he was to provide "the bible of Whiggism" he was no less to be the inspiration of American liberties; and what he had to say—or rather, to do—has its significance for our time also. For history, if it does not repeat itself, has a way of hammering at the same lesson until either it is mastered or the pupils are dropped from the school.

Locke's function was in the literal sense conservative—in the sense that when one is caught in a blind alley the first thing to do is to turn back. It was his job to pick up the old trail at the point where Protestant absolutism had wandered off, and reinstate the law behind the law. He called it "natural rights." It has been called many things.

Neither Hobbes on the one hand nor Bentham on the other had any use for natural rights. Hobbes's nature obviously did not contain them, and the idea savored of the distinction between temporal and spiritual—"two words brought into the world to make men see double, and mistake their lawful sovereign." To Bentham natural rights were "simple nonsense—nonsense upon stilts." He could neither deduce nor infer them; they had therefore no place

7. Bentham, Jeremy, *An Introduction to the Principles of Morals and Legislation,* chap. i, sec. 1.

in a science of government. So much the worse, one may add, for the science of government—since, as Leslie Stephen says, the doctrine of rights confronts a logical theory with a statement of fact. The confrontation has surely at times been dramatic enough!

Locke, a political exile, saw the state mainly as organized coercion; and his concern was to say to it, Thus far and no farther. If Hobbes bequeathed the Austinian theory of law as the command of a sovereign, then Locke's task was to cage that kind of sovereign. In asserting that society is prior to government— logically if not historically—he was reëstablishing the ancient truth that secular power neither may nor can constrain the whole life of personality: that when it presumes too much, revolution is the necessary consequence. Life, liberty, and estate are vague terms—until one begins to lose what they stand for; but between them they cover the dynamic elements of mortal existence; and their very vagueness emphasizes the concessional and conditional character of all coercion, which must continually justify itself by a pragmatic test. And though in his civil constitution Locke will have the executive responsible to the legislature, he also holds that its acts must answer to a moral law which somehow informs the minds of men independently of all government. If this was an arbitrary solution of the problem of the double responsibility, it was nonetheless a real one; for it was designed above all to affirm that force creates no right. Locke unflinchingly carried his contention into the sphere of international relations and their normal mode of expression, organized violence. "A mere aggressor gains no right, *and even a conqueror in a just war can never establish a right which contravenes the liberty and property of the conquered.*" [8]

Professor Laski, in his successive studies, becomes more and more critical of Locke because the natural right on which he put most of his emphasis was the right of property. Locke says: "Every man has a 'property' in his own person; this nobody has any right to but himself. The labour of his body and the work of his hands, we may say, are properly his. Whatsoever then he removes out of the state that nature hath provided and left it in, he hath mixed his labour with it, and joined to it something that is his own, and

8. Sabine, *op. cit.*, p. 536, summarizing the argument of Locke's *Civil Government*, Bk. II, chap. xvi, "Of Conquest." The entire chapter is extraordinarily relevant to current discussion.

thereby makes it his property. It being by him removed from the
common state nature placed it in, it hath by this labour something annexed to it that excludes the common right of other men
. . . at least where there is enough, and as good, left in common
for others." [9]

Anyone who has tried to live by thus "mixing his labour," still
more anyone who has been arbitrarily deprived of the work of
his hands, or his mind, by state action, will incline to agree with
Locke; nor will it seem unreasonable that Locke should make the
protection of such property the root of civil society. What Locke
is defending is property as the extension of personality; and to
complete the picture, we must remember that the extension oc-
curs in time as well as in space. For the property relationship with
genetic nature involves human as well as animal and vegetable
fertility; it is normally bound up with the life of a family; and it
projects itself in time through the labor of the children and their
natural expectation to inherit. A modern exponent of conservatism,
basing his argument on Burke, includes among the limits on political action "the moral obligation on all individuals, and on any
society, not to falsify expectations which it has made legitimate
by express permission or by tacit consent." [10] This is admittedly a
gloss on Locke that raises new and intricate problems; but it may
fairly be contended that in his derivation of the property right
Locke was restoring the organic view of society as against the
atomistic view that other parts of his theory suggested. It is of
interest to recall that Ramsay MacDonald, in 1924, depicted the
socialist as the best defender of private property, since he considered it a good so great that everybody ought to have some.
Not all the members of his party agreed with him.

Laski's case against Locke is a major part of his case against
liberalism, and therefore demands examination. In an early work
of 1919 (dedicated to Walter Lippmann) he has given us a finely
critical appreciation of the good physician; and his subsequent
withdrawal is based not on Locke's theory so much as on its effects.
By putting the preservation of property among the cardinal functions of the state, and committing legislation to men whose prime
interest that was, Locke made himself responsible for a system
that favored privilege and perpetuated inequality: that is the

9. Locke, *op. cit.*, II, chap. v.
10. Butler, G. G., *The Tory Tradition*, p. 56.

charge. To the passage quoted in our first chapter, we may add the following from the same work: "Ireton's state is a society of property owners; and that, at bottom, is Locke's ideal also. The dislike of regulation is a dislike of limitations upon the right of property to do what it will with its own. The good citizen is the man who has achieved, or is achieving, prosperity; the law is to be the law he conceives himself to need. . . . Out of the moral crisis of the seventeenth century there emerged a liberalism, indeed, but one attuned to the implications of the religion of success. That is not a religion which differs very profoundly from age to age. It is the creed of the Pharisee. . . . Its enclosures separate the peasant from the land; its rules of commercial ownership leave the industrial worker with nothing but his labour to sell. Having made inequality an implicit article of its faith, it then invites to freedom those who are denied the means of reaching it." [11]

This line of attack on the institution of private property and on the importance assigned to it, not only by the English Whigs but by the framers of the American Constitution, is at heart emotional rather than historical. It imputes to the founders a foreknowledge of, and responsibility for, later developments that were quite alien to their spirit and purpose. Many volumes have been written—most of them highly technical—on the curious forms and functions of property that legal ingenuity in the service of finance capital has since devised. Stocks and bonds, debentures and trust certificates, subscription rights and priorities, options and futures, patents and trade-marks, processes and designs, licenses and rights of usage, dozens of other intangibles, are the apparatus by which the empire of big business is held together and defended against intruders, private or public. What is really bought and sold, when such things change hands, is economic advantage, actual or prospective. Some of it is predatory, some of it genuinely functional; and the same instrument—such as a holding-company security—may be one or the other according to the particular circumstances. In view of these immensely complex developments, to attack property or property owners in general terms is about as sensible as to confuse water in a stock issue with water in the bathtub. Property as the basis of economic control is as different from the sort of property Locke had in mind as is the

11. Laski, H. J., *Rise of European Liberalism*, p. 156.

stockholder's claim on corporate surplus from the fisherman's claim to his skiff. Indiscriminate talk of property or ownership is now practically meaningless.

When socialists and communists attack the "private property system" what most of them refer to is the highly abstract sort of property from which the concentration of economic power is built up. What Locke and the natural-law school, including the Vatican, refer to is the precise opposite of that. Yet even in its own terms the radical attack is generally naïve; for it accepts the conventional association of property with control, and seldom deigns to notice the extent to which modern governments have changed the situation by divorcing control from ownership. This is the particular defect of state socialism, which—thinking still in eighteenth-century terms—assumes that the only way to get public control is to transfer title from private to public hands; while in point of fact, for better or worse, private ownership is already stripped of the power of control in vast fields affected with a public interest, and many interesting and successful forms of joint equity have been put into practice. Property differs from possession in the legal recognition of an asserted claim. That recognition is granted, or withheld, on terms, and the terms are constantly being revised. While property remains private, there is always some degree—nowadays a rapidly increasing degree— of supervision over its scope, use, and abuse. Should the state become owner, the question *Quis custodiet custodies?* becomes both urgent and unanswerable.

The indiscriminate attack on property as such, so far as it has any meaning, remains an attack on the basis of social cohesion; which is what Locke and his followers, in England, France, and America, so clearly perceived. They were not prepared to allow the political organization of society—which in France and America was obviously a deliberate and late creation—to violate the more fundamental relationship between a man's work and its tangible result; they rightly saw that where that relationship is insecure, all freedom is imperiled; they were close enough to reality to know that it is work, not talk, that makes the world go round; and they did not suppose, or wish, that "the state" could either do the work for them or produce benefits that were unrelated to it. No one would deny that modern developments of the property right, especially in America, have created grave problems as to its scope, its function, and its distribution; but that fact does not impugn the institution as such. If the abuse of an institution is to justify a demand for its abolition, there will soon be little left of law or society. It should not be necessary to remark that Locke was not the author of all the perversions of the property right that a chrematistic society invented, or tolerated; he can hardly be credited with the devices of absentee ownership and fiduciary control that were to make property for power so different a thing from property for use. Nor can Locke—although he opposed the old usury law—be held to have engendered the dominant money consciousness of the century that followed his death: Laski, in the passage above cited, makes too quick a jump from "property" to "prosperity." Certainly there were inconsistencies and limitations in Locke's philosophy that kept it short of a true humanism; but it will support a distributive ideal much better than a capitalist one —as Jefferson realized. And in making secular coercion answerable to moral postulates, and basing the property right on personal effort, Locke cleared the foundation on which liberals of all shades have continued to build. It is significant that Laski now sees Russian communism (or whatever is the current name for it) as the historic successor to Christianity, while the Church of Rome remains the one society that stands dogmatically firm on the private property of John Locke; though its scholars would protest, with some reason, that that is to give Locke credit for what he took at a few removes from Thomas Aquinas.

Pius XII, in his encyclical of September 1, 1944, deals specifically with the question of private property, in a timely endeavor to make clear the Church's position. The need was patent.

Promises of statesmen, and many suggestions and proposals of scientists and technicians, have given rise, in the victims of an unhealthy social and economic order, to a senseless hope of a millennium of universal happiness. This feeling offers a fertile ground for propaganda for a most radical program . . . that does not expect anything from organic reform and everything from subversion and violence.

The pope then recapitulates the philosophy upon which, among other things, the American Constitution was consciously and explicitly founded:

Private property is a natural fruit of labor, a product of intense activity of man, acquired through his energetic determination to ensure and develop with his own strength his own existence and that of his family, and to create for himself and his own an existence of just freedom, not only economic but also political, cultural and religious.

Having thus reaffirmed the position taken by Leo XIII in 1891, as well as that of Pius XI forty years after, the pope proceeds to put private property in its place, in terms so specific that liberals could hardly ask for more. "Whenever," he says, "capitalism arrogates unlimited right to property without any subordination to the common good, the church has condemned it as contrary to the rights of man." "We see small and medium property owners compelled to wage a defensive struggle . . . against those effective concentrations of economic wealth, often hidden under anonymous forms, that succeed in evading their social duties." Workers have a right to the expectation of acquiring some personal property; and when the present distribution of property is an obstacle to this end, "the state should in the common interest intervene, regulate its activities, or issue a decree of expropriation with suitable indemnity." Small and medium holdings in agriculture, trade, industry, and the arts are entitled to special protection. And the pope expressly rejects the argument that technical development automatically makes for bigness and tends to kill off small proprietorship.

No, technical progress will not necessarily and inevitably determine economic life. Too often it has yielded timidly to egoistic calculations greedy to increase capital indefinitely. Why therefore should it not bow before the necessity of maintaining and insuring private property for all as a cornerstone of the social order? Even technical progress must not prevail over the general good, but must be governed by it, and be subordinate to it.[12]

After that, no one will accuse the Vatican of a lack of boldness! But to understand the position, in all its implications, it is essential to remember that it is a logical continuation of what the later Middle Ages inculcated as the natural law, realized as the human part of the larger order.

12. Quotations from the text published in the *New York Times*, September 2, 1944.

§ 5

NATURAL law has long since gone out of fashion; indeed, there was little left of it after Hume. Its obsolescence is partly due to the fact that the "law" it postulates is not the same kind of law as that out of which lawyers make a living. The stubborn absence in English of words such as other languages possess to convey this distinction, and its necessary applications, suggests something peculiar in the English approach to the whole problem.

But natural law, like divine right, had a work to do. It was invoked to fill a vacuum; and even in Protestant countries it was at heart a religious conception. It stood for something both ontologically and axiologically prior to secular actuality, to which when necessary appeal could be made. And as the churches of England and Germany went down the smooth Erastian slope, natural law came up. The life of the Anglican Church after the revolution was more and more a matter of outward conformity—perhaps in consequence of the emphasis legislation laid on conformity, as the one thing it could effect; perhaps also because conformity was required, at least nominally, for the more important administrative and educational positions. The Church was the mart of respectability, and the poor were not wanted; in at least one case the rich departed, locking their pews behind them, when a popular preacher drew the crowd in. "Enthusiasm" was bad form; and despite its Sunday decorum, England seemed to Voltaire the most irreligious of countries. Nonconformity and dissent were becoming stratified, as they have largely remained, on social lines. It was the Wesleys and George Whitefield who took religion to the poor, in field and slum; and the Church could not contain them either, though they raised no standard of revolt.

Such was the religious outcome of the enlightenment, which was now devising, outside the old tradition, its own theology and metaphysics of "nature"—because it had to. Both Catholics and puritans had persistently applied their religious postulates to the problems and practices of everyday life: too persistently, in fact. Now both were rejected. But after the clergy—or the more accommodating part of them—had taken the oath to William, the English Church was in no position to admonish the state. The middle ground was vacant. The theology of nature came in to fill the gap; and as Gierke remarks, the size of the gap it had to fill was "astonishing."

We can watch its progress all the way from Luther to Adam Smith. Here is Luther: "If a judge have love and wisdom, law-books are worse than useless to him . . . Without love and natural right [*Naturrecht*] you will never be in accord with the will of God, though you have devoured the jurists and all their books." [13] Just how true was that? And how useful? Here is Smith, talking about the law which permitted parish officers to seize an unemployed man and send him back to the place of his birth, so as to get rid of him: "To remove a man who has committed no misdemeanor from the parish where he chooses to reside is an evident violation of natural liberty and justice." [14] But was it evident? Evident to whom? Not, apparently, to the people who passed the law.

It is to be noted that the argument, like so much that is strongest in *The Wealth of Nations,* is not economic. Smith has been too rigidly identified with a particular economic doctrine. His plea for freedom of industry and trade was part of his general case for liberty as a natural right; it was not confined, as his German critics have maintained, to calculations of mere economic advantage. Even the great assault on the system that produced the American revolt rests on other grounds than those of mere expediency. "To prohibit a great people from making all that they can of every part of their own produce, or from employing their stock and industry in the way that they judge most advantageous to themselves, is a manifest violation of the most sacred rights of mankind." [15] The conviction, like the language, is religious.

Adam the philosopher would have been very critical of Smith the economist could he have foreseen the full consequences of his doctrine; yet Smith, though he may be the grandfather, is certainly not the father of the "economic man." His deep distrust of the mushroom industrial cities springs from a broader conception of human nature: they would have stayed at a decent level on which the countryside could support them but for the artificial stimulus given to industry and trade. Indeed, Smith's preference for the

13. Quoted in Allen, J. W., *Social and Political Ideas of the Renaissance and Reformation,* chap. vii.
14. *Wealth of Nations,* Book I, chap. x, Part 2.
15. *Ibid.,* Book IV, chap. vii, Part 2.

agrarian interest fits quite awkwardly into his system. Nowadays, he says, the poor man has to pay a price for "the wood of the forest, the grass of the field and all the natural fruits of the earth, which when land was in common cost the labourer only the trouble of gathering them" [16]—and he clearly does not like it; but since property has to be defended, and landlords are owners, Smith gets himself into endless trouble with the theory of rent. It does him credit, because—unlike so many of his successors—he will not sacrifice his facts to the symmetry of his system. He hates the exploitation of tiny children in the new textile mills, and calls on the state to see that they are educated—even if there were no advantage to be gained. Actually, he adds, there is a considerable advantage; for "an instructed and intelligent people are more decent and orderly . . . less liable to the delusions of enthusiasm and superstition . . . not disposed to judge rashly or capriciously" of government policy; and "in free countries" that "is surely of the highest importance." [17]

He has his misgivings about certain aspects even of an unrestricted system. He notes the ease and impunity with which employers can enter into mutual agreements; he sees the bargaining advantage of even the single employer, and sympathizes with the efforts of the workmen to combine. He rejects the mercantilist position that regarded wages simply as costs, and therefore sought to hold them down; and he even goes beyond the criteria of what is now called "the economy of high wages": "no society can surely be flourishing and happy, of which the far greater part of the members are poor and miserable." Nor is it to any narrow economic calculus that he appeals in contending "it is but equity that they who feed, cloath and lodge the whole body of the people, should have such a share of the produce of their own labour as to be themselves tolerably well fed, cloathed and lodged." [18]

Smith opens the door much wider than is generally supposed not only to "public works" but to "those public institutions which though they may be in the highest degree advantageous to a great society, are, however, of such a nature, that the profit could never repay the expense to any individual, or small number of individuals." The Scotsman can look beyond the profit, and character-

16. *Ibid.*, Book I, chap. vi.
17. *Ibid.*, Book V, chap. i, Part 3, Art. ii.
18. *Ibid.*, Book I, chap. viii.

istically gives education special stress. Nor, in the largest issue, does his magnanimity fail. The ideal solution to the quarrel with America, he thinks, is that the colonists should have direct representation in the British Parliament. And if, as is not unlikely, American productivity should one day exceed British, he is willing to contemplate the removal of the capital "to that part of the Empire which contributed most to the general defence and support of the whole." But if such union prove to be impossible, then Britain must face the separation and "accommodate herself to the real mediocrity of her circumstances." Perhaps "by thus parting good friends" the Americans could be induced to enter into reciprocal trade relations, which "might dispose them not only to respect, for whole centuries together, that treaty of commerce which they had concluded with us at parting, but to favour us in war as well as in trade, and, instead of turbulent and factious subjects, to become our most faithful, affectionate, and generous allies." [19]

Despite the limitations of his outlook that Germans and communists take pains to emphasize, liberalism need not be ashamed today to acknowledge Adam Smith among its founders. When those critics can point to a leader as humane, as prudent, and as realistic, liberals will perhaps listen more attentively.

19. *Ibid.*, Book IV, chap. vii, Part 3.

VII

Capital and Labor: Britain

*1. Emergence of a "class" of wage earners. — 2. The state
as a business agency. — 3. Development of English labor
policy. — 4. The abdication of government. — 5. Its rationalization in economic theory.*

§ 1

THE emergence of a "class" of wage earners as a distinct and
separate element of the body politic is generally thought
of as a modern phenomenon; but the novelty lies not in the
economic fact (so far as it is a fact) but in the interpretation put
upon it. A large proportion of the members of society always have
been wage earners, and always will be. It is only a minority, in any
society, that either can or will depend for its sustenance on a noncontractual, fluctuating, and unpredictable remuneration when
there is a chance of something more stable. The fact that in modern societies vast masses of people are enabled to receive for
their labor a steady predictable return, subject to only occasional
changes and rare interruptions that are universally regarded as
disastrous, constitutes a triumph of social organization that all
preceding ages might envy. There is no subject on which power-
hungry intellectuals have written more nonsense than this. If they
or the workers whose backing they bid for have any doubt that
it is a triumph, let them experience for a few years what nature
and the market can do to the farmer, the fisherman, or the crafts-
man working on his own.

The social organization that has accomplished this has been
voluntary, that is to say, in the legal sense private; and when
we remember that it has been accompanied by a steady rise in the
standard of living, a universal extension of education and the political franchise, the growth of religious and political toleration,
a spectacular improvement in public health, a marked lengthen-
ing—apart from war—of the expectation of life, and a very sub-

stantial attainment of the many things that we mean by freedom
—then we may find ground for distrusting those who would subvert the basic principles upon which this much has been accomplished. The onus of proof is on them.

The proletariat is an idea rather than an actuality, precipitated
by that vague and chronic discontent which materialism always
engenders among the half educated. Its factual components lie
in the three following processes: (1) the social separation of those
who depend on the difference between selling price and cost from
those who work for a stipulated rate of return; (2) the identification of national welfare with the prosperity of the former; (3) the
increase in the numbers of the latter for whom the cash income
is all the living there is. In this chapter we shall consider the first
two factors, leaving the third for treatment later on.

The loss of any sense of identity between those who depend on
a margin between selling price and cost, and those who work for
a wage, is even today not nearly so universal as radical theorists
pretend, or desire. Not only in small businesses and professions,
independent shops and service trades, but in many corporate enterprises, especially in Britain, the sense of community survives.
It is being deliberately destroyed by "leaders" who write and talk
as if there were something inherently wicked about a workman
who feels or professes loyalty or obligation to the concern that
provides his income. Such leaders would have short lives in Russia;
but one of their principal weapons is the popular fallacy to which
Marx lent some color, that the distinction between the two types
of return can be eliminated. This is simply impossible. The weather
and the microbes, to say nothing of the vagaries of taste, inventiveness, and greed, make uncertainty as certain as anything can be.
And while it may be to some extent offset by the accumulation of
reserves, some group must always bear the brunt of it, and the
masses will always have to bear some of it. Moreover, when a
high premium is put on economic advance and technical innovation, the degree of uncertainty, and therefore the function of risk
bearing, necessarily gain in importance. Nonetheless, a strong
element in proletarian mythology is the belief that it is possible
for employees to retain the relative stability of contractual remuneration—indeed, to enhance that stability—and at the same
time capture for themselves the gains accruing to those who depend on a noncontractual and unpredictable return; while leaving

the losses to be absorbed by some other entity vaguely called the "state" or the "community" which in this connection means simply "not me." Under no system whatever is this possible; and the readiness to believe that it is springs from our innate disposition to evade responsibility. So well has this disposition been exploited by journalistic demagogues and some trade-union officeholders that a considerable proportion of wage-earning labor in the United States is now socially irresponsible.

A contributory element in proletarian mythology is the notion that somewhere, at some time, the mass of the laborers did in fact receive both types of return, and were ipso facto better off. The myth of a primitive communism has been completely dissipated by modern scholarship, and the idea that the majority of the people ever "owned," either individually or collectively, what are now called the "means of production" is applicable only to a level of sustenance hardly distinguishable from animal life. Beyond the most primitive stage, differentiation of function and conscious coöperation take the lead in social organization. Certainly there existed in Roman times, in Northern Europe and probably elsewhere, recognized common rights of access to wells, running water, and woodlands; it is from these that German historians like to trace the tradition of Teutonic democracy. But the transition from such cases of common rights to the modern conception of collective ownership is illegitimate; as are all such efforts to read modern notions of ownership or other institutional practices into the historic past. The essence of ownership is to keep the neighbors out; the essence of community is to let the neighbors in; it is never wise to confuse the two.

Another supposed precedent lurking in the background of proletarian mythology is the unitary ownership of all the resources of a people vested in the state, or whatever corresponded to it. About the only discoverable cases are feudal—and there is indeed more than a hint about certain forms of socialism of a return to the feudal mentality. William the Norman asserted sole lordship over the land of England, and saw to it with particular care that all tenants-in-chief held directly of him. That was his way of making the connection between land and authority an instrument of completely centralized control; it is not comparable to the assertion by the United States Government of title to undeveloped land, and the subsequent gift of large slices to the railroad corporations.

In all such appeals to the past there is the familiar element of utopian romanticism. It is both safer and more honest to recognize that such notions as collective ownership and economic egalitarianism, whatever their merits or feasibility, pertain to the future; there is then a better chance of looking objectively at the record and distinguishing what has worked well from what has worked badly or been superseded.

Within living memory, in parts of New England, farmers carted their grain at harvesttime to the mill, and left a few sacks with the miller as return for the grinding. That type of transaction is of immemorial antiquity; and if the miller turned out to be a usurer, it meant not that there was something wrong with "the system" but that there was something wrong with the miller.

§ 2

As BACKGROUND to the proletarian problem, the identification of national welfare with the prosperity of the profit seekers is far more important than the confusion of the two types of income; and it has a much longer history. It may be laid down as a maxim of particular importance to liberalism that the proper concern of the state is justice; and that whenever the instrument of justice is identified with a particular economic interest—even that of the nation itself—trouble will certainly ensue.

Now it is loudly asserted by contemporary Marxists that the state is always so identified. "The essential purpose of the state," says Professor Laski, "is always to protect a given system of class relations . . . So long as the state expresses a society divided into economic classes, it is always the servant of that class which owns, or dominates the ownership of, the instruments of production. . . . So far, on the evidence of history, any class which has sought to redefine its position in the state has always had to achieve its ends by violent revolution. In our time the facts give no warrant for concluding that our experience will be a different one from that of past ages." [1] Evidently the immediate task is to transfer, presumably by violence, the control of the state from one class to that to which the writer fancies himself as belonging; and no less evidently it appears that, short of the classless millennium, there can be no such thing as what the ordinary person under-

1. Laski, H. J., *The State*, pp. 293–294.

stands by justice—no more after the transition than before. To this discovery Marxists can no doubt reconcile their consciences, since conscience is also, for them, a class phenomenon; but to the historian there would appear to be some difficulty. For one thing, the whole category of economic classes, invented by Marx in a more-than-usually Hegelian mood, is a generalization so broad as to be less than half true; it gets its modern currency from what Professor Whitehead calls "the abstract level of common thought." And history—except as delivered by a Marxist—is superbly indifferent to it. There are times and places when the state has certainly been under the dominance of a particular economic class; others when it has just as certainly not been; and all along a chorus of innocent people, including the wisest of mankind, insisting that it need not and should not be. It is hard to suppose that such people for three thousand years or so have been entirely deluded. The Marxist will reply that for almost as long a time good people believed that the earth was flat. The allegation is doubtful; but at any rate, they were agreed that the earth was there, and they knew what they meant by it. A reading of history inspired by so thin a conceptual outfit as the theory of economic classes cannot fail to produce chimerical results. The traditional policy of English government, we have said, was from the days of Alfred that of a trust, a stewardship. Not to attribute more virtue to the rulers of England than is their due, we must note that the circumstances of the island kingdom favored that policy. There was less temptation, because there was less opportunity, to buttress authority by bringing in force from outside; and every time that was attempted the results were disastrous to the monarchy. Thus the English crown ranked itself, on the whole, with the people against privilege; the French, with privilege against the people. And for the same basic reason, England was integrated as a living, working society long before France. The hard-shell units of feudalism, the exclusive pretensions of the towns and the gilds, the extraterritorial claims of the clergy, had all been dissolved before the seventeenth century. There was security of life and property under the king's peace, of commerce by the king's measure and the king's coinage, of travel on the king's highway, and of justice under the king's law: none of it perfect or complete, but all of it so well established that the English "revolution" could be a quiet and simple affair turning upon a single issue. The corresponding integration of

France was still lacking at the end of the eighteenth century, and what there was of it had an autocratic, highly centralized character that survived in the post-revolutionary systems, and broke when Paris fell. French unity depended upon Versailles; London was only in a limited way the center of England. And though history has most to say about the doings in the capital—the debates, the royal decrees, the statutes, and so forth—the common law and liberty of England, the sense of fairness that underlay its social and economic relations, were not made there, but in the estates, the villages, the market towns and remote universities of a land that was a community before it became an autocracy.

Lord Bacon, in his history, commends Henry VII for having "changed the policy of the realm from consideration of plenty to consideration of power"; and in the essays he explains his commendation: "howsoever it be for happiness, without question for greatness it maketh to be still for the most part in arms." Systematic economic enquiry takes its rise from certain seventeenth-century skeptics who wanted to know just what this greatness-of-the-nation policy amounted to in terms of ordinary individual welfare. It is high time the question were asked again. But in Tudor times—as now, for that matter—the greatness of the nation was largely a matter of money; and during the centuries in which the money economy was being established, the interests of foreign traders and those of the state had seemed plausibly to coincide. The scramble for "treasure," of which monarchs never had enough, led to a bullionist policy of trade regulation, under which foreign customers were always to owe a net balance payable in precious metal. But as mercantilism matured, it was the great merchants themselves, especially those of the East India Company, who argued that they (and, of course, the nation) would get along better if they were allowed to trade more freely, using gold as needed; and before the seventeenth century was out, there were one or two who saw that the real value of the trade was in the general imports, of which gold was only one. Then came the great campaign of Burke and Smith in the issue of American liberty; and Smith extended the argument for more freedom to a general case. Let trade follow its natural lines—which would be on the whole (he rightly discerned) those of the climatic zones: in that way the nation, rather than one particular class, would get the benefit of the exchange of products—and so would its trading partners. He indicted the existing system of intricate regulation as favoring traders and export manufacturers at the expense of the community; and laid down the famous maxim that since "consumption is the sole end and purpose of all production," the interest of the consumer ought to prevail. So stated, it seemed almost self-evident.

§ 3

THAT principle had in fact been the dominant rule of Catholic England. It permeated the common law, with its abhorrence of extortioners, monopolists, and usurers; and it furnished the general setting within which the relations between government and wage labor were determined. The development of English labor law must always be viewed in conjunction with the constant circumscription of the gilds, and the laws against engrossing, regrating, and forestalling. All are parts of one policy which can be seen in embryo as early as the reign of Edward III: a policy based in the main on the interests of the consumer, for whom the crown felt itself responsible. The Ordinance of Labourers of 1349, and the confirming statute of two years later, do indeed prohibit the wage earners of town and country from using their enhanced bargaining power produced by the great plague to their individual advantage; but they equally enjoin that "butchers, fishermen, hostlers, brewers, bakers, poulterers and all other sellers of victuals whatsoever shall be bound to sell such victuals for a reasonable price . . . so that such sellers shall have a moderate profit and not excessive." It is not the policy of the wage-fixing clauses of the statutes to depress real wages as such; and money wages are controlled as part of the general endeavor to keep prices reasonable. The fact becomes patent when the cost-of-living principle of wage regulation is introduced in 1389. And the earliest anti-combination laws—very severe ones—are directed against the merchants, not the workpeople.

The loosening of gild control in the early sixteenth century was the prelude to a complete transformation of economic society. Henry VIII, in the violence of his assault on an order that was already in process of fundamental change, proved to be even more of a revolutionary than he intended; for the royal irascibility opened the door to a new class who were very generally regarded as usurpers, and a new ethos that rejected the whole Catholic system of economic equity. Not only was usury sanctioned; the traditional criterion of fairness in prices and wages—the *com-*

munis estimatio—was increasingly abandoned in favor of the simple test of profitability. Money began to talk louder than humanity. Money was the backbone of the greatness-of-the-nation policy.

The modern temper appears in administration long before it becomes paramount in legislation; particularly in the administration of the Elizabethan labor code of 1562. The code itself has been described as a backward gesture: a final attempt to reëstablish the status system in the guise of the well-regulated state; and so perhaps it was. But it did not so appear at the time. The right and duty of the state to regulate industry were unquestionable; no overt challenge arose for another century. It is in the application of the code that the determining influence appears. The wage-fixing powers are increasingly used to hold wages down, decreasingly to keep wages fair. Apprenticeship rules are applied sporadically, and finally declared applicable only where "expedient" —expedient, that is, not to the skilled craftsmen but to the new masters of industry. At every stage of the process we can watch the legislature and magistracy hesitating about their duty, wondering what really is the national interest, and being steadily pushed along toward the new policy. And when the final strain approaches, it is the artisans who are the conservatives, looking for justice to a state that used to protect them, only to find that state now in possession of the radicals, their masters.

The same long process is at work in the development of the anti-combination laws. Before the industrial revolution combination is one thing—an upsetting of the order of the well-regulated state; after it, quite another—a questionable interference with the wise conduct of industry by the employers. The Bill of Conspiracies of 1548 was aimed primarily, like earlier laws, at illicit disturbing of the price level: whether by craft gilds or journeymen's associations. But when the London feltmakers get into trouble in 1698,[2] or the couchmakers in 1716,[3] or the tailors in 1721,[4] or the weavers in 1756,[5] the issues are essentially those only too well known today as "industrial disputes."

2. Unwin, George, *Industrial Organization in the Sixteenth and Seventeenth Centuries*, Appendix A.

3. Unwin, George, *The Gilds and Companies of London*, p. 348.

4. Galton, F. W., *Tailoring Trade*, p. 75.

5. Lipson, Ephraim, *History of the English Woollen and Worsted Industries*, chap. iii.

The claim of the masters to be let alone proceeds on parallel lines in respect of their business operations and their relations with their workpeople. But the government, mindful of the older tradition of England, was more reluctant to concede it in the latter case than in the former. As early as 1549 we find the laissez-faire argument applied to the corn trade and the question of land enclosure. It continues, with increasing effect in legislation, right along to the nineteenth century. "It is an undeniable maxim," says an advocate of enclosure in 1656, "that everyone by the light of nature and reason will do that which makes for his greatest advantage. . . . The advancement of private persons will be the advantage of the public" [6]—no need for the state any more to bother about justice! So argued the English clothiers against state regulation of industry at the very time when Colbert was vigorously extending it in France; and by the early eighteenth century domestic trade and production were largely free. Opposition to the principle of control, failure of the machinery to keep pace with the economic evolution, and reluctance of both state and gild officials to use what machinery there was all played their parts in the emancipation.

But so long as there was an important section of the legislature mindful of the old tradition, Parliament was loth to set the masters free to do what they liked with their workpeople. The industrial disputes of the eighteenth century produced a series of anticombination laws for specific industries; but the prohibitions laid on combination are supplemented by wage-fixing machinery in the Elizabethan pattern. The fact that employers appealed to Parliament rather than the courts suggests that the existing law could not be relied on to work in their favor. It is true that the Cambridge master tailors in 1721 got a verdict branding the men's union as a conspiracy;[7] but in that same year the London tailors, similarly harassed, petitioned Parliament and got a law with wage-fixing clauses in its tail; and apparently the law was a more important precedent than the verdict. The clothiers went through a similar procedure, with a similar result, in 1726. "While the state refused to recognize the right of working men to combine together for the

6. Quoted in Tawney, R. H., *Religion and the Rise of Capitalism*, p. 259.
7. Hedges, R. Y., and Winterbottom, A., *Legal History of Trade Unionism*, chap. ii; see also Bryan, J. W., *Development of the English Law of Conspiracy* (Johns Hopkins Studies in Historical and Political Science, Series XXVII), chap. v.

protection and advancement of their economic interests, it still accepted, at least in principle, the duty of safeguarding the economic welfare of the industrial masses. The real criticism of the act of 1726 is that it did not affect equally both sections of the industrial community." [8] The fact that the ideal of the well-regulated state had been virtually abandoned by the middle of the eighteenth century in respect of domestic trade and production, while it remained in respect of labor, now worked to the employers' advantage; but the combination of workmen, if indeed it was a crime, was a crime against a state that was still supposed to see that justice was done them. And responsible opinion was torn between the novel idea of leaving workmen and masters to fight it out, with no confidence that justice would be the outcome, and persisting in the attempt to enforce standards of economic fairness in circumstances that were yearly becoming more complicated—and more inequitable. For in the days of cottage industry and the putting-out system, most families could still get some elements of a subsistence from their own resources, which put a floor under real wages; but when power herded them into the factories, the bottom dropped out.

§ 4

THE British decision to oppose by force the expansive phase of the French Revolution precipitated a social crisis in both England and Ireland for which neither thought nor feeling was as yet prepared. The results followed the usual pattern of war periods: a feverish acceleration of the processes of social metabolism that were already operative, with a compensating debility and slow convalescence afterward. On the land, the position of British and Irish agriculture was difficult enough before the war; when the blockade was broken and the land bubble burst, how was the interest of the consumer to be reconciled with that of the farmer? In the towns, just as trading capital held the lead in the days of the merchant adventurers, so now industrial capital was taking the lead in the rise of the technical adventurers. The situation called urgently for a redefinition of the duty of government to the mass of propertyless wage earners. Mercantilism had demanded cheap raw materials and cheap labor for the export trade: a de-

8. Lipson, *loc. cit.*

mand that the radical manufacturers of the new era insistently endorsed. But how far, when one actually looked at the cheap labor in, say, the purlieus of Manchester and Bolton, did that square with the interests of the consumer? Much of that cheap labor was child labor, because adults were too expensive: they could be trusted to lie on the straw and copulate anyhow, and the tiny tots ate less; so down the mine and into the mill they went, while the parents starved at "home." Now were these people consumers, and if so, were their interests, rather than those of the producers, to be government's primary concern? After thirty years' debate, part of that issue was settled in favor of cheap food for cheap labor. But was that the whole of it?

The climax of English anticombination law followed the French by only eight years; but whereas the latter was avowedly doctrinaire in character, the former was mainly the product of circumstances. The situation in England much resembled that at the close of the first German war, when the deflation policy of the employers' associations that controlled the government was reinforced by latent panic about the influence of the Russian Revolution. In the earlier period, the influence of the American Revolution was already at work in the Corresponding Societies when the French terror supervened; and the anticombination laws take their place in the whole series of repressive acts and actions. But with a unique distinction: they constitute the first occasion on which the interests of the state are legally identified with those of the employers: they write into English law a novel crime—*the crime of interfering with the employer*.

It is noteworthy that all that the particular employers (the master millwrights) asked for in 1799 was a special anticombination law for their own case such as had frequently been granted to other trades. It was Pitt and Wilberforce—both scions of the trading plutocracy—who seized the occasion for a general law. Also noteworthy is the fact that the master millwrights had not troubled to argue anything beyond their interest as employers. They got their act immediately, Parliament refusing to hear the workmen. Pitt's act which followed does not pretend to disguise its partial character. The law of 1799–1800 not only renders criminal any concerted action on the part of the workmen designed to affect the terms and conditions of employment, including the action of attending a meeting; it renders the entering into a combination itself a crime, and further prohibits "preventing or hindering any person or persons from employing whomsoever he, she or they should think proper"; and "controlling or in any way affecting any person or persons carrying on any manufacture, trade or business, in the conduct or management thereof."

The economic power of the workers—what little there was of it—being thus swept away (for the law was pitilessly enforced), there yet remained the protective function of the state itself, which, in the form of the Elizabethan system and supplementary acts, was still the law of the land. It was to that that the wage earners repeatedly appealed, particularly in the hearings of 1813. Even today, despite the far more hideous things that modern civilization does to men, women, and children, it is difficult to read their testimony in cold blood. But in the parliamentary debate that followed, on the motion to abolish the statutory control of wages and apprenticeship, the doctrinaires had a field day:

Mr. Philips: The persons most competent to form regulations with respect to trade were the master manufacturers, whose interest it was to have goods of the best fabric; and no legislative enactment could ever effect so much in producing that result, as the merely leaving things to their own course and operation. . . . *Mr. Hart Davis* could not disguise from himself that the present measure was attended with many difficulties. It would undoubtedly be of great advantage to our manufacturers that the present law should be repealed, and that every restraint should be removed from the rising generation. . . . *Mr. Giddy* thought if any one measure more than another could be said to involve the general rights of mankind, the present was that measure. What was this but the general right of the inhabitants of this country to employ the energies of their mind and body in the way they themselves pleased? . . . *Mr. Thompson* liked liberty; and doing so, he wished to see every man have the liberty of employing his hands and his genius in the best way he could to his own advantage, and for the benefit of the country.[9]

Mr. Thompson's position is both significant and familiar. He would have agreed enthusiastically with the majority of the United States Supreme Court in *Adkins* v. *Children's Hospital* (1923) denying the minimum wage law to women: "To sustain the individual freedom of action contemplated by the Constitution is not to strike down the

9. Reprinted from the Parliamentary Debates in Bland, A. E., Brown, P. A., and Tawney, R. H., *English Economic History: Select Documents*, pp. 582–584.

common good, but to exalt it; for surely the good of society as a whole cannot be better served than by the preservation against arbitrary restraint of the liberties of its constituent members." Mr. Thompson, like Justice Sutherland, achieved in a sentence the transition that English law had been so doubtful about—from liberty to trade without restriction on the treatment of goods to liberty to produce without restriction on the treatment of human beings. In fact, by the time Parliament had made up its mind to the former it was in full retreat from the latter; but in 1800 Mr. Thompson's "liberty" triumphed. The wage earners, already denied the exercise of self-defense, were now deprived of public defense also. The need for a redefinition of the duty of government to the mass of propertyless wage earners was met with the entirely novel contention that it had no duty at all. That, rather than any mere technical applications of water or steam power, was the real industrial revolution.

§ 5

FOR nearly a hundred years in England—for more than that in America—the relation of government to wage-earning labor was mainly determined by the act of abdication with which the nineteenth century opened; and the common attitude to protective legislation is even yet influenced by it. It must therefore be emphasized that the rejection of state responsibility was an abnormal and revolutionary act running counter to precedent, tradition, and Christian justice. It was an outstanding example of what happens when the state as the source of justice is dominated by an economic interest; and the mischief is equally great whether the domination comes from one side (as in the Duke of Wellington's England) or the other (as in M. Blum's France or Mr. Franklin D. Roosevelt's America). In either case the effect is to put the coercive power into the hands of men whose conception of the common good cannot, and in the end will not, be accepted; and a reaction necessarily ensues. The gains made by one group or another in the meanwhile are never sufficient to pay the price of the betrayal. Of course, in the Marxist perspective there is no such thing as disinterested justice, and no "class" of people who will make it their concern; so the best history can offer is a series of actions and reactions until in the end a working unity is attained by the simple process of exterminating the opposition, as in Russia.

The disclaimer of responsibility for the condition of the working people made by the British Government in the Napoleonic period did not last long in its extreme form. The prohibition on workmen's combinations endured for twenty-four years; and in less than twenty years from the repeal of the Elizabethan system, government inspectors were empowered to invade the private property of manufacturers. The whole nineteenth century saw a steady reassertion of the state's traditional concern with social justice, culminating in the minimum wage and social insurance systems of the twentieth. That achievement was the work of all parties and all classes, operating through an amazingly heterogeneous assortment of individuals—tailors, printers, artisans, doctors, journalists, Quakers, atheists, evangelists, theosophists, Episcopal bishops and Roman cardinals, trade-unionists and peers: presumably a Marxist could discover some common class interest among them, but the simple truth would seem to be that a common sense of right and decency could be effectively appealed to, and could assert itself over economic and doctrinaire opposition. For the establishment of minimum standards of safety, decency, working conditions, and wages is not in principle an affair of economics but of ethics. It is a necessary part of Christian justice, which simply forbids the strong to exploit the weak. The employer, vis-à-vis the artisan, is as Adam Smith recognized the stronger of the two; but merely because he can determine the contents of the man's living, within certain broad limits, we no more permit him to exploit his advantage than we permit him to break the fellow's arm and steal his clothes. Inequality is precisely the situation with which government, as justice, exists to deal; and this is a matter of morality, prior to all economic considerations.

That for so long it was not fully recognized as such—or was deliberately refused recognition—was due not solely to economic self-interest (which is present always and everywhere, and by no means a bad thing in its place) but to false belief and false teaching. A lively hold on spiritual and moral truth can always redeem, and often transmute, economic interest; but the hold of the eighteenth century was even weaker than its literary legacy suggests. The ethical thought of the time was saved from vacuity only by a tradition that it neither understood nor cared to understand. While winds of abstraction filled the philosophers' sails, what really bore them up was the current of English life as it had flowed for generations: strongest in the countryside, the village, and the market town, where people knew the meaning of liberty and fairness without benefit of speculation, and custom could still talk back to money. On the whole, eighteenth-century England was still a community; and when the philosophers invoked "nature" in support of political and economic freedom, it was to the human nature of people who had learned to live together that they were really appealing. That learning owed little to law, as we understand law; it was the natural product of life in small working communities. The peculiarity of the factory system was that it lacked this basis of spontaneous mutuality; and the long record of nineteenth-century "humanitarianism" is the story of its restoration on a wider scale than that of personal group relations. The sense of what was fair and reasonable, the "common estimate" on which earlier administration so much relied, was necessarily a local thing: as at its liveliest it still is. But today we have to maintain it among vast masses of people whose social relations are very largely abstract (though they hunger for the concrete, as every radio newscaster knows); and that high responsibility rests mainly in the hands of honest and disinterested reporters.

But it also presupposes a normal human nature unperverted by abstract academic dogma: it is noteworthy that not only the dogmas of current communism but also those of pan-Germanism and Nazi race theory are of highly academic origin. The dogma that held back the growth of community in the nineteenth century was a result of what the French and English doctrinaires did to the conception of "nature." Adam Smith's nature was after all a rather benign old beldam with a very respectable lineage—he was not a Scottish professor of moral philosophy for nothing. It was a very different sort of "nature" that fixed, for Ricardo, "the natural price of labor" at bare subsistence level, and decreed that wages should never rise above it. The absence of any corresponding limit to rents and profits (James Mill) clearly showed where nature's purpose lay. The invisible hand threw off the velvet glove to administer an iron law. If the landlord's share appeared at times excessive, rents "were a most real and essential part of the whole value of the national property, and placed by the laws of nature where they are" (Malthus). Nature, following the merest of hints from Adam Smith, modeled her nineteenth-century garb on the "well-contrived machine." Legislation, if Mirabeau and Bentham were right, was to degenerate from an art to a science; and political economists stood ready to show you the works. J. S. Mill was expressing the faith of 1830 when he wrote, "the laws and conditions of the production of wealth partake of the nature of physical truths." Mill lived long enough to defy the god of the machine; but his American disciple John Bates Clark, in 1890, nailed the thesis to the door of the steel age: "It is the purpose of this work to show that the distribution of the income of society is governed by a natural law, and that this law, if it worked without friction, would give to every agent of production the amount of wealth which that agent creates." [10] Trade-unions were friction: minimum wage laws were friction: the well-contrived machine, if only it were let alone, would produce not only goods —but justice!

It was that idea, embodied in the very phrase "social science," which rendered orthodox economics so sterile in application to the problems of an actual human society. Apart from the metaphysics of marginalism, which was a later development, the main body of that teaching was sound and useful. It showed with irrefutable logic the limits and general contour of the situation within which impersonal economic activity is carried on: a situation that no system whatever can ignore with impunity. But the analogy to physical science applied in the study of human society constitutes the very core and cancer of falsehood; for it excludes the essential characteristic of the subject matter—just as if a physicist began by so describing phenomena as to exclude the fact of inertia. Thus the classical economists by harping on the notion of "science" (as science was then understood) and claiming finality for the results because they were "natural" (as nature was then understood) paved the way for the preposterous contention that by setting avarice free of all restraints from top to bottom of society, a perfectly equitable state of affairs would result without the necessity on anyone's part for either moral philosophy or moral effort.

Any farmhand or factory worker knows that that contention is false. Exclude morality from your calculations and you produce a polity every whit as unworkable as if you exclude rationality. But when farmhands and factory workers raised the cry of injustice,

10. *The Distribution of Wealth*, Preface.

classical economics knew not what they were talking about. Its logic was sounder than that of any alternative scheme they could appeal to; and it had no further answer because it had begun, quite legitimately, by excluding from its field that whole set of values human beings intend when they talk about justice and equity.

Nineteenth-century liberalism came near impaling itself on this dilemma. The ideal of liberty that had come down from Locke, Milton, the Whig philosophers, and Adam Smith was corralled within the iron fence of the doctrinaires and their radical supporters. Disraeli saw it, and rescued a good deal of liberalism for the Tory Party. Political liberalism survived in Britain while continental liberalism died, only because of its empirical character, which readmitted by the back door those dynamic factors that had been expelled by the front.

Laissez faire, as its name implies, was truly a French rather than an English doctrine, and its influence on British policy has been fantastically exaggerated. Even as doctrine, it never reached the systematic perfection of the Frenchman Bastiat or the American Clark; and as policy it was consistently honored in the breach. As we shall see, the "triumph of free trade" involved considerations much more profound than the equations of the classical economists. The work of the neoclassicists Marshall and Pigou harks back to the empirical humanism of Adam Smith; and modern economists have been the first to insist that their studies supply no final criteria for social action. But English laissez faire was reinforced by the hard materialism of the north, into which the dregs of puritanism had now crystallized; by an atheist philosophy which was the speculative counterpart of that; and by certain winds of doctrine that blew over from revolutionary France. These we shall now consider.

VIII

France and Individualism

*1. The problem of unity. — 2. The passion for clarity. —
3. The secular origins of individualism. — 4. Its revolutionary statement. — 5. Contrasting effects.*

§ 1

FOR some hundred and fifty years a major part of the education of an Englishman has consisted in the effort to understand the French. The Spanish are definitely beyond his
comprehension. The Russians do not expect it, the Americans do
not need it. The Germans present a problem, but not an insoluble
one; for there is no such thing as the German mind or spirit, there
are several—the schizoid tendency is conspicuous—and by taking
them one at a time, the Englishman can get some notion of what
the shooting is all about. But there emphatically is such a thing
as the French spirit: not only *l'esprit,* but *la patrie,* which is also
a spirit; and perhaps a part of the English difficulty in recent years
is that so many of the French appear to have lost touch with it
themselves.

The French aspiration to unity, French patriotism, what a
Frenchman means by la patrie, is something that others can approach only intellectually, which is rather less than halfway. Of
course, some part of this passion is due to the difficulty of the historical circumstances; but not all of it. At heart perhaps it springs
from a sense of consecration: the Celtic strain coming through.
While there are millions of French men and women who have
never said an Ave Maria, there are very few for whom Joan is
not a saint. But she dwells in heaven, not in Paris; and if—as is
probable—she sometimes visits her land, an orchard in Lorraine
would be a likelier spot to meet her than the Place de la Concorde.

It would seem as if the aspiration to unity had fallen victim to
that undying illusion in which the meaning of all our mortal life

appears to lie in some human association, or function, or society; while the true France—the home for which the Frenchman has no word—lies on another plane than this. And perhaps it has been the fate of modern France, too skeptical of other planes, to seek in political forms a fulfilment they cannot contain: the security, and the glory, of a house not made with hands. But it is permissible also to hold that the French genius was never more clearly, nor more tragically, displayed than in the fact that when the perennial quarrel of the nation-states approached its bloody climax, there were so many Frenchmen, of both the right and the left, who had outgrown that archaic type of association.

As we said, the integration of France, so far as it was ever achieved, came much later than that of England; and it is note-worthy that the difficulties all along came at least as much from within as from without. The steady development of English com-munity went on for centuries irrespective, on the whole, of what brand of religion the king professed, what his birthright might be, what foreign policy he pursued, what executive machinery he em-ployed. These issues indeed had arisen, but seldom so high as to interrupt for long the process of integration; Britain's greatest war visibly strengthened the ties. Not so in France; one pays a high price for living (or dying) on the continent of Europe. There frontiers were more fluent than the waters of Britain, and local loyalties, like rocks, wrecked many a ship of state. The craving for unity, so often and so passionately manifest, was seldom permitted to make straight for its goal; other issues always supervened. Thus in the wars of the sixteenth and seventeenth centuries, dynastic and national ambition involved the crown in the battle of the faiths. Catholic France fought on the Protestant side: that is, all the king's horses and all the king's men—but by no means all of what was aspiring to be France. Pleas for internal unity were lost in the clamor for external victory; but behind external victory arose internal dissension, temporal and spiritual, and the nascent liberalism of the time was drowned in violence. Its loss not only cost thousands of Protestant lives, but made the very basis of authority a political and religious battleground. The theory of sovereignty itself became an open wound in the side of France, that had never a chance to heal. Well might it seem to the Bour-bons that the commonweal—when at last they had time and en-ergy to set about it—depended upon extreme centralization; and that authority could not be centralized without also being absolute—a fallacy that has disastrously persisted.

Under the absolute monarchy, backed by the Gallican Church, the various elements of French life were visibly pulled together; but it was rather as subjects of the crown than as members of the commonweal. The unity was, and remained, that of a system rather than of an organism. Colbert, says the *Cambridge Modern History*, "defended at every point the cause of monarchy rather than humanity." [1] The verdict is harsh: Colbert saw absolute monarchy as the sole reliable agent of nation building—as at one time the English had seen it—and in his day he was probably right. Along those lines the work proceeded as far as it could go; but neither extensively nor intensively could it go far enough. At no time prior to Napoleon did the areas of political, of legal, and of commercial integration coincide. Despite the work of Sully, Richelieu, Colbert, Turgot, refractory enclaves of authority persisted, the material basis of the commonweal was incomplete, nor—in either the general or the special sense of the term—was there a common law. And it was the price of the past—that past so rich in everything but peace and quiet—that now the time factor became critical. For in the same hour that centralization was nearing its goal under absolute monarchy, forces were gathering that would challenge both the centralization and the absolutism, in both theory and practice. Their explosion destroyed supreme authority itself. Its basis, its rationale, had to be redefined and recodified, late in time, from the foundations. Yet the revolution was unable to establish a lasting liberalism. Its legacy was another centralization with a different bureaucracy, and another absolutism with a different dogma. In due course new challengers appeared—and the pattern repeated itself.

§ 2

HARDLY second to the French passion for unity is the passion for clarity: the heirs of the Greeks have prided themselves upon it, and not without reason. A highly qualified English observer, Wilfrid Ward, writing about 1900, said of this characteristic: "I believe that the French habit of self-analysis and self-expression really belongs to a stage of self-realization radically different from

1. *Cambridge Modern History*, Vol. V, chap. i.

self-consciousness, and which is characteristic in some respects of a higher advance in purely mental civilization than our own countrymen have yet reached." [2] But as Ward noted even then, this particular excellence had its price: the danger of political instability. For in matters of general import the attempt to reach finality of definition divides men more than it unites them; and the more serious the affair, and the keener the intelligence applied to it, the deeper goes the divisive effect. The English always retreat before an absolute; the French advance. The English survived their "glorious revolution" in virtue of their distrust of both glory and revolution; had they seriously discussed first principles, the Lord knows who might now be ruling England. But the critical Declaration of a doubtfully authorized convention was a masterpiece of makeshift, and the fundamental stipulation was not even mentioned, namely, that William had to sign before they put the crown on him.

Such a way of settling a revolution could never satisfy a Frenchman: what a wasted opportunity! To the French approach, the occasion for a constitution would demand that it be made clear and consistent. The basis of authority could hardly escape definition, and some sort of an absolutism would thereby get established— probably in the form of universal first principles (evident especially to Frenchmen). Within a generation or two the French mind, unable ever to desist, would discover, or rediscover, some slightly different basis of allegiance. The matter would begin in the schools, go forward in the journals and the cafés, and end—it has happened before—on the barricades: for the Frenchman is much more likely to act in conformity with what he believes, or thinks he believes, than is the Englishman. On the latter, the sense of solidarity with his class, his people, his tradition is a powerful check (usually mistaken for muddleheadedness); to the former, sheer intellectual integrity—the integrity not only of his own mind but of the French mind as he has received it—is a point of honor; and in both cases the issue may touch the nerve of a very stubborn pride.

If therefore the essence of liberalism is a denial of all absolutes, if it is merely a relativism based on practical expediency, it will always have—as it always has had—rough going in France. Liberals themselves very easily forget that it is only to *political* organization that liberalism denies the sphere of absolutes; it is

2. Ward, W., *Problems and Persons*, pp. 362–363.

because of its supreme respect for personal ends that liberalism keeps the state at a distance. That is a hard lesson for a Frenchman; for while he loves liberty he loves the state too; and it is always difficult to keep two loves under the same roof.

The paradox became conspicuous in the theory of individualism. The French wrote an individualist doctrine into both the constitutional and the criminal law of the revolution, and kept it there for the greater part of the nineteenth century. The doctrine was false; and, in the end, it killed the revolution. The search for an absolute in secular terms encounters the difficulty that there may be more than one such absolute; and between absolutes in conflict who shall define a common ground? The Third Republic found that problem insoluble, as its end bore witness; and once again Frenchmen resorted to violence for the solution of a problem which, in the very nature of the case, violence can never solve. It is worth while to look a little closely at the rise, and the effects, of French individualism; for American thought in this sphere has been influenced more by French ideas than by British, shows the same type of political reaction, and is now visibly heading the state for the same kind of débâcle.

§ 3

THE Black Death evoked in France measures similar to those of England. John the Good—who is credited with debasing the currency eighty-one times in five years—not only tried to regulate prices and wages (1351) but asserted freedom of occupation by abolishing (on parchment) the gild limitations on apprenticeship. The device, however, was even less successful than its English counterpart; and the following century saw the beginning of a policy that was ultimately to prove fatal to the crown itself. The traditional rights and privileges of the gilds were reaffirmed; but with a careful reservation of the royal prerogative. The use of this prerogative came to be concerned less with the economic functions of the gilds than with the fiscal necessities of the crown. As early as the reign of Louis XI (1461–83) we find the sale of mastership being resorted to to raise revenue: that is, the grant of the mastery to outsiders—sometimes untrained persons—in return for a contribution to the royal exchequer. The policy was continued on and off for three centuries, and elaborated by the arbitrary creation of new offices and the direct establishment of royal monopolies (also for lease or sale) in the newer trades. From time to time, notably in 1581, attempts were made at the compulsory extension of corporate organization where it did not already exist; partly to facilitate trade regulation, but partly also to provide new centers of tribute. The increasing financial difficulties of the crown thus committed it more and more deeply to the maintenance of commercial privilege; and although regulations were sometimes enacted to mitigate the pressure of monopoly by the opening of markets, the vested interests proved too strong for their success, while the financial tie-up precluded any statesman from pushing the matter to extremes.

The final outcome was ironic. The state, despite the success with which in certain directions it had furthered the producers' interest, became identified in the popular mind with the economic oppression it had been forced to tolerate; while the oppressors themselves—the gilds and corporations—went bankrupt under the incessant exactions of the royal exchequer. The crown perhaps might have been saved by Turgot's drastic purge of 1776; but after that was rejected, the monarchy itself was doomed along with its ill-chosen allies.

There had been signs for half a century of what was coming: censorship, riots, raids, imprisonments, suppressions. The sayings of Rousseau, of Voltaire, could no more be suppressed than the ideas of the *Economistes* or the wave of popular resentment on which they were riding. Diderot's *Encyclopaedia* was promptly— and ineffectually—proscribed on appearance; it contained, among other things, a frontal attack on the gilds and corporations by Villeneuve, and a statement of the case against Colbertism by Turgot himself: "Les hommes sont-ils puissamment intéressés au bien que vous voulez leur procurer, laissez-les faire: voilà le grand, l'unique principe." [3] For two decades he battled for his principle in that honest, unsubtle, tenacious way of his, with infinite loyalty to France and to his sovereign: knowing that if it were Turgot who must bite the dust this time, it might well be the crown itself rolling there the next. Beaten in 1776, loyal still in disgrace, he dares to write to his king: "They say you are weak, sire, and there have been times when I feared so myself; but I have seen you show true courage in more difficult circumstances than this. You

3. Article on "Fondations," 1757. See Turgot, A. R. J., *Oeuvres*, Vol. I (Schelle).

have said yourself that you lack experience . . . Never forget, sire, that it was weakness cost Charles the First his head." [4] Such was the man who, with a monarch behind him, might at the eleventh hour have averted the revolution!

Turgot's case against the monopolies, like his case against state regulation, rests on specific as much as on general grounds. That there were abuses and a real need of reform, even the Six Companies of Paris, and their spokesman in the Parliament of 1776, admitted. An enquiry into the affairs of the gilds had been started in 1716, and there had actually been half-hearted reform movements before Turgot's time. But the extension of the system by successive royal edicts had not been accompanied by an adequate supervision of their rules and practices. The vested interests of the court and the royal exchequer had stood in the way. Now the gilds as well as the state were bankrupt. Neither the public nor the crown, said Turgot, had really anything to gain by their continued existence: "I do not think anyone could seriously and in good faith maintain that these societies, with their exclusive privileges, and the obstacles they put in the way of enterprise, incentive, and technical advance, are of any use whatever." [5]

In this contention Turgot undoubtedly had the support of the small bourgeoisie everywhere, as well as of the whole group of economists. The decline of agriculture and the pressure of the abominable tax system were rendering life increasingly precarious; the rural population was drifting to the towns, as it has in almost every economic crisis of France; and the restrictions upon the chance of earning any sort of a living were being forced into the foreground of popular discontent. The celebrated manifesto of Bigot de St. Croix, in addition to the usual charges, stresses the effect of gild monopoly on the cost of living. "Once a man has got the exclusive right of selling me this or that article, he becomes from that moment the dictator of the price; I have to submit to his terms. Once a regulation forces me to employ a particular workman, he charges me what he likes. Give me back my freedom, and the monopoly is at an end." [6] The whole case against the gilds is summed up in a tremendous peroration prefixed to the edict of abolition—the denial of opportunity to the mass of willing work-

4. Levasseur, P. E., *Classes Ouvrières*, II, 633.
5. *Mémoire*, *Oeuvres*, Vol. V.
6. Martin-St. Léon, E., *Histoire des corporations de métiers*, VI, 3.

ers, the rigid exclusion of women, the technical obscurantism and social parochialism, the enhancement of the cost of living by all sorts of arbitrary fees and charges levied on the workmen, the everlasting quarrels over jurisdiction, the effective maintenance of a pitiless plutocracy.[7]

So far, so good: it is in the reasoning by which a general principle was extracted from this specific situation that our interest principally lies. In Turgot's abortive policy of 1776, as well as in it resurrection by the Constituent Assembly fifteen years later, the harsh and doctrinal tendency stands out clearly; and it is impossible altogether to exonerate him from some of the charges levied against the encyclopaedists and physiocrats. From their worst faults his practicality and common sense saved him: he was more intent on getting things done than on theorizing about them. As Voltaire said: [8]

> A Turgot, je crois fermement;
> Je ne sais pas ce qu'il va faire,
> Mais grâce à Dieu, c'est le contraire
> De ce qu'on fit jusqu' à présent.

The extreme character of the 1776 legislation is not entirely the result of doctrinaire thinking. As a practical statesman, Turgot may well have felt that the counterproposals of reform brought forward by his opponents were hopeless in the circumstances. In view of the nature of the opposition, he could not afford to temporize; the prompt suppression of their reply to St. Croix's pamphlet shows this clearly. In fact, he seems to have realized that the fate of the monarchy itself might depend on drastic action, and —if a remark of the elder Mirabeau is to be trusted—to have come in the end to despair of that institution. Further, he had never been drawn very far into the a priori theorizing of the physiocrats. His use of the natural harmony theory, for example, is mostly confined to specific instances where the case for liberty could be empirically established on the facts. His application of the doctrine of natural rights is, on the whole, similarly specific. His assertion of the right to work (*droit de travailler*) against the corporations goes nowhere near the danger point of 1848—Louis

7. Text in *Oeuvres*, Vol. V. Complete translation in Shepherd, R. P., *Turgot and the Six Edicts*.
8. Quoted in *Oeuvres*, Vol. V.

Blanc attacked him for it.[9] He was, in fact, well aware of the dangers of political sectarianism, and had more than once criticized the "sectarian attitude" and "fanatical tone" of the economists. "As soon as savants surrender themselves in pride to constitute a body and say 'we,' and believe themselves able to give laws to public opinion, thoughtful public opinion revolts against them, wishing to receive laws from the truth only and not from authority." [10]

The school with which Turgot would never quite identify himself certainly lay open to the implied censure. De Tocqueville, in a very bitter passage,[11] contrasts the intellectual arrogance of the French liberals with the pragmatic moderation of the English and Americans. The work of the former, he says, is supposed to rest on an adoration of human reason; but in truth it was merely their own reason they adored. It is interesting to note that this criticism was also a contemporary one: Schelle gives a lively example of it, emanating from the court party in 1776.[12]

> Ce n'est pas de nos bouquins
> Que vient leur science:
> Eux seuls, ces fiers paladins
> Ont la sapience.
> Les Colbert et les Sully
> Nous paraissent grands, mais fi!
> Ce n'est qu'une ignorance.
>
> Du même pas marcheront
> Noblesse et roture;
> Les Français retourneront
> Au droit de nature.
> Adieu, Parlement et lois,
> Les princes, les ducs, les rois,
> La bonne aventure.

From two weaknesses of the school, however, Turgot was not exempt. One was a lack of the historical sense. In his sweeping denunciation of the legitimacy of the gilds, his persistent regard of them as nothing but predatory parasites upon the body politic, he displays a decidedly a priori view of social process. Behind it lay an ardent faith in the perfectibility of human nature, an ideal-

9. In his *History of the Revolution*. See Say, Léon, *Turgot*, chap. viii.
10. Quoted in Shepherd, *op. cit.*, chap. ii.
11. *L'Ancien Régime*, III, 1.
12. *Oeuvres*, Vol. V.

ism that not even his losing struggle with Louis XVI could quite eclipse. But Seguier, in his weighty speech of opposition to the decree, showed himself more realistically minded. Yes, says Seguier, there are certainly abuses that call for cure; but that is no reason for murdering the patient. Certainly more liberty is desirable; but it must be liberty under law, not anarchy. After all, human beings are far from perfect. They are greedy of gain, and honesty is unfortunately not always and everywhere the best policy. (Marat subsequently made almost an epigram of this: "If from the desire to make a fortune be taken away the desire to establish a reputation, farewell to good faith." [13]) We cannot assume—as Turgot had argued—that competition for trade will prove a sufficient guarantee against fraud, or compel employers to discriminate in favor of the best workmen. And through the protest runs an undertone of fear of disorder and violence once the "turbulent youth" is loosed from the restraints then lying on it. It is true, of course, as the Webbs have pointed out,[14] that Seguier presents a typical defense of vested interests in occupations; but he also shows an appreciation of the role of corporate entities in social life that Turgot and his school fatally lacked.

A second weakness is the tendency toward rash generalization, conspicuously illustrated in the fundamental maxim of Turgot's policy. "The root of the evil," he says, "is in the very right accorded to artisans of the same trade to associate and act together in a body." Accordingly, the decree (Art. XIV) abolishes and prohibits not merely the tyrannous associations of masters but all associations of artisans, companions, or apprentices as well, acquiring thus that purely negative and destructive character that modern French commentators have deplored. And all in the name of individual freedom! The individual was ostensibly being given the chance to seek his own interest; yet if his interest lay—as it was increasingly to lie—in one paramount direction, he was expressly and rigorously enjoined from pursuing it.

§ 4

IT WAS precisely this negative character that subsequent legislation developed and emphasized. Not only does the revolutionary legislation prohibit, in the most detailed and specific way, any

13. Say, *loc. cit.*
14. Webb, S., *Industrial Democracy*, II, 566.

group action on the basis of common employment; it elevates the disintegration of corporate life into a series of maxims that lie at the root of the whole movement and its manifold sequel. The phrases of the Declaration sound plausible enough until one remembers the use to which they were put two years later: "The source of all sovereignty is essentially in the nation; no body, no individual, can exercise authority that does not proceed from it in plain terms. . . . Nothing can be forbidden that is not interdicted by the law, and no one can be constrained to do that which it does not order." [15]

"Fanaticism," said Hegel in a trenchant phrase, "wills an abstraction." The 1791 version of Turgot's policy shows the abstraction triumphant. "There are no longer any gilds in the state, but only the private interest of each individual and the general interest. No one may arouse in the citizens any intermediate interest, or separate them from the public weal by corporate sentiment." [16] In the time and place, Le Chapelier's famous declaration to the Constituent Assembly of 1791 sounded like a triumph of liberty, the climax of half a century's agitation by the pioneers of economic freedom. Actually it turned out to be divine-right monarchy in the dress of the period. The decree of 1791 makes of the sovereignty of law a denial of all group action in social life— not only unfortunately but mistakenly as well. Citizens of the same trade or calling—whatever their status—may form no association, temporary or permanent, may make no joint decisions, may formulate no rules as to their "pretended common interests," may maintain no officers or records, may not even deliberate on common plans to affect the terms of employment. To do any of these things is made a criminal offense; to instigate them involves also the loss of citizenship.

It is comprehensible, of course, that the long oppression of the individual should have led to some overstatement of the case; but it needs more than that to justify the extent to which that case was pushed. It was suggested to Le Chapelier, for example, that voluntary associations of workmen might be permissible when their purpose was mutual help in time of sickness or unemployment. But he would have none of it. That, he says, is the duty of society, acting through its officials, and for it to be done privately,

15. Anderson's translation in *Constitutions and Documents*.
16. Quoted in Pic, P., *Traité élémentaire de législation industrielle*, III, 4.

if not absolutely dangerous through bad administration, at any rate tends to resurrect the corporations.[17] Martin-St. Léon has repeatedly pointed out the sterility of the two extremes of individualism and state socialism. In fact, there were not even two extremes, but only one; for the French state was extraordinarily slow to acknowledge any positive responsibility in the matter. The nation was thus saddled with a half truth that was considerably less than half true. A doctrine of individualism shorn of the right of association is in its nature static and reactionary. The atomic theory of society amounts to a denial of the very forces that create society; it is in fact a theory, not of society, but of sovereignty. The pure individual is a pure abstraction, and a state that is supposed to consist solely of such individuals is an abstraction too. Abstractions are useful in their proper place; but applied to a world of living persons they invariably become tyrannical. The individualism of revolutionary theory, despite its optimistic assumptions, enacted into law the fallacies of Hobbes; and what resulted was Leviathan.

But there were two things Leviathan could not digest, in spite of Hobbes's prescription: the Church and its antithesis, Marxist materialism; for each of these involved an absolutism that was certain to conflict, sooner or later, with the monistic type of sovereignty the revolution had sponsored. Of the two, the Church was likely to provide the acuter bellyache; for there was always a chance that dialectical materialism, working from within, might transform the motivation of the state while preserving, and even enhancing, its monistic character. This was because the type of rationalism the eighteenth century let loose, and the revolution embodied, always speaks for practical purposes the lingua franca of materialism. The most idealistic of rationalists, devoted to humanism and toleration, will readily avow that transcendental ends and concepts are things about which men differ. There may or may not be something in them: in the absence of any way of settling the matter, it is best to let each man decide for himself. So community on that basis can play at best but a minor role in social affairs. But everyone will agree on the desirability of good food and good wine, and plenty of it; that becomes therefore the explicit goal of collective existence. Couple this reasoning with a theory of sovereignty that knows no inherent limits on the scope

17. Martin-St. Léon, *loc. cit.*

of state action, and you have the spurious and pitiless democracy
of economic egalitarianism in place of the true democracy of
Christian humanism. You see also the process that has landed
many excellent people in the camp of the extreme left, wondering
how they got there and where they are going, yet seeing nowhere
else to go.

The Church fought this reasoning all through the nineteenth
century. Religious organizations no less than economic ones were
penalized by the fundamental law of individualism; and Rome
fought all the harder because of the involvement, and the incon-
sistency, of French policy in the temporal affairs of the Vatican.
But under the struggle for power was the enduring issue of principle; and the Church attacked, and has continued to attack, the
pet dogma of the revolution with its inherent trend toward materialism and secular absolutism. The fact that Mussolini attacked
it too does not make the Vatican fascist: even Benito had his insights.

The issue was no theoretical debate. The first important mitiga-
tion of the anticombination laws, confined to the sphere of labor,
came in 1864: largely as a result of the strong lead given by the
Anglophile emperor. But that was the year of the First International; and when French wage earners received a qualified liberty
to organize, their leaders—who were probably more literate than
those of any country except Prussia—were already prepared for,
and largely imbued with, the revolutionary materialism of Marx
and his French precursors. The educational compromise of 1833
had given the Church a place in elementary education at the price
of surrendering higher education to the state; and the Jesuits, who
had foreseen the outcome, fought with every weapon they could
lay their hands on, including some of the most violent journalism
that even France can show. Eighteen sixty-four was also the year
of the famous encyclical *Quanta Cura*, with its Syllabus of Errors,
in which Pius IX took his revenge on the liberalism with which he
himself had started life, which now seemed to have betrayed
both him and his sacred charge.

But the battle into which Pius now flung himself with such fury
had been going on a long time; and for his side he might have
claimed even the august authority of the *Encyclopaedia Britannica*. The *Britannica* had started serial publication in 1768, as not
only a rival, but an antidote, to Diderot's. In the preface to the

bound edition of 1801, dedicated to King George, the editors observe that the French production was "justly accused of having disseminated far and wide the seeds of anarchy and atheism. If the *Encyclopaedia Britannica* shall in any degree counteract the tendency of that pestiferous work . . . (it) will not be wholly unworthy of your Majesty's attention." [18]

Looking back on the papal Caesarism of Pius IX, it must be admitted that no pope since the sixteenth century had been faced with such critical problems or subjected to such complex influences. A papacy that had political territories to defend—and by a polyglot army—could not possibly come to terms with a liberalism that was for the time being necessarily identified with political nationalism. Nowadays it is easy for us to see that the true life of the Church was no more involved in the matter of the temporal power than liberalism was synonymous with the principle of nationality. But people—even popes—fight with what apparatus and what vision they have; and few prelates could discern, as the waves of secular ambition, secular passion, and secular idealism tossed the bark of Peter, the wider waters to which that vessel was being driven in despite of its helmsman. Least of all could Italian and Spanish ultramontanes see with Newman that the Church was undergoing a rebirth, in which its material connection with a doomed world of thrones and dominations was to be severed, that it might live and grow beyond all expectation on a plane more suited to the needs of an era not yet in sight. Newman's own compatriot Manning—so much more powerful for so short a time!— could not see that either; and would hardly have liked the prospect if he could.

Far more important—and Pius knew it—was the ideological struggle; and if he saw it only in black and white, there were plenty on the other side who saw it that way too. Then as now there were liberals who thought it their duty to wage war not only on the Church but on everything it stood for. They had not had time to discover that the weapons of science and sociology were double edged (Mr. H. G. Wells has not even yet had time). In the major issue, the political doctrine and practice of the French Republic were not neutral; and the famous Syllabus, aimed especially at France, was the outcome of fifteen years' cogitation in which Frenchmen had played a leading part. In it Pius took over the

18. "Encyclopaedias," *Encyclopaedia Britannica* (1940).

absolutist thesis that nothing should come between the state and
the individual, and categorically substituted Church for state.
Against the atomic theory of society he advanced the argument—
which Charles Maurras was later to appropriate to the cause of
monarchy—"that authority is something different from numbers
and the sum of material forces." He or his advisers saw that to
make the individual as such the datum for social polity is to exclude from the reckoning all the values that make society safe or
decent; and in a curiously appealing voice he asked (in *Quanta
Cura*), "Who does not see that human society, loosed from the
chains of religion and true justice, can have no other aim than
that of acquiring and heaping up wealth, and can follow no other
law save the desire of serving personal pleasures and interests?"
If you take away *jus* you get mere material force (*vis materialis*)
and then might makes right. The will of the people is therefore
not truly sovereign, save in so far as it is informed and bound by
justice.[19]

If it seem paradoxical to discover a few truths in the Syllabus of
Errors the remedy is to read it again in the light of the full sequel.
The tactical part of it has long since passed into unhappy history;
its immediate impact was to make miserable the lives of thousands
of good Catholics, to widen the breach between Church and society, and to delight the opposition—who were "filled with glee,"
says Debidour: "they would have been really disappointed if the
pope had not published his views, and they were at no pains to
disguise theirs." [20] But the underlying thesis had substance; and
when Pius hurls his final anathema at any who suggest "that the
Roman Pontiff can and should reconcile himself and come to terms
with progress, liberalism, and modern civilization," we can hardly
avoid the reflection that modern civilization, 1944 style, is indeed
pretty difficult for Christian men to come to terms with.

The issue was sharpening while Pius was preparing his thun-
derbolts. On the opposing side, French and Czech freemasonry,
always anticlerical, was fast becoming antireligious; and the
Université, with its pedagogical advance guard in the Ecole Nor-
male, was training a class of intellectuals prepared to sympathize
with, and to further, the rationalistic materialism of the left. Or-

19. Bury, J. B., *History of the Papacy in the Nineteenth Century.* See also *Cambridge Modern History*, Vol. XI, chap. xxv.
20. Quoted in Galton, A., *Church and State in France*, p. 192.

ganized labor, almost from the start, thought of itself in class terms unmitigated by much sense of spiritual catholicity—and not organized labor only, but the mass beneath. The condition of Paris after the national defeat of 1870 showed in lurid light the depth of the chasm already existing in French society: the spectacle implanted a lasting horror in the mind of the radical mayor of Montmartre, Georges Clemenceau. But it was not to be the last time that blood would flow from the fusion of those same two issues: the struggle of a class against the state, and the attack of revolutionary atheism on ultramontane Catholicism. Neither the Communards nor the ultramontanists can be saddled with all the blame; there was something wrong with the state too. Why else, in both spheres, should it resort to such savagery in reply?

When at last the proscription of the Communards was relaxed, and the exiles began to return, the case of the wage earners for full freedom of association was backed by the Catholic Church; for the same individualist dogma that had hampered organized labor was now turned even more vigorously against organized religion. But after the repeal of the Loi le Chapelier in 1884 the alliance, on the whole, fell apart; despite the efforts of liberal catholicism to permeate working-class solidarity. Throughout the many divisions and debates of the labor movement, the class point of view predominated; and the drive for unity proceeded mostly from the left. The intolerance of revolutionary individualism now got its answer in such declarations as that of 1905, proclaiming the socialist party to be "not a party of reforms, but a party of class war and revolution." French labor became the headquarters of direct-actionism: the policy of using the power of organized labor to hold both the state and society to ransom; a power that was used with reckless effrontery against even a socialist premier in 1936, successfully defying the concept of legality itself. By that time the ideological or spiritual disintegration of French society had been steadily deepening for two generations; and the state, dominated for those same two generations by a cynical and frequently corrupt materialism, had lost the key to a synthesis.

§ 5

THIS problem of the synthesis or reintegration is by far the most momentous that modern France has to tackle; and there is no issue to which leaders of thought elsewhere should pay more careful attention. For once again the French aptitude to seize and face a fundamental issue has provided a crucial experiment for all the world to watch, of which—once again—the French have paid the price. They have not complained. Bitterly as they have reviled one another, a sort of defiant pride in the *experimentum crucis* has sustained them, rising tragically to a higher plane than the mere pride of power or possession that other nations tiresomely display. For the problem of synthesis that the French are facing in this twentieth century is far more significant to the future of mankind than the what-we-have-we-hold policies of the British, or the naïve notion of "policing" the world entertained by their trans-Atlantic cousins who have so much difficulty in policing their own polyglot cities. The French have not yet solved their problem; nor can any man say for certain that it is soluble. But other nations may well pray with bated breath that they succeed —and tremble if they fail.

Let us therefore make an attempt, however clumsy it may seem, to segregate the elements of the problem as it has developed in the stress of modern times; remembering that the armed struggle for the control of the European steel industry and the resources of southeast Asia is a part of it—a very recent part—and more a consequence than a cause. At the outset a broad dichotomy is conspicuous between French patriotism, felt and expressed as a spiritual ideal, and materialist internationalism. This dichotomy underlies all the tension in French society since even earlier than the Dreyfus affair. But immediately we are struck by the feud within the internationalist side; for there developed, strictly within this sphere, the fiercest battle between the monetary internationalism of the forces that, on the whole, controlled the Third Republic, and the class internationalism of the proletarian leaders (notwithstanding that several of them, as they succeed in their careers, passed from one side to the other). Jewish influence was strong on both sides of this struggle. German influence, in recent decades, was more effective on the right, Russian on the left; but one has not to look back very far to see those roles reversed, as they may be again. And the picture is complicated by the fact that the nationalist right detested the internationalism of high finance no less heartily than did the Marxism of the left, but used a weapon that the left could never handle: anti-Semitism was an effective political force in France much earlier than in Germany.

On the economic left a secondary struggle was all the while in progress as to tactics; and as the debate between Guesde and Jaurès, and the various splinter groups on each side, went on, rather more than tactics was involved. One could say that the question whether to capture control of the state by political methods or by economic coercion was a tactical issue; but the two sides, in all countries, engendered very different tempers. In France the twentieth century witnessed a steady swing of organized labor toward direct action—at least in theory and statement; though many workers who supported it in their trade-union capacity were also, being Frenchmen, keen politicians. The swing gained momentum from the ostentatiously capitalist interests of a long series of bourgeois governments, and it lacked the brake that the bourgeoisie used to supply. For the bourgeoisie also was changing, or losing, its role. The contest of the Masons and the Jesuits had not left the small towns undisturbed. The centralization of pedagogical training had brought the sharp edge of revolutionary doctrine into the smallest hamlets; and in very many the apostles of ultramontanism were ready to meet the challenge. The state itself was thus involved in the ideological issue because it stood on ideological ground. Further, the influence of Paris was being extended in the monetary sphere. Imperialist ventures and the finance of power politics were reaching out through decentralized banking for the savings of the little people, just as political journalism was reaching out for their votes; and the petty bourgeoisie thus lost its stabilizing influence and tended itself to be divided, as the issues sharpened, between the extremes of left and right. As its economic independence steadily dwindled between wars, the tendency was enhanced, and the countryside became unwholesomely urban in its thinking, its financial interests, and its partisanship.

Even before 1914 the direct-action groups, small as they were, were displaying that hardening of the temper that has since become so conspicuous; and the state was consolidating its defenses with an equally drastic determination. From the ruthless proscription of the Communards to the smashing of the great railroad strikes of 1910 and 1920, the middle ground in the economic sphere also was becoming less and less tenable. Many leading politicians

—Clemenceau, Millerand, Viviani, Briand among them—and still more Catholics shared the distrust of international money, and its growing power over the senate; but no responsible politician could do other than defend the state against the avowed attack of the labor militants. Similarly, the gradualism of Jaurès, like that of Blum a generation later, was made more and more difficult to maintain or to popularize; especially in view of the rival militancy of the nationalists. The situation at this point was essentially similar to that of Germany around 1930.

The flamboyant nationalism of Déroulède's League of Patriots, of the Action Française, the Camelots du Roi, the Croix de Feu, and many more ambiguous groups got its emotional start from the reaction to a military humiliation; just as the same sort of thing was to do in Germany later on. But it found the basis of a more lasting program in opposing that peculiarly abstract form of materialism which operates through the institution of large-scale public debt. The financing of the war indemnity of 1871, like that of 1919, opened the door to financial influences which the national communities could in neither case control or assimilate; and as they became more and more evident the reaction was instinctive and violent. Among the results, in both cases, was a decline in public probity and the sense of social responsibility. To many young Frenchmen of the 1880's it seemed that French civilization was passing into the control of a power that knew no country and had no roots; and conscious as they were that the finest values of a culture attain universality through a specific nativity, their sense of mission took on an almost sacred character. The state, it seemed to them, was ceasing to be master in its own house; the new power was the power of money, and it was visibly corrupting its subjects, high and low alike. That power was in private hands—it gravitated by its very nature toward private hands; and those hands were not particularly clean, not particularly cultured, and above all, not particularly French. And it might be that there was something in the revolutionary tradition itself, or in the ambivalent origins of the Third Republic, that played into them. On that score at least, royalists and ultramontanists would agree.

But what was it these young men (one always thinks of them as young) really wanted? They proclaimed from the housetops, with every variety of fanfare, what they were against; but what were they for? Most of them were *revanchistes*—which was natu-

ral enough, but neither very original nor very constructive; most
of them were anti-Dreyfusards and exalted the army—but more
than that was required for a national movement. They flirted with
royalism, but few were genuine monarchists: there is something
curiously unconvincing about Léon Daudet's late conversion
to monarchy and the Church, and his was one of many such cases.
They flirted with catholicism. Had they seriously endeavored—
as so many of their most gifted compatriots are now doing—to
restore their country to its pivotal position in a reunited Christendom, then indeed a glorious Easter might have dawned on the lilies
of France. But did they suppose they could make the tradition of
Catholic Christendom itself an instrument of their ambition, or
their discontent, or even their ardent patriotism? Apparently they
did, since it became at last necessary to put the *Action* on the Index in 1926. Both Leo XIII and Pius XI were better Frenchmen
than they were. What was left them but a sterile militarism? They
were too intelligent, thousands of them, not to see that if the fate
of their country were to depend on the issue of mere brute force,
cannon fodder, and weight of material, then the dice were so
heavily loaded against France that the game would be worth
playing no longer. Peace, then, by other means—and a chance to
keep on hoping, keep on striving? That would be a very long shot
—but France was older than the Third Republic, or the German
Empire. Or war: and for whose sake? That of a regime they had
so long abused that they had convinced themselves it was hopeless?
As the movement began in confusion, so it ended. Lacking clarity
of purpose, some small part of it was subverted by the very power
it had arisen to defy. But by far the greater part, still bitter and
perplexed, limned in its blood the outline of the France it had
never succeeded in defining. That task remains. . . .

Ironically enough, a similar dilemma was hovering over the
very antipodes of the political landscape. There too eager spirits
were disputing the muddy course of the Third Republic, planning
a cleaner France in a nobler world; and there too the dilemma bore
down hardest on the keenest minds. The position of Jaurès, great
Frenchman and fine scholar as he was, contained an inner weakness that is common to all schools of reformist international socialism. Perhaps his assassination on the very eve of the first
World War was a merciful release for Jaurès. It spared him the
agony of mind he must have undergone in the next ten years; nor

was he likely to have accepted such consolations as were possible
to his British analogue. Jaurès had believed in and worked for
international solidarity via labor organization with a sincerity
rare even in that school of politics—the cleanest of the lot. But
what does the program really have to offer? In general terms,
the ideal of an international fraternity of wage earners, so far
realized that they will refuse any more to slaughter one another,
is a logical and attractive goal; but in political practice—as recent
wars have abundantly demonstrated—it is too negative to prevail
against the more tangible claims of nationality. This is not, as
some have despondently suggested, because the masses are too
stupid to know their own interests; they probably know them as
well as the employers know theirs—though that, of course, is not
saying much. The fact is, international working-class community
is a beautiful but bloodless phantom. There is no such community,
nor is there likely to be. The program rests in the main on economic
considerations, and relies upon them almost exclusively for its im-
plementation; but when it comes to a real test, they have neither
the attractive nor the compulsive power that is assumed. It is an
"erroneous belief," says a brilliant modern economist, "that there
are purely economic ends separate from the other ends of life. The
ultimate ends of the activities of reasonable beings are never economic." [21] We may go farther: the dominance of merely economic
motivation, no matter how logical or how necessitated, always
signifies a decline in human energy, a relapse from the dynamic
spirituality of Western man to the less aspiring ways of a defunct
Orient. Communist materialism is most effective in Jewish hands
because there there is something behind it that is not materialist,
but is inaccessible to the Gentile. For Western man it has only the
blind, though very formidable, force of the appetites. Yet anything
less is liable to get the worst of both worlds. If it is argued—as it
may fairly be—that the aims of international labor go well beyond
the economic, then why rely so heavily on the trade-unions, which
are among the most highly protected groups in modern societies?
In effect, the preponderant emphasis laid by international labor
organization on economic aims, and on an arbitrary abstraction
from the heterogeneity of social structure, removes it from the
sphere of actuality. Compared with the national community, the
ideal is altogether too thin—as the action of the average wage

21. Hayek, F. A., *The Road to Serfdom*, p. 89.

earner shows in every international crisis. The national community has done more for him (good or bad) and means more to him. It is tangible; it has its history, language, institutions, associations; convince him that it is threatened, confront him with a choice (as Nazi propaganda very astutely did) between loyalty to an abstract international class and loyalty to the community he knows by experience, and in nine cases out of ten he chooses the latter. Nor is the tenth case much to count on in practical affairs. As an international community, the Church has far more to show for itself: it is actual: its discipline, its doctrine, its schools and institutions, its language and liturgy, make it a part of concrete experience. And apart from the Church, effective internationalism under the present order can only be that of its opposite: that which is prepared to throw over the national community and all its works, and trains its disciples with a Jesuit thoroughness in that attitude.

The logic of tactics, in this war behind the war, is with the extremists. Armed with the dogma of economic determinism, they alone have the apparatus and the resolution to tear to pieces the national community as a necessary preliminary to the construction of a new society out of selected fragments. But the fate of Trotsky —who alone was consistent—shows how any self-conscious community is likely, in the end, to deal with that endeavor. There is an instructive irony in the position of those intellectuals who thought they saw in Moscow the realization of an international brotherhood, and are now tied to the chariot wheels of a power-politics that has grafted the ruthlessness of the class war onto the old stem of pan-Slavism. It is a safe prediction that that position will not commend itself for long to the majority of the French people; and those who defend it would be wise to take warning. They include many whose display of patriotism in the political executions of 1944 contrasts rather oddly with the amount their logic permitted them in 1939.

At this point, it is evident, we face an impasse. Looking at the logic of the situation as France has revealed it, we have found no clear lead to freedom within community in the fervent nationalism of the Maurras-Barrès school; we have dismissed, on different grounds, both the idealist internationalism of the Jaurès type and the more iconoclastic methods of his rivals; we seem to be left with little more than the status quo. And to close the prospect, it is necessary to add—what should by this time be sufficiently obvious—that the national state itself is a cul-de-sac. National states, as we have seen them at work and at war this fifty years, in every variety of situation and structure, are no more easily to be integrated in a wider community than were the gilds and corporations, the feudal absolutisms and local autonomies of the past; they are not bricks that can be used to build a safer and sounder house for humanity, for there is no cement that will stick. So much we may learn from the teaching and experience of the extreme left. From the extreme right also we may take a hint: just as Catholic Christianity has had, within the past half century, to disentangle itself from the trammels of temporal power—not always realizing what it was doing, or what was happening to it—so now liberalism is called on to disentangle itself from the net of political nationality, before it is choked to death.

"The national community," says Professor Toynbee, "is the social prison-house in which our modern western souls are incarcerated." [22] Now the prison-house is on fire; and men are required to show more intelligence than horses.

22. Toynbee, A. J., *A Study of History*, V, 373.

IX

The Valley of Dry Bones

1. The logic of disintegration. — 2. The nation-state as residue. — 3. The nationalist complex. — 4. Great is Diana.

§ 1

THE individualism that so largely characterized the political and economic life of France, America, and England in the nineteenth century is generally, and rightly, regarded as part of a wider movement; though one may doubt whether "movement" is quite the appropriate term. "Movement" implies a definite direction, if not a conscious goal; it suggests, if not a common program, at least an integral purpose, or philosophy, or point of view. The nineteenth century had none of these things on any scale that could be called common or integral. Its activity was centrifugal rather than linear. Its background, as we have said, was the revolt of ordinary men, in one sphere after another, against external authority; but the success of that revolt in itself settled nothing, it was merely the prelude to a wide variety of possibilities.

Consider some of them. There was the logical extension of the revolt against external authority to a revolt against all authority whatever, as we see it in the anarchist philosophies of the mid-century, especially in Russia, with their profound influence on modern art and fiction. This might perhaps be called the extreme of positive individualism. But there was also a negative individualism of passivity, of subjectivism, that led to the cult of sensation, to "art for art's sake," to the weary quest for anything new in experience—the more exotic or perverse, the better. Along this line, of course, the distinction between vice and virtue lost its clarity; and while some extolled the processes of mass murder as the acme of experience, others—to use Algernon Cecil's phrase—exchanged the beauty of Christianity for the beauties of Christianity on a scale that called for more compassion than they could ever appreciate. They were encouraged to do so by the enormous crop of subjectivist philosophies that the nineteenth century produced: the intellectual counterpart of the cult of sensation. We may gladly acknowledge that in both spheres achievements of permanent value and beauty resulted; but they were located on a pleasant backwater rather than the main stream. To make either the aesthetic or the dialectic activity of the isolated individual a final criterion for the truth of art or knowledge was not perhaps illogical; but it was to commit oneself to a decidedly minor phase of the human adventure. There were brilliant minds, from Stendhal to Artzibashef, who sought to deny that; who proclaimed that the individual, magnified and empowered beyond the common run, was the end and meaning of the whole historical process. Ibsen, stating old truth in new terms, exposed the solipsism of that contention once and for all. The prestige of the individual mind, justly earned in the fields of mathematics and pure science, infected the entire scale of valuation. False analogies were drawn between the abstract phenomenal world of the scientist and the concrete world of personality and society; and because they were false, the nineteenth-century understanding of collective life fell far below that of earlier and less enlightened periods. On the periphery, atheist and ultramontane internationalisms fought both each other and the national states; but the states held the center of the field, becoming more militant and more refractory with each succeeding decade. Into the nationalism of the early century had gone some of the purest passion of the romantics; but Byron, Hugo, Mazzini, and even Fichte would have been appalled could they have foreseen what unbridled nationalism was to do to the body of Christendom. For every triumph of free intellect and imagination was proclaiming the inadequacy of the nation-state as a form of human association; yet the century, so brilliant in so many other ways, failed to meet, even to recognize, its most urgent challenge; and the confirmation, and multiplication, of separate nation-states in 1919 made the crowning disaster inevitable. In the light of that disaster all other achievements of modern civilization must be judged; and the nineteenth century cannot escape the fatal verdict, *mene, mene, tekel, upharsin.*

The heterogeneity of its achievement makes the period an inexhaustible mine for historians, from which some have brought up valuable treasure, and in which others have completely lost themselves. Not to court their fate in this brief essay, let us first define what it is that we are seeking. We seek to show, a little more fully than we have yet done, the nature of the connection between the idea of liberty with which the century opened and the Armageddon on which it closed. For the battle of the nations that now ravages almost the entire globe was of no sudden or sporadic origin. Steadily increasing in scope and intensity, it has been going on with diminishing intervals for over ninety years; and it is not something extrinsic to the course of culture and civil society—that idea is on the face of it preposterous—it springs from something inherent in the type of development historians have witnessed and studied so minutely. For each separate outbreak a specific cause, or occasion, can be assigned; and in a short view, blame can be distributed—very widely distributed—for the failure of each successive "peace." But for the process as a whole, its intensification and acceleration in an era of great intellectual and cultural achievement, no such anecdotal history will suffice. Factors more profound than the conscious aims and interests of rival groups or leaders have obviously been at work: factors of the order Acton had in mind when he spoke of the ruling ideas, or perhaps Paul when he wrote of powers and principalities. Wisely did the legend make the Pied Piper a magician; for there is indeed something nonhuman about the ease with which masses of toiling people who have never seen their alleged enemy are led time after time to mutual destruction—and always for reasons that seem, at the time, to be adequate, even compelling. Does this compulsion really spring from an ancient instinct to hunt and kill? Does it reflect a suppressed need to do violence to life, even one's own life? Hypotheses of that sort rest on assumptions so remote, so unverifiable, that every alternative must logically be exhausted before we entertain them seriously. And there are alternatives on a more accessible plane: a plane on which we can take action, if we can muster the courage of desperation.

At the outset we may hazard a broad, but quite empirical, generalization: In periods when freedom is an object of struggle, or is actively being fought for, it is sufficiently conceived as freedom from. Its specific meaning lies mostly on the negative side—though it by no means appears negative while the struggle is on. The vanguard liberals of France, Russia, America, Britain, Italy, were quite specifically aware of the things they were fighting against, in fact, they often made catalogues of them, with ample documentation. What they were fighting for could be sufficiently described, for the time being, in general terms, broad declarations of rights and liberties. Those things belonged to the future, and the portals of possibility were wide open. But as one enters into the future— as one does with every movement, every breath—its amplitude diminishes, and freedom from has to be translated into freedom for. That is the critical phase of the social adventure. It is inescapable for the simple reason that (as Aristotle argued) a perfectly neutral or inactive freedom is meaningless. In the neutral or inactive sense, a carrot or a cow in a field might feel itself free, in that the conative impulses of its being were adequately realized; but since it has none, the term does not apply. Freedom for man means opportunity to frame and realize intentions, to do something, to speak and act in this way or in that according to choice; and though you may produce volumes to prove that the choice is illusory, any man knows the difference between having and not having it.

Now the influences that determine such choice are profound and complex. What freedom will actually mean to the individual runs the full gamut of human possibility. It will normally mean some sort of intended activity—not even the basic appetites can be satisfied without that; but as to the kind of activity, we can say only two things. One, it will normally mean a chance to work, that is, to devote effort to an anticipated result that will be serviceable to the man and his mate. We can be sure of that, inasmuch as it is the material basis of the relationship between man and nature—as Locke so clearly discerned. Two, it will normally mean activity that wins the esteem of other people—as Cumberland and his successors quite rightly insisted; for that is the practical basis of social cohesion. That is all we can say; and there will be exceptions even to that—oddities for whom freedom means only the chance to vegetate, or to prey on others: abnormalities that present no serious problem. But the manifold activities that freedom will normally mean can never be catalogued. Who does not know of some scientist, poet, artist, contemplative, who contentedly accepts a subsistence that any trade-unionist would scorn, so long as he can be free to burn up his life for the bit of light it may throw into human darkness? Men die not for freedom in the abstract, but for freedom to pursue or preserve some line of activity of whose value to mankind they are utterly convinced. And who has not at least read what a mockery abstract freedom becomes to a man for whom society can find no useful employment—even though it may have arranged to keep him alive?

Now this manifoldness, this richness and variety of free activity, was realized in the nineteenth century on a brilliant and perhaps unprecedented scale. Every sphere of Western culture was enriched by new discoveries, new insights, new tools and potentialities. The power and scope of human action, for both good and evil, were enormously and much too swiftly enlarged. What was lacking was some impulse to integration, some secret of synthesis, that could prevent this dynamic mixture from blowing society into fragments, spiritually and perhaps physically as well. That is no merely retrospective judgment: the lack was evident to many men in many different lands and vocations. Walt Whitman was one of them. "Go on, my dear Americans," he exclaimed about 1880: "whip your horses to the utmost—excitement! money! politics!—open all your valves and let her go—swing, whirl with the rest—you will soon get under such momentum you can't stop if you would. Only make provision betimes, old States and new States, for several thousand insane asylums. You are in a fair way to create a whole nation of lunatics."

There was a Saul among the prophets in the person of Alfred Nobel, the "dynamite king" and donor of the so-called peace prize —for which the original inspiration probably came from his friend and antithesis, Bertha von Suttner. Nobel had little faith in the power of intelligence and good will to control the situation he had done so much to create. "I should like," he said, "to be able to turn out a substance or a machine of such horrible capacity for mass annihilation that thereby wars would become altogether impossible." [1] He had certainly done his best, as one way of making a fortune; but he was not satisfied. To be stopped, he thought, war must be made deadly for civilians also; and since the combination of air power and high explosive was not then in sight, he wondered whether bacteriological warfare might turn the trick. Soon after, as was fitting, he died one of the loneliest deaths in history; and if ever there was a parable for modern times, it lay

1. Pauli, H. E., *Alfred Nobel*, p. 232.

in the fact that the doctors had given him his own damned nitro-glycerin to drink for medicine. It failed. As with his century, the heart had died while the brain lived on. But as most good parables have an undertone of humor, we may recall that while Christian men were expatiating on the wickedness of selling firearms and "firewater" to Red Indians and Hottentots, such men as Nobel and Zaharoff (Sir Basil) were encouraged by every sort of inducement to sell their machines and concoctions to governments of Christian men. Thus in the fullness of time were the benefits of applied science impartially applied to civilians and children, black, white, and yellow. Nobel's dream attained its grand fulfilment. And Herr Hitler decreed a boycott of the peace committee for having awarded its prize to a pacifist. Such is the logic of disintegration.

§ 2

WHEN we wonder how it was that the centrifugal forces got so completely out of hand, despite so many warnings, a curious paradox arises. The enlargement and enrichment of personal activities in every sphere should, it would seem, have led to a corresponding enlargement and enrichment of human association. That had actually been the case in several earlier periods of renaissance. But this time the opposite tendency prevailed. The effective forms of human association became fewer, shallower, and progressively less catholic. Everyone knows how the prevalent type of force organization, the nation-state, came to dominate all other types of association—in fact, it killed off a great many; what is surprising is that, in a period of such promising activity, it met with so little resistance. The notion of geographical sovereignty was itself, as we have seen, a late arrival among social concepts, and when it received recognition it was merely as one type of association among others, by no means the most important. As late as the eighteenth century—in a few cases, even the nineteenth—other forms of society were apt to put it in its place when it presumed too far: the cities and communes, the universities, the Catholic Church, and some of the Protestant sects. Indeed we may say, on a careful reading of history, that even in the eighteenth century it is a mistake wholly to identify secular monarchy with the later notion of territorial sovereignty: despite Louis XIV, there was more to it than that. Then, almost suddenly, the life seems to die out of the manifold forms of human association, and the geographical state has things all its own way; while that state itself, as a basis of association, becomes not only exclusive, monistic, arrogant, and quarrelsome, but spiritually poorer and thinner, less and less significant from the standpoint of full human personality. Not only is the notion of geographical patriotism a pretty thin gruel compared to other bases of solidarity that men have lived by; in our own day, and in spite of the sacrifices we have made to it, it has become admittedly thinner and less satisfying.

But other types of association—*including the family itself*—have become thinner too. The home, the farm, the manor, the estate, as centers of integrated living, have been subject to a progressive dissolution that is not merely, nor even mainly, economic. Compare, for instance, the activities that radiated from an Episcopal see in the sixteenth century, or even the restricted group that focused upon the cathedral itself, with what remains today. It is trite, and not quite accurate, to point out that the activities have largely become specialized—a good many have ceased altogether; others, of course, have undergone an autonomous development with an enlargement of scope that was not necessarily an improvement. But take the whole range of administration and local government, the cameral economy, the chapter, school, and seminary, the associated crafts, the music and other arts, the library and record offices, the social services and minor ministries incidental to the main functions—it is a sample of very varied activities integrated. as far as was needful, not so much by pattern as by purpose or central direction; and while some of those activities have been improved as well as extended in the process of detachment, they have also become fragments of a whole that is not there any more, in that fundamental sense, and has not been replaced by any equally significant form of synthesis. In generalizing the functions a good deal of the integration was not extended but lost.

Or consider the scope and content of integral association represented by a well-developed gild, for comparison with that of a modern organized industry. Of course, the industry can boast a greater variety and quantity of product, a wider market, technical and managerial efficiency, specialization and subdivision of labor and all the rest of it; but what strikes one, in most cases, from the associative point of view is that the concern is split right down the middle by the struggle over the division of the income, and that the effective basis of organization on both sides is exclusively economic. The productive function has largely ceased to be a basis of significant community, and that basis has not been supplied by anything else. The gild type of association, as we see it in Roman as well as medieval life, allowed the community of coöperative work its natural expression on other planes of social activity, including a good deal of art and festivity, mutual aid and collective benevolence, and a sense of significant purpose that spoke the same language as other kinds of association. A generation ago students were afraid of idealizing the nature of gild society, and tended to represent its passing as an inevitable phase in the "evolution" of modern enterprise. Now a more serious risk lies in the opposite tendency to minimize the radical contrast, and deny its significance. A strong case can be made to show that the decline of gild society was by no means inevitable, nor due solely to the operation of technical and economic factors. The kind of fatalism that so easily besets certain schools of historical interpretation has its roots in an impulse to evade fundamental issues.[2]

We must not, of course, be led into supposing that earlier types of community could in any case have continued without change, or that they can be re-created in close semblance of their original form. Such questions are not our present concern. What we have here to notice is the broad fact of the loss, or attenuation, of the spirit of association itself, the drying up of its sources, above all the comparative shallowness of the type that came to dominate or devour all others, the territorial nation-state. Yet here too we must make a careful distinction between the national community as a concrete fact of cultural, historical, and functional experience, and the political state of the later nineteenth century that claimed to represent, or even to be, that community in its organized and external aspect.

The validity of that claim varied very widely between different cases. In some, of which perhaps Denmark was the best example, it had substantial justification; in others, of which Ireland under British rule was an extreme instance, it was a none too polite fiction; but in no case whatever had the political association a legitimate title, in the natural order, to supplant or supersede other forms of community; and the more it did so, the less was the like-

2. Cf. Somerville, H., *Why the Gilds Decayed* and references there cited (Paulist Press, New York).

lihood of a liberal, peaceable, and fruitful development of humane society.

This fact, which recent history has so horribly vindicated, is grounded not in the purpose but in the nature of the national states. The current distinction between "peace-loving nations" and all others is, historically and factually speaking, a piece of transparent political cant. Classed by that criterion there is little to choose, over the past century, between Britain, France, Russia, and Germany; and even peace-loving America indulged in the most extraordinary diplomatic contortions to get itself involved, for a second time, in the Anglo-German war. National states, in their external aspect, are power organizations pure and simple— or at any rate, simple: offensive or defensive, according to circumstances. Indeed, when a state sets out to be more than that, and manifests a missionary ardor like France in 1799 or Russia in 1918, it is very firmly stepped on by all the rest, regardless of their internecine rivalries. The game of national states is well understood and consistently played, in peace or war, on the power basis, and cannot be played—as Americans are now discovering—on any other basis, because the pieces are not adapted to any other sort of game. It is an error to attribute any differential characteristics in the way of purposes or conscious aims to the various pieces; because their very nature renders such attribution meaningless— it is literal anthropomorphism. What, for example, makes American advice on India or Palestine so exasperating to the British who are actually involved in the situation is not its content, not even its tone, but the fact that it speaks for the most part in terms and categories that are not relevant to the vast impersonal reality of the British state and its administrative functions. When Gladstone tried to make the state behave in foreign affairs as he thought a Christian gentleman ought to behave, the results were disastrous: not because there was anything wrong with his standards but because the state is not a Christian gentleman: it is not a person at all, and therefore not the sort of entity (alas!) to which personal criteria and valuations apply. His biographer and disciple, John Morley, learned in bitter experience the same lesson. Americans have been encouraged to think of their own foreign policies as different from all the rest, a pure evangel of culture and good will; but what their state is actually doing in South America is what any state would do in its expansionist phase; and if they wish to exercise moral judgment in this inappropriate sphere, they might as well do it from anywhere south of the Rio Grande as from the banks of the Tigris, the Ganges, or the Irrawaddy.

A poignant illustration of the nature of the nation-state is afforded by Czechoslovakia. That highly synthetic entity, with its Slavs, Poles, Hungarians, and Germans, its Catholics, Jews, Freemasons and agnostics, was the product of politics, not history; but its founders, recognizing their problem, set out undaunted to make of it a genuinely integrated community. They knew that this would take time, and that it could not be done arbitrarily; as Masaryk said, "Liberty is strengthened by freedom, not by blood and iron." A federal constitution was promised on the Swiss model, minority guarantees were willingly accorded (in sharp contrast with Poland and Rumania), and a liberal measure of cultural as well as economic decentralization was planned. Had the little state been an island in the Pacific, it might within a few generations have become a true and exemplary society; for there was abundant courage, intelligence, and sincerity. But it was a state in a jostling arena of such entities; and the inherent nature of the political state asserted itself even against the will of the founders. Beneš saw himself forced to make it increasingly monistic, centralized, and military, notwithstanding that no man in Europe worked harder to transform the jungle of nation-states into a community of communities. At last its fate depended on the impersonal calculation of its allies as to whether, or when, its continued existence was worth another war; yet it is futile to propound that issue in terms of good people and bad people. People did what they did, things were as they were, because the blind stresses of a system of nation-states could not, and cannot, shape the issue otherwise. This is not to deny that state policies may be affected, within quite narrow limits, by voluntary and personal pressures; but modern history gives unanimous evidence that the radical change in the interrelation of societies which life now urgently requires cannot be achieved without radical change in the very nature of the structure in which they are predominantly cast. Said Bertrand Russell, thirty years ago, "Every increase in the strength of the state has been a new disaster to mankind." It would seem to follow that every policy which tends in that direction has the weight of evidence against it.

§ 3

THE political state as an agent of widening human community is fatally handicapped by the fact that it is not, and cannot be, human enough. It is too abstract, too impersonal, too monistic. The one sphere in which a monistic, impersonal institution is clearly necessary is the enunciation and execution of law in a settled community. Law must be the same for everybody, and must have a central source, because we cannot get along with several different systems of organized coercion, nor admit several different kinds of authority to coerce. In the formulation and execution of law the state is bound on the one hand by principles of justice that spring from the true nature of man; but it is also bound, on the other, to the active life of the community in which, and through which, those principles are continuously articulated. This is the process we paused to watch in ancient Rome. As here expressed, it corresponds to Stammler's "natural law with changing content," and is in opposition to pragmatic, instrumentalist, or deterministic definitions.

But communities engage collectively in a vast number of activities besides the formulation of law—activities ranging all the way from the maintenance of lighthouses and harbors to the education of children and the care of the insane; there is no limit to them, and there is no general principle that can be used as a limit: it is all a matter of expediency and efficiency, in the widest sense. At some points in the execution of some of these activities, an issue will arise as to which those concerned desire the power of law behind them. At the moment, for example, in the writer's community, the need for a new isolation hospital is being discussed, and some neighboring communities are coöperating in the project. We shall in all probability set aside funds for this purpose, and it is possible that some amendment or extension of law will be required. The appropriate law-making body will then be approached, and presently the courts, if its action is challenged, will see that whatever is enacted conforms to the basic rules and principles of justice. That is the normal type of connection between collective activity and law.

Some activities are of such a nature that rules made in connection with them must apply to every single member of a big nation. If you want to mail a letter you must put the proper stamp on it, whoever and wherever you are; and if you label your envelope "Printed Matter" when it contains manuscript, and so stamp it, you are liable to punishment. Everyone trading in the United States must use the standard kinds of money, weights, and measures. Indeed, in the latter category, we have the beginnings of a wider community; for though not all nations use the same units, a yard is a yard and bears the same relation to a meter or an arshin whether you happen to be in New York, Paris, or Moscow. Whether it is either desirable or possible to achieve a similar result in regard to units of purchasing power, the nations have not yet decided. All such activities, however, are open ended, in that they are not designed to exclude anyone or monopolize anything for the national group, and in many cases are entirely suited to cooperation that ignores political nationality completely. There is nothing, for example, in the nature of our hospital project that would make us decline or repel the advice of qualified Frenchmen, Germans, or Chinese, official or unofficial. The American Government, in its reforestation or soil conservation projects, remains free and willing to give or take assistance to or from Russians, Japanese, or Argentinians—so far as the nature of the enterprise is concerned. For here we are dealing with humanity at work, and work is the foundation of community.

But when we turn to consider the United States or Russia or Japan in its corporate capacity as a nation among nations, we find that we are suddenly talking about a quite different kind of creature. Now we are watching a suspicious and desperate poker game with the revolvers under the table. Are these the same entities that we were just now considering? No, they are not; even though they go by the same names and wear the same clothes. These are states; those were communities; and between the two there is a great gulf fixed. It is the nature and the origin of that gulf that we have to consider. The history of psychology contains many cases of what is traditionally known as demoniacal possession. This is one of them.

The process by which the closed nation-state came to dominate or devour all other types of association was long and intricate. We have seen in earlier chapters how conditions were set for it in the natural integration of the local communities, coupled with the rejection by several of them—those that were to become the most militant—of all idea of allegiance to a more inclusive form of association. For more than a century their leaders have tried from time to time to re-create such a form; but no more today than at any other time can they afford to admit what the facts so plainly teach, namely, that the very nature of the segregated states makes that aim impossible. Neither conservatism nor collectivism will face this stark reality, for both tend to maintain and reinforce the national state, and quarrel merely as to who shall control it. Contemporary governments of both the extreme right and the extreme left maintain the pretense of constructing an "international order" out of the national units, but their daily actions show plainly which set of interests they take seriously. Only liberalism dares to strike at the root of the matter (thereby offending both adversaries) because liberalism alone inherits a tradition powerful enough to do so.

No explanation that is solely or mainly economic can fully account for the monopolization of the associative tendency by the nation-state complex. Factors much more profound and general than the economic played a decisive part in concentrating human sociality in this dead-end type. Morever, the increasing strength of the economic factor has itself to be explained. It is well known, of course, that the trading organizations of the mercantile period contributed a great deal to, and received a great deal from, the consolidating national states. It is also true that when their rivalries happened to run along national lines (which was not always the case) they received, and welcomed, diplomatic and even military assistance. But it was by no means taken for granted that their economic advantage coincided with that of the entire national community. On the contrary, a very fruitful economic debate sprang up over that very question. Nor were they willing, without a struggle, to merge their identities with that of the state which gradually absorbed them. The extent to which, for example, the East India Company, the Hudson's Bay Company, or even (and that is a test case) the Anglo-Persian Oil Company, can be regarded as the originators of the militant nationalism that pervaded their areas is easily exaggerated. The state brought its own purposes to bear over, or through, such organizations, and its purposes went beyond the economic: the drive for power had deeper roots. The trading companies had, on the whole, made economic expansion very profitable; it is more than doubtful whether the process showed a net profit to the nation-states. India might be the brightest jewel in the British crown, but the British people have never ceased paying for it; on direct account it is now a heavy liability; but even in good times, if the total cost of imperial strategy and "preparedness" could be computed, including the diversion of resources, the margin of economic gain would be small or nonexistent. Similarly, the cost to the United States, before December 7, 1941, of holding and defending the Philippines and the complementary naval bases, would probably exceed any economic advantages that either the nation or any of its citizens acquired. For it must not be assumed that in the absence of political and military control there would have been no trade and no investment.

Nor again can it be argued that militant nationalism, and its accompanying tendency toward a totalitarian type of social organization, represents the successful effort of an interested minority to stimulate and exploit national sentiment in the interest of private capitalists. That is a popular version, but it covers only a small part of the facts. Many times in the Western nations during the nineteenth century, popular opinion was more chauvinistic than that of bankers, investors, politicians, generals, or monarchs. It supported the most saber-rattling postures of Palmerston, and overwhelmed the efforts of Bright and Cobden to avert, and then to terminate, the most ill-advised war of modern history. "The most disingenuous democrat must admit, if he is honest," says Sir Henry Slesser—himself a leading member of the Labor party— "that the war fever which seized the nation in the fifties . . . was the direct fruit of popular emancipation." [3] Cobden wrote to a friend in a letter of April 13, 1857: "It does not follow that we should be nearer the realization of our pacific principles if we had universal suffrage tomorrow. In the present general elections the most warlike returns have come from the most popular constituencies, the least warlike from the most aristocratic counties." [4] The jingo election of 1857 that brought Palmerston his greatest personal triumph was a true precursor of the khaki election of 1901 and the coupon election of 1918. German Liberals supported Bismark's foreign policy as all but a handful of British Liberals sup-

3. Slesser, H., *History of the Liberal Party*, p. 81.
4. Hobson, J. A., *Richard Cobden*, p. 208.

ported Palmerston's; even Napoleon III recovered a brief popularity with the Paris mob in July, 1870. In America "manifest
destiny" evoked the missionary ardor of innumerable Main Streets,
and refused to be satisfied with a merely diplomatic victory over
Spain. "Every Congressman," said one of them, "has two or three
newspapers in his district—most of them printed in red ink . . .
and shouting for blood." [5] Those newspapers were not bought nor
subsidized by bankers; they were giving the public what it wanted
—and its foremost want is very seldom peace. "In almost every
crisis," says Walter Lippmann, "the tension is increased by the
newspapers"—naturally enough, since newspapers are made to
be sold. The increasing influence of the masses, and the extension
of the means of popular appeal, have created the most serious
problem with which the advocates of international coöperation
have ever been faced. The extension of democracy has brought
with it the extension of war, of war-mindedness and war preparation; and the influence of women, so far from opposing, has reinforced the tendency. Does anyone suppose that the national
leaders of our time would have obtained their extraordinary fol-
lowings had their policies been consistently pacific?

§ 4

IN THE year of our Lord 1742, Jonathan Edwards looked out on
the rest of the world from the little town of Northampton, Massachusetts, and found it sadly in need of salvation. And as he looked,
comparing in his mind the spiritual apathy of the old continent
with the fervor of his New England congregations, it was revealed to him by many prophetic signs that America was the pre-
destined agent of the world's conversion. The text of Isaiah,
"Surely the Isles will wait for me, and the ships of Tarshish first,
to bring my sons from far," evidently referred "not to the British
Isles, nor any other isles near the continent of Europe," but to
America. The advent of Joseph, who was born of the younger sis-
ter, separated from his brethren, and saved the world from famine;
the healing of Hezekiah, when the sun went from west to east and
the Lord prophesied great things for his church; together with
many another portent and parallel passage, clearly foretold the
high destiny of the new world. The course of latter day events,

5. Beard, C. A., and M. R., *Rise of American Civilization*, II, 371–372.

laid open to the eye of faith, showed further confirmation: "Whereas till of late, the world was supplied with its silver and gold and earthly treasures from the old continent and now is supplied chiefly from the new, so the course of things in spiritual respects will be in like manner turned . . . and if we may suppose that this glorious work of God shall begin in any part of America, I think if we consider the circumstances of the settlement of New England, it must needs appear the most likely of all the American colonies to be the place whence the work shall principally take its rise."

Edwards was neither the first nor the last to recognize the moral mission of America. A full century before he penned his meditations, the spiritual apathy of the English had drawn the censure of devout colonists. Says Roger Williams (*ca.* 1640):

> The very Indian boys can give
> To many stars their name,
> And know their course, and therein do
> Excel the English tame.

The enactment of the Constitution was widely interpreted as proof of the divine favor specially reserved for God's own country; and appreciation still abounds in clubs and places where they sing.

> Beneath the Constitution's shade,
> A boon and shield of priceless worth,
> We stand erect and unafraid,
> Unmatched in all the teeming earth.

Recognition of the fact has not been confined to the native born. Thus William McDougall, the psychologist of the occult, observed in 1915: "It may well seem to us that there was a land reserved by God for one great purpose, and a people developed and guided by Him to occupy that land in order that they might realise that purpose . . . to lead mankind onward and upward toward the realisation on earth of the City of God." [6] And another psychologist, Hugo Münsterberg, commented with hardly the hint of a smile: "There is something jubilant and something final in American patriotism, and every outsider must feel what a tremendous power for the good of the country is generated by such triumphant confidence. . . . Can it be denied that all the modern discussions

6. McDougall, W., *The Indestructible Union*, p. 105.

on peace and disarmament, on arbitration treaties and the causes
of righteous wars, get a good deal of their steam from the confident belief that it is the duty and mission of America to be the
preceptor of Europe in the department of higher morality?" [7]

Unfortunately there are those who fail, or even willfully decline, to recognize this duty and this mission; and the number
includes not merely individuals but nations and the representatives
of nations. The English have been notoriously obtuse in this matter.
The claims this peculiar people has advanced on its own account
would of course hardly merit consideration but for the fact that
it has proceeded, with sublime effrontery, to act upon them. Says
one of their early chronicle plays:

> Lust dwells in France, in Italy and Spain
> From the poor peasant to the Prince's train,
> In Germany and Holland, Riot serves,
> And he that most can drink, most he deserves:
> England I praise not, for I here was born
> But that she laugheth the others unto scorn. [8]

The use of the stage as a vehicle of conscious nationalism even
antedates that peculiarly English manifestation, the chronicle
play; and the playwrights knew what they were doing, and for
whom they were doing it. Says Heywood, in the *Apology for
Actors* (1612): "Plays have made the ignorant more apprehensive,
taught the unlearned the knowledge of many famous histories,
instructed such as cannot read in the discovery of all our English
chronicles; and what man have you now of that weak capacity that
cannot discourse of any notable thing recorded even from William the Conqueror, nay from the landing of Canute, until this
day?" In exactly the same mood, Ford commends to the audience
his tragedy of *Perkin Warbeck* (1634)—a piece of more, or rather
less, than questionable accuracy—as

> A history of noble mention, known
> Famous, and true; most noble, 'cause our own;
> Not forged from Italy, from France, from Spain,
> But chronicled at home.—

"Most noble, 'cause our own": there you have it, the sole sufficient imprimatur! There was no David Starr Jordan in those

7. Münsterberg, H., *American Patriotism*, pp. 3, 4, 16.
8. *Cromwell*, III, 3.

days to question the veracity of these "famous histories" in which
the "unlearned and ignorant" were thus instructed; and we may
doubt whether, even had there been, he would have had much of
a welcome from either players or audience. "As was right and
necessary," remarks J. A. Symonds, "the authors of our chronicle
plays made history subservient to art." Nash advertised the fact:
said he in *Pierce Penniless* (1592): "Tell them what a glorious
thing it is to have Henry V represented on the stage, leading the
French king prisoner, and forcing both him and the Dolphin
swear fealty." The reader will not need to be reminded of the
continuance of this tradition by other writers, such as Shakespeare,
Henley, Kipling, Punch, etc. Its consequences have been conspicuous through many centuries. Innes, for example, observes of the
Tudor period that "men quickly learned to look upon themselves
as the chosen people of the Lord of Sabaoth who gave them the
victory over their enemies, and to whom with entire sincerity they
gave the glory; while they found a satisfying warrant in the scrip-
tures for spoiling the Egyptians and smiting the Amalekites,
symbolising specifically the Spaniards and the Irish." [9] Other
primitive peoples, the historian will remark, have proceeded
on much the same assumption; but none other has succeeded in
establishing by such methods an empire upon which, if the sun
never sets, it is doubtless because they are not to be trusted in
the dark.

For a more impartial examination of the question of national
merits we naturally turn to that nation of critics, France. And
certainly no one (or at any rate, no Frenchman) can fail to be
convinced by the unanimity with which the Gallic genius is acclaimed. Among many who have attempted to define it, few have
approached the clarity of Desiré Nisard. The accuracy of his work
is attested by the fact that it held a premier place among French
histories of letters in the last century, running into at least seven-
teen editions between 1844 and 1880. The differences, he shows
us, almost beggar description "entre l'esprit français et ce qui se
manifeste de l'esprit" in other nations. Others have, he admits,
their points and their local patriotisms, like that of the mountain
dweller for his mountain; but the love of France is of a larger
kind. "Nous l'aimons, parce qu'elle nous paraît la meilleure patrie
pour l'homme en général; nous voudrions y donner le droit de

9. Innes, A. T., *England under the Tudors*, p. 425.

cité à tout le genre humain. Nous l'aimons, parce que toutes choses nous y paraissent plus conformes à la raison." Traces indeed of the spirit of humanity are everywhere; but "notre privilège à nous, c'est d'en représenter le plus de traits essentiels." In short, "c'est le christianisme qui a fait de l'esprit français l'image la plus complète et la plus pure de l'esprit humain." [10] That, as the followers of Maurras were prompt to recognize, was an excellent translation of the old promise that the meek should inherit the earth.

A different version, it is true, was popular east of the Rhine; but what could one expect of a people that had learned, not merely from its politicians but from its moral philosophers, from Fichte to Eucken, to regard itself as "the people of the Soul," and saw the 1914 war as part of "the civilizing task which the decrees of Providence have assigned to us"? "The depth of feeling common to us Germans," said Eucken, "has become a power controlling our activity and permeating our history to a degree unknown to any other people. In this sense we have a right to say that we form the soul of humanity, and that the destruction of the German nature would rob world history of its deepest meaning." Surely no one would accuse the Germans of being clannish about it; for as their philosophy broadened out from precedent to precedent, the claims of mere political nationality were superseded by the great discovery of the master race. They did not demand sole credit for that contribution to human brotherhood; they were only too willing to share the honors with a Frenchman, an Englishman, and a couple of Americans. Said one of the latter:

The backbone of western civilisation is racially Nordic, the Alpines and Mediterraneans being effective precisely to the degree in which they have been Nordicised and vitalised. If this great race, with its capacity for leadership and fighting, should ultimately pass, with it would pass that which we call civilisation. It would be succeeded by an unstable and bastard population, where worth and merit have no inherent right to leadership, and among which a new and darker age would blot out our racial inheritance. Such a catastrophe cannot threaten if the Nordic race will gather itself together in time, shake off the shackles of an invertebrate altruism, discard the vain phantom of internationalism, and reassert the pride of race and the right of merit to rule. [11]

10. Nisard, D., *Histoire de la littérature française*, I, 15, 18.
11. Stoddart, L., *The Rising Tide of Color*, p. 201.

Thus the matter was put on a sober scientific basis, and all previous or competing claims to the role of chosen people were disposed of. There was, it is true, some subsequent argument about membership in the great race; but since everyone admitted that the Germans were first-rate scientists, and German scientists discovered (to their great surprise) that the German nation was its purest embodiment, there was obviously no more to be said. It was just another case of manifest destiny. And at that we must leave the matter, regretting particularly to exclude the comments of some of the other vertebrates who have long since learned to refrain from destroying their own species. Typographical difficulties unfortunately preclude the publication of their opinions.

By this time it is surely evident that what we are dealing with is a tremendous upsurge of innate primitivism, a break-through of the mass mind, that has captured control of the means of communication and the death-dealing appliances of modern science. Under these conditions mankind must either foresee or forestall its own destruction: there is no third option. Within a single generation the wildest power dreams of Nobel and the later psychopaths will be exceeded. Even now the process of mutual extermination may be beyond control. This fair earth will be fairer far without us. And millions of suicides will attest the human shame. A report of the British Information Services of New York, published in December, 1944, contains this passage:

British people are frightened, but theirs are not present fears; they are for the future. The possible future—or the absence of it—which the flying bomb portends. The first intimation of the next war may be an ultimatum or a threat that "some of our cities may be blasted next morning" said General Sir Frederick Pile, chief of Britain's Anti-Aircraft Command, recently. "That is what the flying bomb has brought us to. It is the beginning of a new type of war." That is what frightens the people of Britain—the beginning of a new type of war. It would indeed be a war to end all war, and possibly all human endeavour.

Yet there is no more evidence today than there was in Nobel's time that increasing frightfulness diminishes the war impulse. On the contrary it has acted on both sides to intensify the struggle; and it does so in a sort of geometric progression, as the impersonal competition of the guarded and sequestered scientists goes on. There is nothing in the nature of modern war to stop war, and very much to perpetuate it; for the belligerent societies will see to it that whatever happens, scientific "progress" is continued.[12]

12. "John Hays Hammond, Jr., noted inventor engaged in secret work for the Army Air Forces, predicted today that World War III is inevitable but that it will last only hours instead of years. He said: 'Another war is bound to come unless human nature changes—and I don't think it will. The people have little to say about whether there will be a war. It's the leaders who plunge a nation into battle. If the matter were put to a popular vote, wars would occur very seldom—if ever. We must be ready next time.'"—United Press dispatch appearing in *New York Herald Tribune*, March 1, 1945. Mr. Hammond is optimistic in assuming that negative considerations will ever mitigate the popular predilection for force.

X

The Problem of Reintegration

1. The arithmetic fallacy. — 2. Impoverishment of community. — 3. Pluralism versus nationalism. — 4. Return to pessimism. — 5. The religious synthesis.

§ 1

LET us return now to the question posed in the previous chapter: Why was it that the vast extension of intellectual and spiritual activity in the nineteenth century was not accompanied by a corresponding extension of the manifold forms of human association, but fell almost completely under the domination of the one form that was to prove the most dangerous and destructive of them all? For part of the answer, as we have seen, we must look backward over a couple of centuries to note the growth, or abuse, of that pervasive materialism which had seduced intelligent people to deny the transcendental nature of man and the true bonds of human solidarity.

So much has been written, especially in the past two decades, on this theme that its further development is perhaps unnecessary. The consensus of modern thought points to a thesis so radical, and yet so elementary, that scholars have hesitated to give it the emphasis it deserves. It is a thesis in elementary arithmetic. Professor Whitehead, philosopher of mathematics, remarks that our everyday awareness of life and nature "is disclosed to us as one complex of things. But the seventeenth-century dualism cuts straight across it. The objective world of science was confined to mere spatial material. . . . The subjective world of philosophy annexed the colours, sounds, scents, tastes, touches, bodily feelings, as forming the subjective content of the cogitations of the individual minds. . . . But actuality is through and through togetherness."[1] The supposed objective world—a very abstract world, as Whitehead reminds us—was now to be the scene of many

1. Whitehead, A. N., *Science and the Modern World*, pp. 209, 251.

triumphs. Located in a space and a time that were the projection of very simple methods of measurement, it revealed such regularities as were describable by simple counting and computation. There were a lot of them, and some turned out to be very useful in the hands of inventors (others not so useful). So spectacular, indeed, were the results of early quantitative method, that practical people tended more and more to assume—at first tacitly, then explicitly—that the sort of reality it applied to was all the reality there was: that what could not be measured was not, so to speak, really "real," but had a subjective, fugitive, romantic, illusory quality that you could take seriously or not just as you pleased: it would make no great practical difference to a world that was now going to be run by steam and electricity. Thus the poets, artists and men of imagination were gradually herded off in a sort of public reservation where people could spend a pleasant hour or two when they had the time; and if occasionally, in the dead of night, one could catch a queer wailing and roaring out there as if something primeval yet lingered—well, there was always the morning's work to attend to, and business was business.

But the method of enumeration had its own surprises in store. For one thing, as it gained refinement and complexity, and to every new method of measurement some fresh pattern of regularity was disclosed, some people began to suspect that the trick was done with mirrors; and a certain doubt arose as to who was doing it. The world of the empiricists took on a sort of Pirandello quality, as objectivity itself threatened to turn into radical idealism. For another thing, the observed regularities were seldom quite complete, quite final; they showed a tantalizing imperfection that suggested not only endless refinements of measurement, but a possibility of substructure that knew nothing of the regularity science was seeking. And just as Dirac advises us not to try to form any visual or spatial image of what his equations refer to, so other scientists now speak of merely statistical laws and probabilities.

Despite Whitehead's stern warning against the mathematical observations of nonmathematicians,[2] one may perhaps remark that as the methods of measurement and enumeration have been refined and expanded, the world they reveal has come to bear less and less resemblance to that "objective world of science" which

2. Whitehead, A. N., *Introduction to Mathematics*, chap. ix.

the seventeenth century so confidently set out to explore. Far from being the same world, we cannot even be certain that it is the same sort of world. The supposition that what cannot somehow be measured does not truly exist never had much encouragement from the great scientists; today very few would maintain that the concepts of number, quantity, time, and space are enough to describe more than a little of the universe in which we live. In so far as the idea of number implies the discreteness of things, there are too many entities it can never encompass: cases in which no sort of an aggregate of discrete elements will give us the whole that we know.

Such was the case, in fact, of the atomic theory of physics applied (or misapplied) as an explanation of "matter." For so long as matter was supposed to consist of material particles, then however small you made your particles, the problem was confronting you just as solidly at the end of the analysis as at the beginning. Such was the case with those psychologists who set out to describe the psyche as an aggregation of sensations, stimuli, or instincts; who, when Gestalt psychology insisted on looking at the forest as well as the trees, complained that it was not really scientific. Such was the case, above all, with the atomic theory of society that corresponded to the atomic theory of matter. No important truth about society could ever be arrived at by representing it as a mere summation of individual units; for the only aspect of the units that permits one to apply an aggregative process, namely, their spatial discreteness, is precisely that which ignores all characteristics that make them human individuals. The felicific calculus that was expressed in Bentham's "greatest happiness of the greatest number" is the world's prize example of the arithmetic fallacy. Under a mask of specious objectivity, it offers a formula that can have no significant relevance to the nature of society. And so far as the idea of simple enumeration has governed the theory of democracy, it has done more than any other factor to render that theory abortive and dangerous.

It is interesting to notice that even Rousseau was in some degree aware of the danger. What he meant by the "general will" he never succeeded in making clear, even to himself; but "there is often a great deal of difference between the will of all and the general will." [3] At one moment he speaks of the general will as a

3. Rousseau, J. J., *Social Contract*, II, iii.

mere aggregation of individual wills conceived as all alike except for the plus and minus signs. Next moment he is telling us that the "resolutions of the people" may be wrong, especially when private associations are permitted to exist among them, while the general will is always right. He gives the general will an absolute sovereignty from which there is no appeal—not even a right of rebellion—because it is supposed to be absolutely moral; but where it gets the intuition of morality is never explained. This is the same dilemma that we meet in Hobbes, who never tells us where Leviathan went to school. And the source of it is the same in both. Rousseau, like Hobbes, starts his specious logic with the assumption of a *total* surrender of personality to the collective existence —"the total alienation to the whole community of each associate with all his rights"; [4] it follows that whatever each associate may get out of it will be something less than free personality. In practice, as both Laski and Acton agree, the general will comes down to the rule of a bare majority; and "once we deal with modern problems our real enquiry is still the question of Locke—what limits shall we place upon the power of government?" [5] In the light of recent events we can focus that question more sharply: Are there questions of such a nature that simple arithmetical enumeration fails to give a sufficiently authoritative solution; and if there are (as the framers of the American Constitution believed), what other or supplementary methods can we apply?

We can now see why the theory (and practice) of individualism gave so great an impetus to the rise of a monistic and tyrannical form of social organization acting on a very primitive cultural and psychological plane. A type of social control which came to rely more and more on a simple aggregation of supposedly similar individuals could not possibly express much more than the appetites and impulses individuals actually have in common, at the level at which they are common; it was naturally bound to become the instrument of those impulses as realized on that level, attaching far more importance to the size of the aggregate than to the quality of the collective intention; and those aspects of personal intelligence and aspiration which do not admit of, or rely on, a merely additive process were bound to appear incidental or irrelevant to the main pattern, discounted from the start by the fact

4. *Ibid.*, I, vi.
5. Laski, H. J., *Political Thought from Locke to Bentham*, p. 75.

that, arithmetically, they could never muster more than a small minority. Some type of general social control was, admittedly, necessary; but its very generality required that its sphere of operations be strictly confined to those of the most elementary character; and in so far as it impinged on the activity of free personality, its influence could not be other than retrograde and atavistic.

But, it will be asked, was not that the very point of the laissez-faire philosophy that grew out of individualism? The answer is both yes and no; but rather no than yes. The antistate attitude of laissez faire rested, as a whole, on much narrower ground. There were liberals—of whom Acton represents one type and Herbert Spencer the other—who saw the problem in its broader aspects; but the liberal case for civic freedom is much older and stronger than the argument of laissez faire, and the latter, as a historical movement, hardly touched the central issue. For laissez faire was characterized by an absorbing preoccupation with the expansion (not merely the maintenance) of economic activity. It opposed state action in certain spheres on exclusively economic grounds; it similarly opposed all types of corporate life except those which represented organized capital. But its nineteenth century exponents were, in most cases, quite willing to tell the state what would be, as well as what would not be, commendable activity from their point of view; and they gladly recognized—again, with one or two exceptions—the idealization and personification of the state as rather useful than otherwise to their main interest. For the prospect of material aggrandizement has an almost universal attraction; the inflation of the ego by identification with the group is one of the most primitive impulses; and the two together make an almost unbeatable combination, easily able to swing into its orbit other constituents of common consciousness—legend, history, tradition, even religion—in the most wildly distorted forms.

The process by which this is accomplished is itself worth noting. The normal function of the more literate and vocal members of a community is to reflect and articulate what is already in the public mind in more or less inchoate and latent form. Their doing so not only enables them to exercise their skill, but serves the purpose of the many social and economic interests that are embedded in the established order of ideas and institutions. So long as they do this, therefore, writers, lecturers, preachers, commentators are not only rewarded, but honored and esteemed far beyond the anonymous craftsmen who minister to the welfare of the community without adding to its self-esteem. It is natural in such circumstances that the orthodox intelligentsia should be profoundly convinced of their own sincerity, and even originality, and conceive of themselves as luminaries rather than reflectors. But let one of them step too far out of line, and he will incur a double odium. He must expect no further remuneration or esteem; he will cease to be respectable, becoming instead "a traitor to the cause"; and his fellows in the trade will see in him a disturber and a rogue, seeking only to push them off the bloody treadmill on which they earn their economic and psychological living. His only consolation will be that in so far as by the sweat of his brow he unearths a facet of truth, the people will some day see it for themselves; his only hope that some may look before it is altogether too late.

§ 2

THE quality of the nationalist complex became progressively cruder since about 1860 in all the Western states. Just as the integration of a personality may be brought about on various cultural or axiological levels, so it is with a group. The steady decline of the value plane on which the national aggregates cohered was manifest in an increasing materialism coupled with increasing irrationality, of which the growth of racial intolerance inside the various communities was, and remains, a striking symptom. Under these circumstances, the mere increase of numbers was a depressing influence; for in the absence of strong counteracting forces, the highest common factor was bound to fall. The extension of elementary education was not, as it turned out, to be reckoned among the counteracting forces. A general ability to read and write may merely implement the maxim that evil communications corrupt good manners. Universal literacy as such is an axiologically neutral extension of human potentiality, like any other offshoot of applied science. It is only because the transcendental drive is so deep rooted in ordinary human nature that society got some good, as well as evil, out of the greatest revolution of our era—the revolution of the rotary press.

A factor of primary importance to the cultural quality of the national aggregates was revealed in the fine study made by Thomas and Znaniecki of *The Polish Peasant in Europe and America.* This important work, published in five volumes in 1918, was the forerunner of many studies in the nature of social process of which the Lynds' *Middletown* is the best known. The investigators hoped to derive, from their work on this special case, some observations of general import; and to a remarkable extent, they succeeded. One of their observations, empirically established beyond question, especially concerns us here. It may be sufficiently indicated by the following quotation (Vol. I, chap. iii):

The pace of social evolution has become so rapid that special groups are ceasing to be permanent and stable enough to organize and maintain organized complexes of attitudes of their members which correspond to their common pursuits. In other words, society is gradually losing all its old machinery for the determination and stabilization of individual characters.

If that was true of the era that preceded mass journalism, mass movies, radio, and the cheap car, it is infinitely more significant today; and it is true not only of Polish peasants transported to America, but of all of us. The social effects of applied science, unrestrained by positive factors of community, have been extremely unfavorable to psychological stability, individual or collective. The habit of reflection, of recollection, of interior tranquillity, has been eliminated by the insistence of a perpetually changing set of violent stimuli. The accelerating shifts in the material and social environment have monopolized the common consciousness; and even academic education is seized with an absurd predilection for the contemporary, out of which no stable system of values can possibly be derived.

The effects are most marked, of course, in the case of recent immigrants to America from very different cultures; for it takes more than one or two generations to give much depth of content to the sense of community, and the process cannot be very greatly expedited by indoctrination at the informational level. Least of all can a real rooting be hastened when the new environment is itself gyrating at the tempo of boogie-woogie. But the effect is not confined to the new immigration. The older population also has exhibited a very marked geographical, as well as social, mobility; and since the home and family can no longer be regarded as effective agents for the transmittal of value systems, the same spiritual rootlessness is increasingly in evidence.

A further tendency toward the impoverishment of the communal idea arises strictly within the economic sphere. Modern states, in proportion as their mutual competition has increased, have also been internally afflicted by the growing disparity of economic interests. This is an aspect of the matter that we shall presently examine; but it may be said at once that while the notion of economic "class" has proved quite unable to generate a fruitful and constructive form of human association, it has been extremely effective in dissipating the strength and content of the sense of national community.

All these, and certain further influences we shall review, have conspired toward the same result, namely, that while the external situation has enhanced the monistic and refractory character of the nation-states, the sense of community on which they rely has become shallower and more sensational; so that their continued integration calls for policies that are bound to become more arbitrary and coercive, less and less favorable to the development of free personality.

§ 3

THE twentieth century saw a marked revival of European interest in the theory of society, especially that part of it which concerns the nature of group life. The contributions of Gierke and Troeltsch were outstanding; they aided the work of Le Bon, Duguit, Romains and the French pluralists, and of Maitland, Figgis, Laski, Cole, and many others in England. Among many exiles whose work has helped to extend this interest in America, the name of Arnold Brecht deserves especial mention.

Very broadly speaking, this revival of interest had two related objectives. First, it sought to clarify the distinction between community and state, and to rescue the former from the latter; second, it explored and deepened the historical, legal, and psychological bases of corporate life as contributory to the one and at odds with the other. The whole effort was consciously directed against the assertive monism of the secular powers; the outcome of which, in both internal and external situations, could be foreseen long before 1914. The movement developed a strongly Catholic trend.

The Church was the outstanding example of a society that ante-
dated all the monistic sovereignties, and had more or less successfully resisted assimilation. Moreover, the failure of Bismarck's
Kulturkampf had not discouraged the French Republic from
starting another that contributed both to the isolation of France
and to the revival of interest in the whole subject.

The Church offered a philosophical as well as an institutional
challenge to the state. It claimed to be a form of association that
promised a fulfilment, instead of a frustration, of personality; and
it maintained that the principles in virtue of which it did so could
be specifically applied in political and economic life. That contention appealed to a good many organizations that were resisting
on their own account the claim of the state to dominate, control,
or restrain their activities. An interesting and rather fruitful liaison
was thus established between Catholic right and economic left:
the only one of its kind.

It was significant that the pluralist movement went farthest—
in theory—in the two newest states of the European imbroglio:
and was most effectively quashed there. The circumstances of
Germany in the Europe of 1919–24 could hardly have been
better calculated to ensure a resurgence of nationalism. That,
after all, was the principle on which Woodrow Wilson had essayed
to redraw the rest of the map of Europe; and for a moment it
seemed as if, in a league *of nations,* a united Germany might regain what she considered her rightful place. No such prospect was
open to the Italians. A good deal more thought and study went
into the planning of the "corporate state" than is generally recognized, and Mussolini's interest in it was genuine—up to a point.
That point was probably reached when *Il Duce* discovered that
such a state, if sincerely and completely enacted, would be incompatible with the *Führer-prinzip;* and the 1930's seemed to
offer such a unique opportunity for the latter that the corporate
state became merely another disguise for *sacro egoismo.* The
Italian case, however, was merely an extreme example of what was
happening in all the Western communities. Everywhere the movement to enlarge the autonomy, and enrich the content, of other
forms of group life was overwhelmed by the increasing monism of
the political states. We see it in the growing centralization of
power in Austria, Czechoslovakia, and Russia; in the government
of Germany by decree after 1930; in the British labor law of 1927

and the policies of the Tory governments that followed; in the sequel to the Popular Front in France and the NRA in America.

It would be interesting if one could relate this recent movement of concentration to the nationalist *mystique* of a generation earlier; but on the whole, it will bear no such interpretation. The work of Maurras and Barrès probably had some influence on modern German nationalism, especially in the more conservative and aristocratic circles; but such organizations as the Stahlhelm marched into the National Socialist camp holding their noses, and the Hitler following, for all its frantic efforts, produced nothing worthy to rank with the higher expressions of national consciousness. Integral nationalism had rather more effect in Italy; but the posturings of d'Annunzio and Mussolini were a crude and cynical caricature of the Barrèsian attitude. In the meantime many of the finest spirits had followed Charles Péguy into the Church; as if realizing that the concept of the nation, no matter how exalted, had not breadth nor depth nor height enough to contain their aspiration. Nor is the *mystique* of democracy upon which American writers, broadcasters, and film producers have spent so much money and ingenuity, a more finally satisfying thing. Even at its best, as in the work of MacLeish, it suggests rather the ballyhoo of a popular newsreel than anything Walt Whitman would have recognized—and Whitman was no stranger to ballyhoo. It is too intentional, too conscious, too forced. The best work in this field is local and regional, like that of Bernanos; and nothing in the utterance of modern America has approached the sublimity of Lincoln, who spoke so simply and so humbly.

§ 4

SOCIAL theory, after World War I, took a decidedly pessimistic turn. The being who was only a little lower than the angels now saw himself, not altogether falsely, as governed by "herd instinct." Human sociability, on which the eighteenth century had relied so optimistically, was now analyzed into elements drawn from the animal kingdom. The mood of the time, and the determination of American sociologists to approach the study of humanity with the concepts and methods of physical science, produced another demonstration of the additive fallacy. Once again it became evident that if you insist on regarding mankind only in terms of numerical aggregates, the uniformities you discover will have a subhuman quality. What was perhaps unfortunate was the carefully inculcated belief that all other characteristics are unreal and imaginary.

The social implications of this viewpoint have been under attack from several quarters. Bergson, for instance, long before his conversion, was insisting on what he called the fallacy of discreteness. The notions of time and space, he pointed out, by which we make the external world intelligible and manageable, do not necessarily give a complete account of it; and when we "borrow them back" from the world on which we ourselves have bestowed them, and attempt to explain our own existence in those terms, we cannot help missing its reality.[6] It is of interest to notice the effect of this criticism, or the expression of a similar thesis, in recent stream-of-consciousness fiction, especially that of James Joyce. The tendency of Bergson's work as a whole, like that of Whitehead, is toward a revendication of personality against the encroachments both of a mechanically conceived universe and a collectively conceived society.

Modern sociology has an inherent disposition to regard the human individual as a mere by-product of social or cultural process, a mere overlapping point of innumerable groups; and so to deny him any significance or efficacy in his own right. A large body of fact supports this view: the sort of fact that the methods of sociology are adapted to discover. But even among the sociologists are some who warn us not to take it for the whole prospect. Trotter, the philosopher of "herd instinct," will not allow that the whole of personality is exhausted in its social aspects; and all those who, like Sorokin, are determined to steer clear of determinism have to find elbowroom somewhere in their systems for you and me, as recognizable entities. A considerable number, following Pareto, have us classified into active "elites" and more or less passive masses: again, with much justification. But the ground of the classification is exceedingly abstract; any attempt to apply it in specific terms leads to difficulties. It is evident, of course, that any reader of these lines belongs to some sort of an elite—either in virtue of his interest in the subject, or his having the price of the book, or his wife having friends from whom she has borrowed it. A fortiori, therefore, the writer belongs to the elite. He devoutly hopes, however, that the reader will refrain from mentioning

6. Bergson, H., *Time and Freewill*, passim, especially chaps. ii and iii.

the fact if ever they have the good fortune to meet St. Francis.

Berdyaev, in an important work [7] that comes to hand as this chapter is being written, remarks that "there is nothing more repellent than the pride and contempt of a closed élite." There is obvious truth in the view that intellectual and cultural values are most clearly realized by minorities, through whose influence a process of diffusion continually goes on; but to think of these minorities as actual numerical groups is quite misleading. Here, as everywhere else, the quantitative aspect is less significant than the qualitative. Similarly, Berdyaev points out, it is a mistake to identify the "masses" with the working class or "the people." "A lack of expressed personality, an absence of personal originality, a disposition to swim with the current. . . . A man with such characteristics is a man of the masses, to whatever class he may belong." Such people are just as frequent in colleges as in coal mines.

The dominance in our civilization of mass standards and mass psychology is therefore a qualitative, not a quantitative, phenomenon; and Berdyaev has some interesting comments on its origin. The characteristic products and potentialities of our era, he observes, are such as to be available in just the same way to the barbarian as to the man of the highest culture.

The masses appropriate to themselves the technical side of civilization and eagerly equip themselves with it, but it is with great difficulty that they assimilate spiritual culture. The masses had indeed in the past their own spiritual culture and it was based upon religious belief. The masses in the present transitional period, on the other hand, are devoid of all spiritual culture, they set store by nothing but the myths and symbols which are instilled into them by demagogues—national and social myths and symbols, of race, nation, state, class and the like. With all this the making of idols is always going on. [8]

Idols of that sort, embodying values of a lower order, have an inherent tendency to subject to themselves values of a higher order—those of knowledge, of art, of the spiritual life; a constant struggle is embodied in the very nature of social culture. But it is a reflection of the struggle that is embodied in the nature of man himself; for example, the conflict between sexuality and love. The

7. *Slavery and Freedom,* pp. 124, 121–123.
8. *Ibid.,* pp. 121–122.

sexual impulse operates, arithmetically speaking, on a very common plane (that is why Hollywood cannot do without it); it permits the substitution of one object for another. Love is a relation between complete personalities. The historical issue, as Berdyaev and many others now see it, is the defense of personality against the forces of a material civilization that tend to crush and annihilate it. This issue is different from, and much more profound than, the current controversies about democracy versus dictatorship, socialism versus capitalism, and so forth; its argument proceeds on a deeper level.

One does a student no real service by allowing him to think that he can get at the value of an important work without the trouble of reading it; we shall therefore not try to summarize Berdyaev's treatment of the main issue. We may briefly notice his approach to that part of it in which liberalism is particularly concerned. Nineteenth-century liberalism, he thinks,[9] actually developed into capitalism because it incorporated in its tradition a false individualism. "It is remarkable that great creative men have in fact never been individualists." They have often been solitary, unrecognized, or rebellious, but that is different; their valuation of themselves has not been egocentric, but evangelistic. Individualism is really the same sort of thing as collectivism viewed from the other end. The individual who thinks of himself as in contrast to the universe has already a mistaken apprehension of both; the quantitative relationship of part to whole does not, or should not, apply. The individualism of modern times, springing from Renaissance sources, was essentially "an escape from the world and society to the self, to its own soul, to the lyric, to poetry and music. The life of man's soul was much enriched, but the processes of dissociation of personality were put in train." True personality has no use for atomistic nor aggregative conceptions; it is unitary, and therefore free, creating a world of freedom. It naturally tends to establish communal and fraternal relations among men. It does not fight the state, as individualism pretended to do, insofar as the state exercises necessary and useful functions. The hour at which it must fight arrives when, *owing to the condition of the people*, the state becomes hypostatized and assumes the garb and trappings of sovereignty. "The idea of sovereignty in all its forms is slavery for man. The very seeking after sov-

9. *Ibid.*, pp. 135–136, 145–146.

ereignty is a great delusion. . . . There does not exist any sovereignty at all."

§ 5

WHAT is this condition of the people? Berdyaev calls it "a fallen
condition." We have surveyed a good deal of its background, and
certain of its economic and social aspects. Let us return for a moment to those more fundamental considerations at which we
glanced in Chapter III (§ 5). The Christian doctrine of man, it
was suggested, takes account of the fact that the mind can never
define the life that is both mind and so much more than mind.
It offers therefore an open-ended description of human nature
that is both more complete and more dynamic than analytical
methods can give; but it cannot present this, by the nature of the
case, in terms of the natural sciences. In what modern philosophy
calls existential terms, however, religion deals with the integral
nature of man in relation to the integral nature of the universe;
and it thus operates as a discipline that preserves in man a sense
of proportion. It saves him from *hubris*, self-conceit, on the one
hand, and endows him with a certain dignity on the other. We get
a hint of this when we compare the undertone of assurance in the
art of the Catholic era with the clamant arrogance of modernity.

Catholic religion is the historic form of man's total response to
total being. It places the whole of man—body, mind, spirit—and
the whole of society in their true relation to that which informs,
sustains, and so evidently transcends them. It is that element of
our human heritage which ceaselessly—*ohne Hast, ohne Rast*—
draws the endless variety of action, thought, and feeling toward
a central order and coherence. It is the only element that does
this; and in its absence all flies to pieces. It is the integrating factor
of life, personal and social; and its mode of operation is, by analogy,
quite familiar.

Consider the lover at odds with his girl. He is not sure of her,
there has been a misunderstanding, something has come between
them. His energy flags, his work becomes poor, he is exhausted,
nervous, and tiresome. But they meet again, the situation is cleared
up, they understand one another: suddenly he is vigorous, buoyant,
alert; his work becomes light, confidence returns, courage rides
high—life has meaning again, including all those parts of it that

really have nothing to do with the young lady. Or consider the artist, the engineer, or the scientist, confronted with a difficult problem. While he is baffled, while experiments fail, while hypotheses break down, everything seems wrong; the weather is vile, his family is a nuisance, the bills are a burden, his health is poor—nothing is as it should be. But when the way suddenly becomes clear, things take on a different aspect. Now purpose is set, the means are at hand, the goal is in sight—and matters that have nothing to do with it slip into place and cease to bother. The sun shines, the family is pretty good after all, he is not going bankrupt, he hasn't got stomach ulcers: God's in his heaven and life is integrated about its central direction. Moments like that are all that sustain the torture of artistic creation. In some sphere or other we all know them; too few of us know how dynamic integration of that sort can be achieved for the whole of a life, including that in us which binds us to our dead and lives beyond our dying.

We have alluded to religion as the discipline which preserves in man his sense of proportion. That sense operates as it were in three directions, which we may call upward, outward, and downward. First, it places the whole of man, the whole of humanity, in right relation to what we call God—and also, let us remember, to all in the universe that is not-God, that is anti-God. That is an aspect of the matter, and of the human obligation, which the nineteenth-century optimists too glibly ignored. What is this right relation (it is necessary to our argument that we put the question)? It is that which natural man has known since the dawn of history, it is simple worship: the attitude that propounds no theorem, makes no petition, but lies open like a leaf to the sun of being. Second, the sense of proportion places man in right relation to his fellows through its application to family life and collective action of all sorts; it underlies therefore the philosophy of government, of political economy, of sociology and jurisprudence. Third, it establishes a right relation between the faculties and attributes of bodily life, the appetites, passions, powers, and rational will; without which inner harmony neither the individual nor the society can ever know peace or freedom. And it is the very essence of religious teaching that these three modes of integration are intimately related in the order in which we have placed them, that all swing upward to, and all depend on, the one supreme perception. If that is clear, then the living truth will inform the second and third spheres also; and if that is wrong then all else will be wrong—that is, disorderly, chaotic.

No church or sect has, or claims, a monopoly of this perception. But in the general eclipse that accompanied the rise of technical civilization, a certain advantage lay with what is now quaintly termed "institutional religion." That had, at least, a toughness of tradition, of dogma and liturgy, that could protect the essentially religious impulse until the smoke began to lift. The Protestant sects, within whose membership was some of the purest piety, were more exposed to the individualism of the era; and popular religion tended more and more to become identified with individual morality. But any religion conceived primarily as a system of individual ethical sanctions is bound to be largely anthropocentric, and will probably end by losing, or discarding, its religious content altogether with no serious sense of loss. The ultrarespectable religion of Victorian times—Matthew Arnold's "morality touched with emotion"—was not religion at all, and it was never quite clear why there should be any emotion. We have since heard a good deal about "scientific ethics"; and it is evident that sects whose major emphasis has been on individual conduct are running more and more to ethical culture, amateur psychiatry, and social reform—in which fields they are neither fish, flesh, nor fowl. They find themselves competing with, or trailing after, the secular agencies of field work or research, and losing their way in the welter of economic and social programs; so that those who want to retain what religion they have become uncomfortably aware of the lack of connection between the topical discourses they hear from the pulpit and the sentimental terms and associations in which those discourses are set. Religion becomes mere uplift and humanitarianism, and in such worthy causes the Protestant churches are merely one type of organization among many—not a very effective one at that.

One may ask further what this residual religion really has to say about the work of the world. In point of message it is apparently seeking to blend the virtues of puritan individualism with a vaguely collectivist ideal, drowning the technical difficulties in a flood of fraternal sentiment. One should work hard and be thrifty (or should one? Both the Gospel writers and the Keynesian economists are a bit doubtful); one should do things that are socially useful (which implies a criterion, either dogmatic or prag-matic); one should be a good worker, a good employer, a good citizen—how trite it all sounds! Any brand of religion can exhort; but can it inspire? Can it give new meaning to the suffering of the soldier, the toil of the housewife, the work of the farmer, the riveter, the teacher, the artist, the administrator? Yes, apparently it can—on one condition: that it goes nationalist. Modern na-tionalism has actually superseded Protestant religion over a very wide area of Western society. It has taken over the drive, the emotionalism, and much of the technique. The drive is toward death; but people willingly ignore that in their satisfaction at finding something that can fully absorb them, something with a kick in it. The modern cathedral is the battleship. Thus, since both individual and society yearn for integration of some sort, a false and partial synthesis usurps the place of a true one.

The more strictly ideological forces at work either tended to confirm that result, or proved too weak to avert it. Protestant re-ligion, in becoming individualistic, also became highly subjective. Apart from its ethical bearing, religious apprehension became an affair of mood, sentiment, emotion, romanticism: religiosity rather than religion. In such circumstances it was easy for people to for-get that while the ontological assertions of religion are necessarily matters of faith, the reality it deals with is matter of fact. And the laws of that reality operate just as surely as the laws of physics, whether or not we choose to take note of them.

In thus withdrawing, or being forced back, behind the closed door of personal privacy, popular Protestantism more and more lost touch with what had been the central integrative factor of European culture; almost instinctively therefore it clung all the closer to its Bible. Ever since the puritan revolution there had been a strong tendency, harking back to old Jewish practices, to treat the Bible as a magical book surrounded with all sorts of tabus. Even today many people, when they hear or speak of the Chris-tian revelation, believe more or less consciously that the phrase refers to the authorized version of the Bible as printed and pub-lished in London by order of King James I in the year 1611; and knowing neither the French, German, Latin, Greek, nor any other version, they are unaware of the peculiarity of their position. They suppose too that the familiar order of the books was the order of composition, and never regard, for example, the obvious variations between the gospel narratives as constituting a literary or historical problem. An objective approach to the text therefore strikes them as impious.

This objective approach, in modern times, aroused the first shock about chronology. The work of the historians—many of them quite orthodox—in extending our knowledge of the pre-Roman world made it evident that by no possible interpretation could the chronological scheme of the Old Testament be made to tally with the record. This was received by many who should have known better as an attack on religion.

The habit of regarding the Bible as a magical history book was matched by the habit of regarding it as an encyclopaedia. The growth in popular knowledge of the natural order therefore created another commotion. Scientists found themselves compelled to choose between adhering to what they indubitably knew, or honestly thought they knew, and accepting a literal interpretation of Semitic cosmology. The legends of the creation, of Moses and the Red Sea, Joshua and the sun and moon, Jonah and the whale, thus appeared as religious issues. Most of the scientists, as both the Church and the Gospel enjoin them, preferred to continue using their minds. Darwin brought on the climax. It must be emphasized that the main responsibility for the ensuing crisis rests neither on the scientists nor on the Church, but on Protestant bibliolatry, which in certain backward parts of the world, by the twentieth century, had degenerated into rank superstition.

The advance of scholarly criticism into the literature of the New Testament was mostly carried on by Christian scholars, for the simple reason that they were familiar with and interested in the field; but their results were eagerly seized upon and interpreted by men working in other fields whose minds were already made up about the religious issue. Some of these interpreters had, or professed to have, extraordinarily naïve ideas about religion. For instance Conybeare somewhere picks up the biblical phraseology about "the right hand of God" and has a lot of fun with the notion of a god who had right and left hands. Of course Conybeare knew far better than that (he was an Oxford don who specialized in Armenian archaeology) but he had a motive.

The famous battle between science and religion had its comic aspect, inasmuch as very few actual scientists took part in it, and what was being defended had very little to do with religion. Most of the triumphs of scientific method have in fact been accomplished by men who recognized the validity of religious apprehension, such as Newton, Kepler, Pascal, Leibnitz, Faraday, Harvey, Priestley, Pasteur, Darwin, Wallace, Mendel, Romanes, the Thomsons, Rutherford, Jeans, Eddington, Compton, Einstein, Whitehead, Planck, Millikan, Langmuir, James, Bergson, Münsterberg, Jung, and a hundred others. On the other hand, the warriors of the American "Bible belt" in making a totem of their sacred book, had really blinded their own eyes to the magnificence of the heritage they had there. Under these circumstances, wooden swords and tin helmets could put up a tremendous clatter; until it began to rain in earnest.

Nonetheless, there was something far from ignoble about the mountaineer with his shot gun and his Bible (especially if one forgets that he occasionally went on a lynching bee). And if puritanism had lapsed far into bibliolatry, at the opposite extreme the religious synthesis was effectively obscured by a rigid institutionalism. It is possible, from a secular standpoint, to explain, and even in some measure to condone, the policies of the Vatican in the 'sixties and 'seventies, and again in the opening years of the present century. It is not possible to ignore the fact that the influence of those policies extended far beyond the great events and the critical years, out into the seminaries, the bishoprics, the schools and parishes; so that even today, in thousands of out-of-the-way places, the altars of the Church resemble rather the armed outposts of a great empire than the skiffs and dories of the fisher of men. A sacramental religion, in virtue of its inherent power, can the more easily become to untutored minds a vehicle of superstition; and though the truth it conveys be all-sufficing, that does not dispense with the need for a teaching apostolate. No human failing, we know, can quench the light that shineth in darkness; but not all the darkness is outside the walls, and many a little sacristy contains a good extinguisher.

Thus, a generation or so ago, at both extremes of expression, the integrative effect of the religious tradition was being frustrated. And it was just at that time that the full-scale assault on religion got under way. That assault was organized and led by able men who knew what they were doing and why they were doing it. They had fashioned a new faith—or at least, had mustered new materials to reshape an old one—in whose service they displayed a missionary ardor as sincere as that of their opponents. The name of that faith was positivism. Its avowed enemy was Christian religion. It appeared at first as an ally of liberalism. But it was to prove a most potent factor in reducing political liberalism to its recent state of bewilderment and ineffectiveness. For the core of liberalism is free integrated personality; the expression of that is its goal and program. Positivists say precisely the same thing; but the integrative formula they offer is radically different from that which lay at the heart of European culture. So much the worse, they reply, for European culture; and the rejoinder cannot be casually dismissed. Thus the contest involves the soul of civilization; and it is an open issue in both Western Europe and America.

XI

The Positivist Attack

1. *Comte's new religion. — 2. The apostolate of Mr. Wells. — 3. Progress to utopia. — 4. Determinism: economic. — 5. Cultural. — 6. Biological. — 7. Psychological. — 8. Moral.*

§ 1

THE nature of the positivist attack on religion may be indicated by one of the chapter headings in a leading American textbook of sociology: Myth, Magic, Religion, and Science. The implication is that these terms describe a progress; that religion is merely the anachronistic survivor of a primitive (i.e., inferior) type of mentality, manifesting itself in totemism, animism, devil worship, witchcraft and other modes of superstition; and that the whole caboodle, religion included, is in process of being superseded by the development of "rational knowledge." "It would seem possible, with the greater development of the sciences of life, mind, and society, for man actually to acquire a scientific basis for an ever more and more perfect individual life and social organization . . . The question arises, however, whether this progressive naturalistic view leaves any basis for the religious attitudes." The answer plainly given is that it does not. "In spite of many soft words and hopeful assurances to the contrary, there is an irreconcilable conflict between the modern spirit, which is scientific and practical, and the spirit of orthodox Christianity, which is mystical and other-worldly. . . . The combined effect of all these modern influences is to produce a process of secularization of both individual and social life. Secularization is a process of replacing the sacred by the secular, of replacing theological postulates of thought and belief by rational ones and mystical-supernatural controls over behavior by social-naturalistic ones. Our own is undoubtedly the most secular culture the world has yet seen." [1] It is. It is also by far the bloodiest and most destructive; but that is presumably because science has not yet "progressed" far enough. It will be noted that the author, like most modern rationalists, is willing to make an act of faith in Science as absolute as any theist ever made in God.

The attitude to religion of which this is a sample is not, of course, confined to sociology, nor is it characteristic of all schools of sociology; but there is a reason why sociology should be its stronghold. The natural sciences and the disciplines of economics, political theory, law, and jurisprudence have their special fields of concentration; and though at certain points they must and do refer to more general views, their main concern is not with them. But insofar as sociology, following Herbert Spencer, aspired to become the synthetic philosophy, it was bound to encounter what it quite rightly regarded as the other synthetic philosophy, namely, religion; and its omnium-gatherum therefore drew together the various lines of intellectual enterprise that bore on the common antagonist.

The influence of the natural sciences is abundantly evident in such pronouncements as those just cited, and little more need now be said about it. A good deal of the ground had been cleared by Descartes, with his *cogito ergo sum*. The maxim might just as well have been put the other way round; but Descartes was so proud of that *cogito* that he could see no further significance in the *sum*. The real founder of positivist sociology was Auguste Comte (1798–1857). Comte was no ordinary man. Both his intellectual stamina and his psychotic disposition are noteworthy, as is also the fact that his work had much more influence on American thought, with its historic propensity toward French rationalism, than on English, with its persistent Catholic undertone. Comte was in fact a logical successor to Calvin.

According to Comte, every sphere of effort and enlightenment "progresses" through three stages: "the Theological, or fictitious; the Metaphysical, or abstract; and the Scientific, or positive. . . . Hence arise three philosophies . . . each of which excludes the others." [2] The third and final stage is that of empirical research and scientific inference already reached by the natural sciences: a stage that dazzled Comte's generation in Europe, and continued

1. Hankins, F. H., *Introduction to the Study of Society*, pp. 541, 543, 546–547.
2. Comte, *Positive Philosophy*, Vol. I, chap. i (Martineau).

to dazzle the next two in America. The whole life of society, as
well as of the individual, falls under this law of the three stages;
and the main thing, therefore, was to hasten the advance toward
the third stage by getting rid as fast as possible of the other two.
Comte did his best.

The idea of a law of progress in human affairs did not of course
originate with Comte; it had been a favorite notion of the eighteenth century, and French liberalism in particular had been affected by it. Earlier writers, however—Condorcet, for example
—had not been altogether clear about what they meant by "law."
Comte was explicit: he meant no more and no less than what is
meant by the physicist in the laboratory. Now anyone who discerns that kind of a law in history will have to be very nimble
to avoid running into some sort of determinism; it may be an
optimistic determinism, but it will amount to a denial of freedom
nonetheless. And Comte's followers, as we shall see, though some
of them ran very fast, were not able to avoid the trap. So far as
Comte himself avoided it, it was owing to the schizoid character
of his personality rather than the logic of his thought. He was a
highly emotional and inhibited person, naturally responsive to a
much wider range of experience than his intellectual system allowed for. He left, for instance, a significant record of how his
passionate but platonic love for a much younger woman led him,
after her death, through what was almost avowedly a cult of religious adoration, to a retrospective appreciation of his own
mother. He knew, and could not get away from, the power and the
necessity of a religious apprehension; but since his system condemned all historic forms of religion, he went ahead and invented
a new one, complete with a priesthood, ritual, hymns, sermons,
sacraments, and saints' days. He worked very hard at perfecting
it and making converts—it was eventually to be the only permitted form of religion in the new society; and toward the end
of the Victorian era, earnest intellectuals would gather in dreary
lecture halls surrounded with plaster busts and aspidistras, trying
to breathe a little life into the "Great Being," hypostatized Humanity.

§ 2

MR. H. G. WELLS, the best-known of Comte's modern disciples,
has followed his example in this as well as other respects. Since Mr.

Wells boldly proclaimed himself an atheist at the mature age of fifteen, he has written more pages about God and religion than almost any living theologian. If he now repeats a youthful gesture by spitting like an elderly gamin in the face of Mother Church, the passing generation will nonetheless remember how his magnificent zest for life bore them across the mud flats of an ebbing tide, and hold him ever in affectionate regard. For Wells loved mortal man as few have done since Chaucer; loving greatly, he could laugh as Comte could not; and many a time the God of compassion has laughed with him.

Mr. Wells's latest religion—if our information is up to date—centers upon what he calls the World-brain. Rumor has it that a marriage is being arranged between Mr. Wells's World-brain and Mr. Bernard Shaw's Life-force; the progeny will doubtless be a promising brood of Brave New Worlds. This new religion, worth a little scrutiny, is adumbrated—as Wells says, "in prophetic mood"—in the final chapter of his *Outline of History:*

. . . a common world religion, very much simplified and universalized and better understood. This will not be Christianity nor Islam nor Buddhism, nor any such specialized form of religion, but religion itself pure and undefiled—the Eightfold Way, the Kingdom of Heaven, brotherhood, creative service, self-forgetfulness. Throughout the world men's thoughts and motives will be turned by education, example, and the circle of ideas about them, from the obsession of self to the cheerful service of human knowledge, human power, and human unity.

The anthropocentric character of this idealism is conspicuous and common to all types of positivism and secular rationalism. On what premises does it rest?

It assumes that the ultimate ends of human existence on this planet can be defined, and eventually encompassed, by the same type of mental procedure that has so signally enlarged man's knowledge of, and control over, his physical environment; and that apart from such ends as can be so defined and encompassed all the rest is mere "myth, magic, and religion"—illusion, in short. That is certainly a bold venture of faith, in face of the illimitable cosmos: "When I consider thy heavens, the work of thy fingers, the moon and the stars, which thou hast ordained: What is man, that thou art mindful of him? and the son of man, that thou visitest him?" To some minds that might seem the more reasonable attitude; but not to the positivist. The heavens, the moon and the stars, are just brute matter swinging in meaningless mechanical routine (never mind how or why); and the "thou" of the psalmist is nothing but the mind of man, which does not hesitate to limn its own millennium:

Animal and vegetable life, the obscure processes of psychology, the intimate structure of matter and the interior of our earth, will yield their secrets and endow their conqueror. Life begins perpetually. Gathered together at last under the leadership of man, the student-teacher of the universe, unified, disciplined, armed with the secret powers of the atom, and with knowledge as yet beyond dreaming, Life, for ever dying to be born afresh, for ever young and eager, will presently stand upon earth as upon a footstool, and stretch out its realm amidst the stars.

Glory to Man in the highest. And on earth . . . ?

This boundless confidence in man (which is, be it noted, a product of circumstance rather than of reason) necessitates a special reading of history and of psychology. Since rational man is, by hypothesis, the goal and prize of the whole process, history has to be a one-way street, leading up, despite a few blind alleys and some rather rough ground, to the utilitarian temple of this Admirable Crichton. (Curious what a resemblance he seems to bear to those who write about him! The gospels strike a different attitude.) [3] Whatever the past has wrought in the way of beauty, philosophy or wisdom must by hypothesis be inferior to what man is now doing—or is assuredly going to do when he gets round to it. If history does not obviously look that way, so much the worse for history: let us have a "New History." It involves some surprising value judgments, but they are all necessary consequences of the a priori value judgment about man—about the peculiar kind of man postulated at the outset. And the root of the trouble with that kind of man is that he is not man at all, but only the ghost of that part of man which reflects the material environment: disembodied brain. Put him in sole charge of affairs, and he becomes the platonic tyrant; worship him, and he becomes not a god but a monstrosity. It is noteworthy that none of the younger writers and poets who share Wells's positivism also shares his optimism.

Without in any way belittling the importance of science, it is possible to hold that its net contribution to the good of humanity,

3. Cf. De Tocqueville's observation, see p. 144 *supra*.

especially in the applied field, has been overvalued, and secured at a far higher price than is generally acknowledged. Were the men of Versailles in 1919 intrinsically better or wiser men than the men around Metternich, or the men of the Augustan age and many other ages, merely because the former could ride in aeroplanes whereas the latter could ride only on horses? Is the Parthenon inferior to Rockefeller Center because it has only one story whereas Rockefeller Center has goodness knows how many? Has the balance of good and evil forces in the world, or in the heart of man, been perceptibly altered by the achievements of "rational knowledge" as such? Or has such knowledge merely endowed the human creature with far more powerful tools for use in either direction, without materially affecting that inner citadel where the use of the tools is determined? Does the increased expectation of life furnish demonstrable ground for an increased expectation of wisdom?

Dr. Irving Langmuir, Nobel Prize winner and associate director of the General Electric Research Laboratory, in an important address on December 26, 1942, issued a plain warning against the current overvaluation of science.

It is often thought by the layman, and many of those who are working in so-called social sciences, that the field of science should be unlimited, that reason should take the place of intuition, that realism should replace emotions, and that morality is of value only so far as it can be justified by analytical reasoning. Human affairs are characterized by a complexity of a far higher order than that encountered ordinarily in the field of science. In the complicated situations of life we have to solve numerous problems and make many decisions. It is absurd to think that reason should be our guide in all cases. Reason is too slow and too difficult. We often do not have the necessary data. Or we cannot simplify our problem sufficiently to apply the methods of reasoning. What, then, must we do? Why not do what the human race always has done: use the abilities we have, use common sense, judgment and experience.

Our morality is a kind of summation of the wisdom and experience of our race. It comes to us largely through tradition or religion. . . . The philosophical, metaphysical or even scientific analysis of the principles of ethics has not proved particularly fruitful.

The difficulty for the modern positivist of accepting even so temperate a caution is twofold: it seems to take the meaning out

of history, as he understands history; and it too painfully deflates
the rationalist ego insofar as that has nothing left to fall back on.

§ 3

As BERGSON has remarked, "our intellect has its instincts." There
is an inherent tendency in every naïve intellectual to regard himself as the heir of all the ages. It probably arises from an unana-
lyzed experience of time as a directional flow, and it makes very
plausible the notion of history as a secular progress culminating
in himself: culminating, that is, pro tempore, in a "specious present," through which history is supposed to be moving forward
toward a still bigger-and-better future. From the mass of philosophical criticism that this idea has evoked, two points may be
simply presented.

i—History does not support it. Certainly human knowledge and
technique relating to the physical and biological world have ac-
cumulated to a degree never before known; though whether man's
inherent powers, even in this field, have expanded is at least
debatable. But the "straight-line theory" seems to hold good of
technical processes only; in no other sphere is there evidence of
such an accumulation. Other aspects of human life do not seem
to admit of an accumulative process—those, for example, in which
"values" such as beauty, insight, wisdom, are attainable. And the
progress of rationality in respect of the physical setting by no
means validates any general view of history as a continuous
"onward-and-upward." The "idea of progress" which was current
in eighteenth- and nineteenth-century rationalism, and has even
been used by some modern sociologists as a stick to beat the
Church, has by this time been so battered by the course of events
that it is broken past all mending. Instead, we are now offered
pessimistic cyclical theories, revivals of ideas that have found
currency for millennia when things were going badly. But in fact
the pessimism of the latter view is as fantastic as the optimism of
the former. Both alike rest on foundations far too shallow to be
deemed historical, and can be made plausible only by doing the
utmost violence to the record of events.

It is true, of course, that looking backward we discern periods
of high attainment, very various in quality, followed by periods of
decline, of transition and confusion; but the attempt to see in

these any formal pattern, especially a pattern of deterministic character, involves a degree of abstraction and generality that is dangerous to the integrity of historical study, and much too thin to substantiate any philosophy of either collective or individual life. Furthermore, all such efforts involve and rest upon a conception of time that has been rendered invalid, not only by the development of modern philosophy since Kant, but also by the achievements of modern science itself. No student who is looking for a trend or a meaning in history will ever find it in the theories of positivist sociology, because the very postulates are such as to exclude the kind of trend or meaning he is looking for.

ii—A purely secular interpretation of social life, either historical or contemporary, has an inherent tendency to become utopian, in terms of the only category that it knows—the material. Early Christianity found here its first and most formidable obstacle. All the discussion of the nature of the Kingdom of God is intended to lift human hopes and aspirations to a plane on which they would not be doomed to endless and bitter disappointment. Modern Christianity has had precisely the same task in confronting both the rationalist utopianism of Frederick Harrison, H. G. Wells, Julian Huxley, Lancelot Hogben, J. T. Shotwell, and scores of others, and also the more dogmatic version current everywhere among the Marxists. The issue is well described by Professor Niebuhr:

Our modern culture since the Renaissance has not taken the Christian faith seriously because it had a simpler answer to the problems of life. It agreed with Christianity in regarding human history as meaningful, but it assigned a simple meaning to history. . . . Any culture or any religion that is deficient in the "tragic sense of life" is certainly inadequate to give us light and guidance in a day in which the very securities of a technical society have been transmuted into evil. We need a faith that throws light upon the importance of every historical task and responsibility. But it must on the other hand reveal the limits of all historical striving. Without such a faith, the modern man remains an inveterate utopian, disavowing all religious ultimates in one breath and in the next breath affirming his faith in some incredible utopia, some impossible heaven on earth . . .

If we engage in the task of world reconstruction without a disavowal of the utopian illusion, which has informed our culture particularly since the eighteenth century, we shall ask for the impossible by way of world federation or some world superstate; we shall not get it, and then we shall be tempted again to despair and disillusionment.[4]

Modern positivism does in fact reflect not only the utopian illusion, but the utopian disillusion; and it is brought to the latter by an intellectual as well as a circumstantial nemesis.

The foundation of Herbert Spencer's work was laid, and a good deal of the structure erected, before the publication of the Darwin-Wallace theory. Spencer was confident he could achieve what to Comte had been only a distant possibility, namely, the reduction of all individual and social phenomena to a single unitary principle. His principle lay in an extremely arbitrary identification of social with biological and ultimately physical processes. Taking the theory of evolution—or his own idea of it—in his stride, Spencer laid down the laws of progress with what he conceived to be scientific finality. So sure was he not only of the power but of the ultimate beneficence of the natural laws governing the "social organism" that he became the outstanding opponent of state interference; not because he liked anarchy, but because he was certain that the cosmic process, left to itself, would do a better job. As a critic of statism Spencer has not even yet been equaled. Much of his comment has proved prophetic; for example:

If the present drift of things continues, it may by and by really happen that the Tories will be defenders of liberties which the Liberals, in pursuit of what they think popular welfare, trample under foot. . . . Probably, however, the Liberal, and still more the subspecies Radical, who more than any other seems under the impression that so long as he has a good end in view he is warranted in exercising over men all the coercion he is able, will continue to protest. . . . The function of Liberalism in the past was that of putting a limit to the powers of kings. The function of true liberalism in the future will be that of putting a limit to the powers of Parliaments.[5]

Spencer is acutely aware in his later work of the conflict between voluntary and coercive coöperation. He opposes not only Hobbes and Austin, but Bentham, in asserting the priority of individual rights to collective authority. He thus comes round to a defense of the traditional natural right (*Naturrecht*) basis of political theory.

4. Niebuhr, R., "A Faith for History's Greatest Crisis," *Fortune*, July, 1942.
5. *The Man Versus the State* (1940 American ed.), pp. 19, 21, 209; see also Preface by Albert Jay Nock.

But Spencer's conception of the human being as all of a piece with other products of biological evolution let him down in the end. In his old age he was not so sure that the cosmic processes which had hitherto been on the side of humanity might not, in some later turn of the cycle, be against it. To stake one's all on the sort of nature nineteenth-century science had revealed was to take an awful gamble; there are pages in Spencer that are curiously prescient of the coming horror. Having no other ground for hope, Spencer stuck stoutly to his evolutionary hypothesis; but if from that hypothesis the optimism be removed, what is left? Nothing, alas, but the notion of an ineluctable process to which neither goal nor meaning can be assigned. Then determinism comes into its own.

§ 4

It is hardly necessary nowadays to argue seriously about the common forms of determinism. Modern science and philosophy have knocked away the flimsy scaffolding of such views; and in any case, determinism is not, and never was, a working philosophy of life. One can conceivably die by it; no one ever consistently lived by it. If people would reflect more simply and sincerely on their actual experience of living they would be less vulnerable to a great deal of academic nonsense, and philosophy would be the gainer. In essence determinism is one of those theories which, as Professor Broad said of behaviorism, "are so preposterously silly that only very learned men could have thought of them." But it is worth while to examine the few simple notions that underlie it because, properly understood, they help to define the true nature of human freedom.

There are five species of orthodox academic determinism: the economic, the cultural, the biological, the psychological, and the moral. Of the first, Nicolai Bukharin was the leading, and, for some years, the official spokesman. Since his death in the Russian "purge" of 1938, and the subsequent disavowal of Marxist doctrine by the Soviet Government, American communists have had to adapt their utterances to strategic rather than dialectic considerations. They are not the only Americans who have found the transition from dreams to actualities somewhat bewildering. It must be remembered however that some sort of determinism is the logical outcome of materialism. The element of Spencer's system that can obviously be fitted into a materialist view of society is the notion of internecine struggle; and the false biological analogy is therefore still of service in providing an excuse for the class war, and a rationalization of subhuman ethical practices. The determinism of Marx had a strongly Hegelian and idealistic bias, and was in essence more humane than its modern derivatives. The theoretical basis of these latter is to be sought not so much in old-style economic determinism as in the four other species we have listed; and the influence of those species is by no means confined to the organized groups of avowed communists.

§ 5

CULTURAL determinism is directly descended from the "law of nature" of the natural philosophers. Nature had been kept pretty busy by those elegant gentlemen; and the temper of the coal age was rather trying for an eighteenth-century beauty. When Shelley died, nature was undoubtedly a little tired; by the time Darwin had finished with her, she was definitely not what she used to be. It became necessary, at last, to find some other patron saint—or at least, some other patronymic—for the determinism of the industrial era. "Culture" saved the day: a daughter of nature who had been to college, and acquired some of the sophistication her mother so obviously lacked when she took up with Rousseau.

Culture—to quote a standard definition—is "that complex whole which includes knowledge, belief, art, morals, law, custom, and any other capabilities and habits acquired by man as a member of society." [6] It (if such a conglomeration can have a pronoun) comprises practically the whole "social heritage"; and this "social heritage" is represented as controlling and determining the behavior of the individuals from whose mutual relations culture arises. The circular argument involved here is innocently set forth by a well-known American sociologist: "Culture is not inborn but acquired by every individual in social groups; but this culture of the group dominates the behavior of the individual and so the behavior of human groups. Human social life is thus dominated by culture; and culture is a matter of habits of thought and action acquired by interaction with other members of one's group." [7]

6. Tylor, quoted by Ogburn, W. F., *Social Change*, p. 4.
7. Ellwood, C. A., *The Psychology of Human Society*, pp. 10–11.

This is an example of the characteristic fallacy of "social science" and is worth noting on that account. Such descriptive generalizations as the one above, and the abstract concepts of which they are composed, may have their uses as guides to intellectual or even practical procedure; but there is no confusion more common than to speak of the generalization or abstraction as if it were a thing with an independent existence, and then attribute to it a causal role in the world of actual events. This slip over the line from intellectual abstraction to ontological postulation is the more dangerous because, as in the case above, it is usually unconscious; and its necessary result is a sterility or perversion of thought which no abuse of language can disguise. How far such abuse can go is evident in this attempt of a social psychologist to describe higher education: "In our age no personality can be regarded as properly developed and molded if it has not been trained in the higher type of conditioning of adjustment behavior responses to abstract language stimuli, because the latter transcend in breadth and depth the content of concrete personalities." [8] As Humpty Dumpty said, there's glory for you!

Insofar as an intelligible meaning can be got out of this passage, liberalism has to reject it. It is not true that "abstract language stimuli" transcend the "content" of personality; and the whole theory underlying this type of approach is one that liberalism has an urgent duty to oppose. Much modern speculation about the "course" of history, the "evolution" of culture, the "progress" of civilization, and so forth, has had the practical effect of persuading the individual that the significance of his particular life and character, his particular moment, his particular generation, subsists only in reference to the condition and future of society as a whole; and that apart from that prospect, he and his here-and-now are devoid of anything that can really be called meaning. The circular argument involved here is commonly ignored, as is also the opening it provides for Hegelian theories that reduce the individual to nothingness before the secular state. This is, in fact, one of those notions which, seldom rising into explicit consciousness, tend to color the outlook of a whole era; and it is probable that no other fallacy of our time has done more to corrupt manners and morals, to corrode assurance, and to destroy mental and spiritual health.

8. Davis, Barnes *et al.*, *Introduction to Sociology*, p. 433 (L. L. Bernard).

For it is, by both liberal and Catholic doctrine, a fallacy, and a cardinal one. It is one of the central tenets of both that every person great or small, cultured or lowly, every moment of time, every human generation, partakes of a significance that is absolute, second to no other; that to maintain the contrary in contemplation of a God who is supposed to be outside human time, or the divine Presence, which is supposed to be inside human time, is morally speaking, presumptuous and philosophically speaking, ridiculous. What any individual—even the weakest and meanest—is and becomes in himself, what he does by himself, with himself, to himself, is not to be held of no account merely because, as is probably the case, it will make precious little difference to the state of society, the course of history or the fate of civilization. This is the true and fundamental basis of democracy; and if that institution tries to perpetuate itself on any other foundation than this, it will assuredly collapse—for there is none.

Perhaps Berdyaev has defined the issue more clearly than any recent writer. The modern doctrine of progress, he says, is spuriously messianic and millenarian, projected in a false "time," in which every generation becomes a mere means, an evanescent accident in

the incessant extermination of past by future. . . . There is no such thing in history as progress from good to perfect on a single plane of development. . . . Every generation has its own goal, its own justification, its own meaning, its own values, its own spiritual impulses whereby it approximates the divine life. It cannot be merely an instrument and means of future generations. . . . There is no reason for making one's optimism, creative energies and prospects depend on the modified values of later generations. There is no ground for the conviction that these are more authentic than those which obtained in the past. . . . From the standpoint of the present, the future is no richer in reality than the past, and our efforts should be with reference, not to the future, but to that eternal present in which both future and past are one.[9]

Liberal philosophy therefore refuses to let the concrete reality of the here-and-now be as it were intellectualized away into the thin air of any sociological *Weltanschauung;* and by the same token it will not allow the separate specific human personality to be reduced to the phantom "individual" of abstract political or

9. Berdyaev, N., *The Meaning of History,* chap. x.

statistical generalization. It does not deny that there are some things one can learn about living creatures by studying them in statistical aggregates; but it stoutly opposes the tendency of modern collectivism to *treat* them as if they were no more than arithmetical units. It does not assert that personal life is separate, or separable, from the collective; but it refuses to regard you and me, our friends and relations, with all our troublesome characteristics and idiosyncrasies, as a mere precipitate thrown off from something vaguely called the "environment" by a sort of biological catalysis. Where positivist theory talks about "individuals" liberalism talks about "persons": meaning human beings taken one at a time, each as valuable as every other. In so doing, it recognizes, perhaps more clearly than other creeds have done, the differences of function and capacity on the plane of social and material events; but if all valuations are to be derived from, and confined to, that plane, then much that we regard as finest and truest in human experience and achievement is excluded from the system. It is rather difficult, for example, to fit the essential quality of Dante's *Vita Nuova* into that sort of world.

§ 6

FOR its more solid justification, cultural determinism falls back on economic determinism on one hand and biological determinism on the other. Fortunately for science, biological determinism has little to do with biology. The theory that conduct is finally determined by the structures and processes revealed in the laboratory is entirely extrinsic to the research itself; it is made plausible only by an a priori exclusion of the phenomena and possibilities that conflict with it. Very often this preliminary exclusion passes unnoticed. It is then easy to convince the unwary that what a man feels, thinks, and does is what he is compelled to feel, think, and do by his biological heritage and constitution; that apart from these, mental and spiritual activity are simple delusions; that the kind of response a man will make to a given situation is "determined" by the biological factors. Well, of course it is—in the sense that one does not get flute music out of a bass viol; but however this notion be elaborated—and it is elaborated in the most varied and ingenious ways—all the meaning in it is that a man behaves like a man because he is a man, and that if he were some other kind of creature he would behave like that other kind of creature. That is about as much in the way of a general theory of man as modern cytology will support. Proof of this profound theorem is constantly accruing as enterprising "researchers" discover new tricks to play on him, new bits to cut out of him and new drugs to squirt into him; for when these things are done, behold the man acts, feels, and even thinks differently from what he did before! It is even possible, to a certain limited extent, to catalogue the differences and relate them to the means employed; and it is demonstrable that if enough of these means are employed, the man will cease to be human at all. Some knowledge of the mechanisms of the body is arrived at in this way, as are some useful devices for the correction of functional abnormalities; but to suppose that it sheds light on the nature of the human being as such is possible only to those who have made up their minds at the outset that the human being is *nothing but* an assemblage of biochemical reactions. There are questions one must not ask of these pundits: Why, for instance, does the man make any response to the situation in the first place? To answer that, one has to drag in theories like "vitalism" which savor of philosophy or even religion—and what a theory is that which begs the entire question in the name it gives itself! Or, granting the profound theorem that a man acts in such and such a way because he is a such-and-such kind of creature, what kind of creature really is he? Answer, by your leave: he is the kind of creature who acts in such and such a way because he is a such-and-such kind of creature. If you insist beyond that, the nothing-but fallacy will poke its inconvenient head out of the laboratory slop pail.

§ 7

THE psychological version of biological determinism was furnished by Doctor Freud. The patient and voluminous work of that curious personality has without doubt been a stronger enemy of Christianity than all the naïve atheisms fed to the very young; for it founded a fellowship of devotees who considered themselves so exceptionally mature that they were not so much hostile as superior to religion. They had their own; and a very potent cult it was.

Like all cults that amount to anything, it had a core of genuine insight and efficacy, which it proceeded to embody in a system of myth and symbol so well worked out that the apostles, initiates and fellow travelers completely forgot that the entire conceptual outfit was in fact only myth and symbol. Indeed, as the system developed, the Doctor forgot it himself; and his attitude toward heresy, persisting in many of his followers, plainly showed that something more than a purely scientific motivation was at work. That was what gave the thing its power: it satisfied, at least for a while; it reached the soul, and effected a real conversion.

The exploration of the atavistic strains in human nature paralleled, and supplemented, the biological dogma we have been discussing; and the practitioners had no difficulty in showing how strong and how dynamic these strains were. It seemed to follow —and this was the therapeutic secret—that to give adequate recognition to these chthonic powers and come to terms with them (the terms being theirs—for what else was there?) spelled integration, peace, and success in life. On such terms (with the aid, perhaps, of Dr. Steinach) Faustus could be young again; and that —as the manners, the diversions, even the dress of the period indicated—was the obvious *summum bonum*. Thus the practice of psychoanalysis rapidly expanded from a useful approach to genuine psychosis into a popular panacea for all who were so minded, and could afford it.

Now the type of conflict with which this procedure is properly concerned—naturally a very frequent type in a materialistic culture—lies between what may be called normal and subnormal motives; whereas the type of conflict with which religious psychology is concerned lies between normal and supernormal motives: between the "natural man" and the urge toward spiritual perfection. This latter conflict is just as real as the former, and for some minds just as urgent; but the Freudians were noticeably reluctant to give it either attention or recognition. The school of Jung always acknowledged its existence (and was solemnly excommunicated therefor); Jung and many others have written wisely and sympathetically about it; and at last the Freudians manifested a certain curiosity. Freud's clumsy construction of the "superego" was a belated attempt to fit this phase of experience into his analytical system. He announced that the superego was

. . . a genuine structural entity . . . the vehicle of the ego-ideal, by which the ego measures itself, towards which it strives, and whose demands for ever-increasing perfection it is always striving to fulfill. . . . The super-ego is the representative of all moral restrictions, the advocate of the impulse toward perfection, in short it is as much as we have been able to apprehend psychologically of what people call the "higher" things in human life.[10]

But if we ask from what source the superego derives its "impulse toward perfection" the answer is not very satisfactory. The derivation of the "lower" impulses was quite plausibly traced back to our animal heritage—to the deep and powerful roots by which our nature is grounded in the material world. In seeking a derivation for the "higher" impulses the system, owing to its original bias, could look only in the same atavistic direction. Thus Freud tells us that "no doubt the ego-ideal is a precipitation of the old idea of the parents."

One of his ablest exponents is more explicit.

The Super-ego is the composite of identifications with the authoritative and prohibitive attitudes of other personalities, especially the prohibitors of what the child would like to do. . . . The resulting blends of identifications determine those standards of caste, of religion, of race, of culture, which are so decisive in the social configuration of the adult. Still later, identifications with personified ideals, those of art and philosophy, for example, add their components to the final character. . . . [But] not only are the basic elements of the Super-ego the "precipitate" of identifications with parents, but the unconscious guilt and "fear of conscience" are shown to be similarly derived from the actual original fear of the power and the punishments of these grown-ups . . . If the child disobeys he is punished; if the adult disobeys he experiences conscious remorse or neurotic suffering.[11]

Voilà tout! That is the whole works; and it brings us back to the same moral relativism and social determinism that all materialism necessarily lands in.

There is a further and more obvious flaw: as an explanation of the creative impulses that inspire art, poetry, virtue, religion, and all historical achievement, the atavistic theory is totally and ridiculously inadequate. It is in fact being everywhere abandoned: sur-

10. Freud, S., New Introductory Lectures on Psycho-Analysis, pp. 92–93.
11. Hendrick, I., Facts and Theories of Psychoanalysis, pp. 163–167.

reptitiously in the case of the Freudians, overtly in the more liberal schools. When Freud, in his later years, was more or less compelled to broaden the individualistic basis of his system, he found himself forced to reckon with factors he had always avoided taking seriously. His instinctive response was an attack on religion in general, and Christianity in particular, that went far beyond the logic of his own position. Religion, he averred, was *nothing but* an illusory compensation for the severity of the discipline which social life imposes; but whereas most of his followers show a patronizing tolerance of religion as an opiate for the people (or the patient), not so the master. (It is noteworthy that this part of the exposition is cast by Freud in the form of a dialogue, in which a puzzled enquirer puts the questions, and Freud supplies the answers. "May I ask you to enlighten me?" "With pleasure. I was only waiting for this invitation.")

The enlightenment provided by the master consists in the proposition that religion is "the universal obsessional neurosis of humanity. It, like the child's, originated in the Oedipus complex, the relation to the father. . . . This historical residue has given us the conception of religious dogmas as, so to speak, neurotic survivals, and now we may say that the time has probably come to replace the consequences of repression by the results of rational mental effort, as in the analytic treatment of neurotics." One needs a deep breath, and a moment of historical recollection, to grasp the full sweep of this pronouncement. For Freud the contemplation of a neurotic world was tempered by an act of faith in human rationality, which was really an act of faith in his own intellectualization, à la Comte. "Culture has little to fear from the educated or from the brain workers. In their case religious motives for civilized behavior would be unobtrusively replaced by other and secular ones; besides, for the most part they are themselves supporters of culture." That was written in 1928, when things looked a little brighter: little did Freud know what some of the educated brain workers of his own nation were going to do to him! So he could go on to extol the recognition of man's ignorance and impotence before the cosmos as "irreligious in the truest sense of the word" and find assurance in the thought that "the problem of the nature of the world irrespective of our perceptive mental apparatus is an empty abstraction without practical interest. Science is no illusion. But it would be an illusion to suppose that we could get anywhere else what it cannot give us." [12]

Nonetheless, his followers have had to reckon with the fact that we do go on looking, and they are increasingly interested in what we seem to find. It is an open question, however, how far that interest can be intelligently pursued with the postulates, and the techniques, inherited from Doctor Freud; and it is certain that the equipment for the cure of souls must include in future a wider training than he envisaged: notably, and emphatically, a training in philosophy.

§ 8

MORAL determinism is so obvious an outcome of the foregoing that it scarcely needs illustration. It leads inevitably to that moral relativism which is almost a hallmark of positivist sociology. Ideal absolutes are barred: they cannot be empirically established. What people want is what their circumstances make them want, and in the circumstances it is right—so far as there is any right—for them to want it. Different groups want different things, and therefore formulate different value systems. Each group thinks and does what it must, and that is all there is to it. If the other group can be persuaded, or "conditioned," to want the same things, and therefore formulate the same ideals, as we do, there may be peace; if not, since each system is right for each group, we shall find ourselves in conflict, and superior force will solve the ethical problem.

This goes right down to the plane of individual behavior. Here also positivism achieves a grand simplification. Conscience itself is socially determined: a thesis which tallies with, and is to some extent indebted to, that of Doctor Freud. "The mores," says Professor Kimball Young, "consist of the codes of social conduct which grow up in any community or society. The mores are the generally accepted and expected forms of conduct which are assumed to be necessary for group welfare." They frequently acquire therefore a religious sanction; and Dr. Young is inclined to be tolerant of this trimming, since it gives a man "surcease from worry and considerable faith in himself. . . . In contrast therefore to the common sense material world we find a world based on fantasy and wishful thinking, particularly in religion, art and play. This

12. Freud, S., *The Future of an Illusion*, pp. 39, 76–77, 68, 57, 97–98.

world helps to fulfill life, gives it a richer, more pleasing, and more personally satisfying meaning" [13]—at which perhaps the artists will join the priests in praying to be saved from their friends! Professor Hankins, more strictly consistent, will tolerate no such nonsense: "It is here that appears the sharpest contrast between the rational and the supra-rational sanction to conduct. As man emerges from the dogmatic-emotional morality of religious tradition into the critical-intellectual morality of scientific knowledge, he acquires freedom and power." [14] The power we recognize; the freedom seems daily to grow less; for as the power increases it cuts loose from its creator and makes man himself its slave.

It is noteworthy that the positivist position is now being increasingly attacked by psychologists and sociologists themselves. Sorokin's sweeping indictment is well known. He sees all this mechanization of mind, and the meaningless materialism to which it leads, in terms of a major historical crisis underlying, and provoking, the current outbreaks of physical and cultural destruction.

If science and technology remain morally and socially indifferent, serving with the same equanimity the God of Creation and the Mammon of Destruction, they will be ruined. . . . If they cease to be morally and socially indifferent, they will have to stop being what they are; they will be obliged to recognize some universal—and in this sense absolute—norms and values. They have to choose. . . . Sensate Western culture and society are given a categoric ultimatum: either persist on the road of overripe sensate culture and go to ruin, to a life uncreative, devoid of any genius, painful and inglorious; or shift, while there is still a possibility of doing so, to another road of ideational or idealistic culture. [15]

Among many other protests that might be cited is that of the distinguished Gestalt psychologist, Kurt Koffka; it is the more significant in that Koffka had an almost obsessional horror of wishful thinking and a priori generalization. The concluding passage of his major work contains the following declaration (with which the present writer would humbly associate himself):

If there is any polemical spirit in this book, it is directed not against persons but against a strong cultural force in our present civilization for

13. Young, K., *Sociology*, chap. xix.
14. Hankins, *loc. cit.*
15. Sorokin, P. A., *The Crisis of Our Age*, pp. 270-271.

which I have chosen the name positivism. If positivism can be regarded as an integrative philosophy, its integration rests on the dogma that all events are equally unintelligible, irrational, meaningless, purely factual. Such an integration is, however, to my way of thinking, identical with a complete disintegration. Being convinced that such a view is utterly inadequate in face of the facts, I had to attack it, and that the more since its hold over our generation is strong. It makes a difference to one's life whether one is a positivist or not.[16]

Every systematized body of thought, including the skeptical and agnostic schools, has an inherent tendency to become dogmatic; and science and dogma are incompatible. The only sphere in which dogma is both permissible and useful is that in which dogma is expressly recognized as defining faith, not knowledge; and it is to faith alone that the language of absolutism is philosophically appropriate. The exhaustion of the materialist doctrine is patent when that doctrine itself dons the robe of dogmatic absolutism which it so strenuously denies to every other discipline.

But in denouncing this pose the critic must not overlook the elements of truth that lie behind it. The idealist, for example, will deny that conscience is socially determined in a fundamental or total sense; he does not thereby deny that part of its specific content is so determined. A distinction is made between the inherent drive toward spiritual wholeness and the manifestations of that impulse under any particular circumstances. Thus the notion that the separate individual conscience is an autonomous and final court of appeal is as misleading as the opposite error. In recognizing the validity of the appeal to conscience, one does not thereby assert that conscience is beyond and independent of all guidance and enlightenment. Similarly, when the idealist disputes the identification of morals with mores, and maintains that there is more to morality than meets the sociological eye, he does not assert that the specific dictates of morality are all immutable. The teaching of Jesus is especially illuminating on this point. Seventy years ago, in some parts of New England, smoking was a more damnable vice than drinking; today both habits are largely outside the scope of specific moral precept, and parts of the sex ethic are probably undergoing a similar transition. On the other hand it must be recognized that the blatant insincerity, vulgarity, and sensationalism of certain aspects of American life are now within the scope

16. Koffka, K., *Principles of Gestalt Psychology*, pp. 684–685.

of the sternest moral judgment. The essential distinction is that between the behavioristic approach to morality, which finds only shifting and pragmatic standards, and the religious approach, which recognizes an ideal norm. Religion is concerned with the quality of the total life and culture; it looks beyond the letter which killeth to the spirit which giveth life; its standards are therefore higher than those of individual or social expediency. Christian courtesy, for example, goes beyond mere morality into positive beauty of act and demeanor; so with Christian virtue in many another matter. Much of the weakness and ugliness of Protestantism comes from the assumption that the main concern of religion is with behavioristic morality, and stops there; whereas beyond that plane there is a whole culture to be purged, ennobled, and rededicated.

Yet a final caution is needed. Before giving up the assorted myths of social determinism, a man must recognize that he may be letting himself in for a much less comfortable, indeed an appalling, alternative. Under the spell of agnostic or atheistic teachings, modern life has become largely a technique for the deliberate evasion of moral responsibility: a phenomenon that now characterizes public as well as private life in an amazing degree. Alike in its restless and centrifugal tendency, the absence or denial of critical standards, the shortness of popular memory, the shallowness of popular convictions, this evasion is manifest; and nowhere is it more evident than in the refusal to reckon with the fact, or even admit the conception, of individual and collective sin. Deterministic theories, sociological and psychological, are popular because they offer people a plausible excuse to go on fooling themselves and ignoring or denying their own experience. It is a simple fact—and everybody knows it—that when we refuse to fulfill the demands of our higher nature a sense of failure and remorse besets us: we feel and know that we have sinned and come short of the glory of God. Since this feeling is uncomfortable, an age that has made a god of comfort will not admit it; it is barred as far as may be from consciousness, and the word sin is banished from polite usage. Instead, we invent all sorts of elaborate disguises for the fact to which it refers. A deterministic dogma comes in very handy as an escape from responsibility. Sociology proffers a variety of comfortable excuses for human failure. You can blame, according to the school of your choice, either the "environment" (ignoring the circular argument involved); or the "culture"—that commodious *Ding an sich* suspended in a logical vacuum; or your genes, hormones, and chromosomes; or that poor old scapegoat, the "subconscious"—you can blame, in short, almost anything except your self; because you have been taught that you really have no self. If there is a quicker way to weaken the moral fiber of a democracy, it has yet to be discovered; for in all these subterfuges the root impulse is to escape the more exacting and uncomfortable aspects of human responsibility, individual and collective. Catholics, as individuals, know how hard (and how salutary) it is to utter a sincere *mea culpa*. The masses of mankind have always found it easier to strike their enemies, real or fancied, than to strike their breasts. Yet a return to sanity and realism requires that men be made to face the fact, and the consequences, of their own wrongdoing before they deal with that of other people; and the Church is the only organization that tries to make them.

Twenty-four years ago, in his first book (a history) the writer penned at least one sentence that has stood the test of time: "Nations may choose, if they will, the method of trial and error; but the trial is apt to be long, and the error is punished." No one who knows his Bible will attribute any originality to that; but the frightful truth of it lies on a plane that we persistently refuse to recognize. Yet if deterministic dogma is abandoned; if human freedom of choice, and therefore human responsibility, are acknowledged; if it is held that there are absolute, not merely relative, standards, of what is proper to man; if the concepts of freedom, personality, and deity have any meaning: then we are forced to face the possibility—yes, and the actuality—of sin on a sustained and colossal scale, such as the prophets of Israel so courageously discerned and denounced. The stress of an armed struggle breeds forgetfulness, and victory breeds complacency; but no matter how total the victory, if any lasting good is to come of it man must set out in penitence and humility, remembering the long record of selfish folly and willful blindness, and the abrogation of all human decency to which it led.

XII

The Retreat from Liberalism

*1. Two liberal principles. — 2. Both are abandoned. —
3. Theory of intervention. — 4. Intervention in practice.
— 5. Ethics versus politics. — 6. The world policeman's
beat.*

§ 1

BRITISH liberalism, in its international application, rested on
two fundamental principles: Nonintervention in the internal affairs of other nations, and freedom of trade. These
principles were explicitly recognized by liberal statesmen as complementary to one another, being the negative and the positive
conditions of peace and freedom. Their abandonment in our generation effectively dispelled the hope of either.

The principle of nonintervention was magnificently defended
by both Burke and Smith in regard to the leading issue of their
time. It was further defined by Castlereagh in 1815, and followed,
against ever-increasing opposition, by Canning, Huskisson, Peel,
Cobden, Bright, Gladstone, Campbell-Bannerman, and Morley.
In the course of that long defense, the nature of intervention received exhaustive definition. Public abuse and provocation were
recognized as a leading form of it. Peel courageously repudiated
the old fallacy—now being urged on the Americans—*bellum pari
si pacem velis.* Cobden in 1850 attacked the business of international moneylending with a candor that has seldom since been
equaled.[1] He refused to allow that the principle of free trade sanctions the lending of money wherever it can get the highest return,
irrespective of the purpose and probable effects of the loan. So
the press and the City of London denounced him, and the transactions of the moneylenders have continued to evade public scrutiny even where public as well as private funds are involved.

1. See Morley, J., *Life of Cobden*, chap. xix, and speeches there cited.

The liberal statesmen of the mid-century had to defend the rule of nonintervention even in cases where the grounds of a proposed intervention were such as to command widespread popular support—to check a tyranny, or to aid the causes (then allied) of nationalism and representative government. "Peace, retrenchment, and reform" demanded that the interest of the home parish be balanced against even the most deserving of foreign missions; and the occasions on which Gladstone departed from his principles turned out less fortunate than those on which he adhered to them. In the sort of world the great powers were creating, the consequences of even the best-intentioned intervention might be difficult to foresee or to control; and while no doubt Russian interest in the Christians of Constantinople, British sympathy for Armenians and Bulgarians, French protection for Lebanese Catholics, were all disinterested at the outset, the pattern into which they fitted has an old familiar look. Nothing more clearly demonstrates the need for caution than the way in which history transforms the schemes, both good and bad, of those who pin their faith on force; and it must always be remembered that resort to coercion creates a new situation that cannot be revoked when the occasion or the mood is past.

Liberal policy relied on opinion, moral as well as intellectual, both to restrain the impulse toward force and to mitigate the tyranny of the oppressor; and it rather took for granted the existence of a will to peace. In fact, that was hard to discover. We have already noted (p. 172) Cobden's observation on the state of popular opinion toward Palmerston. That observation needs to be supplemented by another, made when he was striving to quench the chauvinist panic worked up on both sides of the Channel in the 1850's:

We cannot disguise from ourselves that the military spirit pervades the higher and more influential classes of this country; and that the Court, aristocracy and all that is aping the tone of the latter believe that their interests, privileges, and even their very security are bound up in the maintenance of the "Horse Guards." Hence the very unfashionable character of our movement, and hence the difficulty of inducing influential persons to attend our meetings.[2]

2. Letter of September 19, 1853. See Hobson, J. A., *Richard Cobden*, p. 94; Morley, *op. cit.*, chap. xxi.

Cobden goes on to describe the general attitude of his country-men as "arrogant, dictatorial and encroaching toward foreigners"; but it must be remembered that most of Palmerston's foreign adventures were conceived, or at least presented, in terms of a certain idealism: idealism and arrogance being, of course, not incompatible.

The idealism of the masses is in fact a greater obstacle to peace than their chauvinism; for while the latter is latent and sporadic, the former is constant and more flattering to self-esteem. The United States, in virtue of its immigration policy, has become a giant sounding board for the plaints of every oppressed or thwarted minority on earth. In Britain that effect was tempered by a proximity to the scene of operations from which Americans are fortunately shielded; and idealism is naturally more eager when it is accompanied by a consciousness of great strength and great resources. In these circumstances no general will to peace may be assumed—for disillusion is by no means the same thing—and in the absence of a genuine philosophy of peace, the use of force can always be presented as ethically superior.

§ 2

BRITISH liberalism, as we said, saw freedom of trade as an integral part of the policy of peace; but it was a tragic circumstance that nonintervention and free trade had so little chance to pull together. No sooner were the ports made free to shipping and the customs barriers pulled down than foreign affairs fell into the hands of Palmerston; and it is noteworthy that the same mob sentiment that cheered him on raised an unprecedented uproar against the establishment of Roman Catholic bishoprics in England. In the long duel between popular peer and dogged commoner, Cobden scored one great success in the commercial treaty that dissolved the danger of war with France. If ever a man could claim to have achieved "peace with honor" it was Cobden in 1859 rather than Disraeli in 1878; for he pulled that pact out of the very teeth of Mars. But it is significant that he had to do it by extraconstitutional means, and at his own expense. After the achievements of Palmerston and Disraeli, the role of free trade in the policy of peace was circumscribed by the fact that an ever-growing area of the world was not open to free settlement or free investment. Britons may well be proud of the establishment, during the next half century, of the liberal empire; but it was not entirely the fault of foreigners that the liberalism was confined to the empire.

Nonetheless, the long adherence of both parties in Britain to the principle of free trade cannot be dismissed as a manifestation of mere self-interest. True enough, the preëminence of British shipping, insurance, and finance had been largely the outcome of that policy: the liberals of the mid-century had frankly, and rightly, emphasized its practical advantages to the western island. But Gladstone had made a tremendous moral impact on national policy which was not confined to his party or his generation; and the connection of free trade with international peace was deeply embedded in it. It was that factor, quite as much as the influence of the City, that defeated the power politics of Joseph Chamberlain, and kept Britain, almost alone, on the trail of a forlorn hope. The effort made by Britain and the Scandinavian states at Geneva in 1927 to check the economic nationalism of postwar Europe was a last-ditch fight for economic disarmament. The finishing blow was struck by the United States Congress in 1930; and any lingering disposition to renew the struggle was dispelled by the aggressive isolationism with which Mr. Franklin D. Roosevelt wrecked the World Economic Conference of 1933.

No sooner had Britain, with bitterness and misgiving, abandoned the general principle of free trade than the American Government began to discover its merits. The reciprocal trade treaty program of Mr. Cordell Hull was certainly, in the mind of that statesman, associated with the cause of peace; but it was also an effort to counter the bargaining campaign launched by Britain two years earlier, and the system of empire preference established at Ottawa. Nonetheless, the political benefit was at least as important as the economic, so far as it went; it was a reminder of how much more might have been accomplished had circumstances permitted the governments of Britain and America to work in coöperation while there was yet time. But the American refusal to follow the British in negotiating with Germany in 1934, and the subsequent failure to reach agreement with the Argentine, proclaimed in ominous tones that the time was past.

Meanwhile the principle of nonintervention had lost its authorit as the result of a process started by Woodrow Wilson. Wilson, following the course of events from the banks of the Potomac, discerned a distinction between the German people and the German Government; and as soon as he got the chance, he acted on that professorial vision. He was the prime mover of the "wicked Kaiser" theory, and he brought the full force of his eloquence, his humanitarianism, and his position to encourage—one might say, to demand—a political revolution inside Germany as a preliminary to the cessation of hostilities and the preparation of peace. Having duly produced the revolution, and enacted a model democratic constitution, the Germans of 1919 were unable to follow the logic which nonetheless saddled them with the retroactive war guilt clause of the treaty, on which the reparation demands were made to depend; but if Wilson's logic was somewhat confused on that point, the blame was not wholly his. Still following his dream, in which nationalism, self-determination, and democracy were all vaguely synonymous with peace, he enacted a Palmerstonian policy in a professorial garb; and the condition for entry of a state to the League of Nations was that it should be "fully self-governing." (How the Italians managed to get a seat for Ethiopia is one of the minor curiosities of history.)

In thus imposing stipulations about the type of government as a condition of international comity, Wilson and his fellow ideologues were harking back to the principles of the Holy Alliance, which British empiricism had flatly and consistently rejected. The result was to start a widening divergence between British and American ideas of foreign policy, which reflected the divergence between ideological groups within each country. Not only the extreme left, but the extreme right, wanted an interventionist line. The extreme right got its way, by entirely illicit means, in Churchill's war on the Russian Revolution, and made an attempt—frustrated by British labor—to back the Polish attack of 1920. The reaction of radical groups all over the world is still an active factor in politics.

The Italian issue sharpened the divergence between interventionists and their opponents. Eden's courageous effort to make the League effective was based on the official condemnation of Italy by the Council; the United States, not being a member of the League, was not committed to action, as Britain was. But the entire left in both Britain and America insisted that Britain ought to attack, not merely Italy, but fascism. This Eden quite correctly denied. Britain was accordingly denounced for not following a policy whose application would have been just as hotly denounced had the shoe been on the other foot.

Then came Spain. Once again, Eden stated in the most explicit terms that the Foreign Office would not fight, nor recognize, an ideological war; and once again, the radical intelligentsia of America damned him for it, and made believe that Britain had no policy but reaction. Actually, the nonintervention committee represented a much more consistent and authentic policy than that of the crusade for which the American left was clamoring; nor was the argument for nonintervention weakened—it might just as well be strengthened—by the fact that three European powers had openly intervened. Britain was perfectly free to decide whether to start a European war on Spanish soil; but such a decision must be governed by military considerations, and the state of Britain was not much stronger than that of America. The embargo on the sale of arms to the Spanish Government was another matter. That measure, in which America joined, can be justified, if at all, only on grounds of expediency; the question however should not be examined without reference to the British definition of neutrality in the American Civil War. The American embargo issued from the new American neutrality law of 1935–37, which forbade the export of arms to belligerents in international or civil wars. It was this law that President Roosevelt urged Congress to repeal on September 21, 1939, on the ground that it might operate unfairly as between "an aggressor" and "the victim." The President was already an interventionist, though perhaps he did not know it, since he assured the Congress that "this Government clearly and definitely will insist that American citizens and American ships keep away from the immediate perils of the actual zones of conflict." But perhaps he did know it. He had made no state secret of his opinions, nor of his desire that all Americans should share them.

Once again, some five years later, the divergence of policies became evident as Americans who sincerely believed that they were participating in an ideological war were frankly informed, by both the words and the deeds of Mr. Churchill, that they were not. If anyone had misled them, it was certainly not the British. It is doubtful whether, in all these years, a finer exposition of British policy has been given than that which Harold Nicolson offered in November of 1939; the sincerity as well as the authority of his little work commend it especially to Americans at this time. He wrote:

Until March 15th last [occupation of Prague, 1939] it was believed by the Prime Minister [Neville Chamberlain] and his intimate advisers that if we could only avoid a head-on collision our own life might be preserved. After March 15th they cherished no such illusions. . . . Hitler was out for loot. And since the British and French empires offered the richest loot in the world, it was probable, it was even certain, that in the end we also should be attacked. It is this realization which accounts for the sudden change of policy after March 15th. . . . He would attain to such gigantic power that even the British fleet might be unable to restrain him. German armies might reach Istanbul and push on to the very confines of India . . .

For 250 years and more the British people have known instinctively that their safety depended upon preventing the continent of Europe, and therefore their sea communications, from falling under the domination of a single Power. It was this instinct which prompted them (at great cost to themselves) to fight Spain, Holland, Louis XIV, Napoleon and William II. They called this instinct by varying names. Sometimes they called it "The Balance of Power"; at other, and more sentimental moments, they called it "The protection of the smaller Nations." Yet whatever names they may have given to the instinct it was there as a durable, firm and recurrent element in their national destiny; it is a sound biological instinct; it is the instinct of self-preservation. It is conditioned by hard and inescapable facts.[3]

The preservation of what Britain has organized and accomplished in this world is a motive that needs no apology; it is a cause in which the people of the Empire will offer their lives whenever occasion requires, and in which Americans may most honorably stand and fall beside them. There might perhaps, on a most searching historical analysis, be valid and unselfish reasons why the United States, as a nation, should resist involvement; there could be no reason for Americans to deceive themselves as to the nature of the enterprise. Nor should they be allowed to. Any nation that deliberately embarked on an ideological or religious war would be guilty of a crime against civilization; and a stupid crime at that, since ideas are not to be disposed of, as are human beings, by the use of high explosive.

3. Nicolson, H., *Why Britain Is at War*, pp. 131-134.

§ 3

YET, as the Western conflict ends, the contrast between American idealism and Anglo-Russian empiricism threatens again to impede constructive work for peace; and as it happened twenty-five years ago, the Wilsonian tradition may invite another disillusion.

Mr. Roosevelt, in contrast to his predecessor, had throughout the gathering European crisis taken a strongly partisan line; neutral in thought, he said, was precisely what we could and should not be. After the outbreak of hostilities he showed no hesitation in condemning "the totalitarian powers in their war against the democracies." [4] The United States would "continue to help those who resist aggression." [5] Hitler was branded as the "enemy" of "our fundamental rights—including the right of labor." [6] His attack was "aimed at the form of government, the kind of society that we in the United States have chosen. . . . It is not an ordinary war." [7] Throughout the earlier stages of official American participation, it was customary to speak of the powers on the same side as "the democracies" resisting "powerful and resourceful gangsters (who) have banded together to make war upon the whole human race." [8] But so broad an application of the term democracy entailed embarrassments, and the term "peace-loving nations" was substituted. This term, to which we shall return, received official status in the Moscow declaration of October, 1943.

The exegesis thus offered by the President was seconded by statements as to the defense of "the whole Western hemisphere" [9] which mark an important, and probably permanent, change in American policy. With the latter we are not here concerned; but the effect of the former was to encourage the conception of the war as a crusade for certain ideal ends; as many members of Congress maintained, and many good citizens believed, "we are fighting this war for the Atlantic Charter." This in turn fostered a species of interventionism of which neutral states in Latin America were to receive the full impact. Whether or not such states, though

4. Speech of October 12, 1940.
5. *Ibid.*
6. Speech of September 1, 1941; see also speech of December 15, 1941.
7. Inaugural Speech, July 19, 1940.
8. Speech of December 9, 1941.
9. Speech of October 12, 1940 and statement of April 29, 1941.

officially neutral, were to receive the benefits of classification as "peace loving," or whether they were to have the entire battery of propaganda, black list, boycott, and blockade let loose on them, depended on whether their governments and policies conformed to the aims and policies of the United States; the justification being that in a war of absolutes neutrality as such was entitled to no respect. By contrast, it is interesting to observe that the American proposals to Japan of November 26, 1941, laid down "the principle of noninterference in the internal affairs of other countries."

The theory of what might be called absolute interventionism has been set forth in an important essay by Professor Karl Loewenstein.[10] The situation to which Mr. Loewenstein's proposals have reference may be interpreted as follows: The common notion of the functions of a resuscitated League of Nations or comparable body is that it would deal with "aggression" in the manner of a police force or a fire brigade. Aggression is thought of as an overt act, or series of acts (the constant use of the term "aggressor" has fixed that notion) and the general idea is that the League or council would wait until somebody set the house aflame and then summon the apparatus. Improvements in procedure proposed since 1924 suggest only that in certain circumstances the fire brigade might dash to the scene as soon as it saw the smoke, without waiting to be summoned. But the idea that an international authority could ever act effectively on the principle of waiting for overt events on which to pass judgment is now hopelessly out of touch with reality. Overt acts on which judgment could be passed in accord with some quasi-judicial formula do not, in fact or in theory, constitute an adequate basis for international action: the powers do not act, and will not act, on so limited a view of the case. The United States has frequently taken action in Latin American without waiting for the sort of critical event League theorists have in mind; and on the other hand, Britain did not go to war with Germany merely *because* German armies crossed a frontier, nor did America fight Japan *because* Pearl Harbor was attacked. In all such cases, on both sides, the resort to force exists on a much broader basis of policy.

Nor can it be held that merely to punish, or as it were, cancel the overt act solves the problem. For the fact of forceful intervention creates a new situation, it does not restore the preëxisting

10. *The Nation* (New York), August 26, 1944.

one; this was conspicuously shown following the application of sanctions to Italy in 1935. To be effective, intervention has to become control, and that involves comprehensive action. In other words, the juridical quality of specific acts furnishes a safe criterion for intervention only to the extent that considerations of general policy, past and prospective, warrant the belief that such action will be truly constructive. An international tribunal armed with force must either get farther in (to the extent of becoming a superior diplomatic and political agency) or keep farther out (to the extent, probably, of dropping the force).

International action that goes farther into a situation than a policy of watchful waiting would take it runs, of course, head-on into the Wilsonian doctrine of self-determination, as well as the British principle of nonintervention. It is here that Mr. Loewenstein's proposals boldly take the bull by the horns. He begins by noting the disparity between the ideals of the "Atlantic Charter" and the developing realities of the international scene, and finds Article 3, which promises every people the right to choose their own form of government, "particularly objectionable." He claims that

. . . there is no absolute right of internal self-determination, and consequently, that the victorious states must be prepared to claim, and must be permitted to exercise, the right of intervention in the internal affairs of any state which "chooses" a "form of government" constituting by its nature and potential development a threat to their own security and to universal peace.

The logic of the idea is compelling; and as Mr. Loewenstein reminds us, there is historical precedent. Napoleon applied it without scruple, and the Holy Alliance fashioned it into a policy—which England rejected; the rejection being amplified in the Monroe Doctrine. "Political laissez-faire," says Mr. Loewenstein, "became the credo of liberalism" and persecution of national or racial minorities failed, on the whole, to dislodge it. Nonintervention is further guaranteed in several Latin American treaties, and was followed in principle by the League of Nations. The result was that "under protection of the dogma of internal self-determination" despots were able to subvert their own nations and then to turn their "loathsome practices" against others.

There is indeed more historical precedent even than Mr. Loewenstein cites. The earliest instance is perhaps in the agreement made by Philip of Macedon with his Greek allies in 346 B.C.; and the Old Testament preserves numerous cases in which the profession or practice of obnoxious systems was quite actively discouraged both by Jahveh and his chosen people. More recently, the Anti-Comintern Pact of 1937 (Germany, Italy, Japan) was a good replica of the Holy Alliance. Professor Loewenstein is perhaps overgenerous in holding that "only governments are aggressive, not peoples," and that "since the Napoleonic period all major international wars have been started by authoritarian monarchies or dictatorships."

The author points with effect to current difficulties in applying the "Atlantic Charter." He compares Roosevelt's statement of February, 1943, that self-determination does not permit any government to make slaves of its own people with Churchill's hands-off-Spain declaration of May, 1944; [11] and he asks whether royalist or antidemocratic governments-in-exile have an unconditional right to reinstatement. He endorses Roosevelt's affirmation that no free people will voluntarily adopt a Nazi or Fascist form of government; and in order to implement that postulate, he makes the following proposals:

1. Each defeated nation must hold elections for a constituent assembly to draw up a Constitution, which must be of the "democratic-constitutional type." Elections will be under the control of the United Nations or an international police force. Collaborationists, Nazi sympathizers, etc., will not be allowed to vote, and parties with antidemocratic platforms are prohibited.

2. The victorious powers will scrutinize the constitution, which must contain a democratic bill of rights; and they will have veto power over objectionable provisions.

3. Ratifying elections are then to be held; and "if a nation should fail to elect a National Assembly whose majority is sincerely

11. Mr. Churchill: Internal political problems in Spain are a matter for the Spaniards themselves. It is not for us—that is, the government—to meddle in such affairs.

Dr. Haden Guest: Is not a fascist government anywhere a preparation for an attack?

Mr. Churchill: I presume we do not include in our program of world renovation any forcible action against any government whose internal form of administration fails to come up to our ideas, and any remarks I have made on that subject referred only to enemy powers and their satellites. (House of Commons, May 24, 1944.)

pledged to democracy, or to write for itself a democratic constitution, or to ratify it by at least a two-thirds majority, it would
indicate beyond reasonable doubt that such a nation is not qualified for self-government."

§ 4

PROFESSOR LOEWENSTEIN has rendered a real service in venturing
thus to challenge a doctrine so dear to American idealists; and
he suggests a line of action that has not only been followed before
but will probably be followed again where circumstances permit.
Britain has been cautious in conferring the right of internal self-
determination upon India, and is not likely to be indifferent to the
type of regime established in Burma and other colonies and de-
pendencies, nor in her (and other) mandated areas, however these
may be described. The same holds good of all colonial powers,
including the United States. Russia may possibly show some interest in the constitutional provisions of neighboring states; and
if the treatment of certain Latin American countries is any indication, the American State Department will not draw too fine
a line between external and internal self-determination. The good-
neighbor policy is not subject to the old-fashioned limitations of
the Monroe Doctrine.

There is one type of intervention in modern history that has attained a limited recognition under international law, namely, intervention for humanity, occasioned by such oppression of racial
or cultural minorities as to affront the civilized conscience. The
action of the United States in bringing diplomatic pressure to bear
upon Rumania in 1872 and Russia in 1880 comes under this category; [12] though no forcible coercion was attempted. These cases
are subject to the theoretical criticism that the American action
was unilateral; but the point is more than offset by the fact that
the United States was beyond question disinterested. The extreme
difficulty of securing disinterested action when more than one
great power is involved is evident in the handling, during the last
quarter of the nineteenth century, of the problems of the Armenian
and Cretan Christians and the Rumanian Jews. It may be con-
jectured that had any active steps been taken to implement the
minorities treaties imposed in 1919–20 on Poland and Rumania,

12. Moore, J. B., *Digest of International Law,* VI, chap. xix, 351–367.

similar difficulties would have arisen. One must further bear in mind the obvious fact that intervention takes on different aspects according to the status of the power that is to be dealt with. The interest of well-meaning Americans in Indian affairs has received no very marked encouragement from the British premier or his government, and Englishmen have shown a superior tact in their studied ignorance of conditions in Puerto Rico.

Another type of intervention has not infrequently arisen from economic causes. Whether the debt-collecting activities of European powers in the cases of Venezuela and Santo Domingo could be called intervention is perhaps doubtful; but the era of dollar diplomacy furnished conspicuous examples of the way one thing leads to another. That of course was long ago; yet the extension of loans and credits to sovereign states or their central banks is always liable to have political repercussions; for lenders are apt to impose political stipulations in the interests of security. Thus not only the French loans of the interbellum period, but the League loans to Austria, and certain private loans of great moment and magnitude, had political clauses. Whether stipulations thus arising tend to be of the same nature as those which political idealists would desire is a highly interesting question. The financial principle of legitimacy, like its predecessor, has a strong preference for the status quo.

While these considerations suggest that the dogma of nonintervention has not been quite as sacrosanct as Professor Loewenstein implies, they are all of an *ad hoc* nature in contrast with the systematic basis of his proposal. That basis would furnish a ground for multilateral action in pursuance of a policy known and declared in advance. It would supply an objective criterion for deciding which states were, as the Nazi theorists used to say, "*staatswürdig*," and which were not; and it might be reasonably expected that the great majority of states, after due consideration of the prospects, would be found worthy. There might however be states in which the initial supervision of the setup and the establishment of an approved "form of government" would have to be supplemented by a continuing supervision of the use made of it; for it is surely evident on the record that despite Mr. Loewenstein's assurances, democracy is as much a matter of the spirit in which institutions are worked as of the letter on which they are founded. But if the establishment and maintenance of a democratic-constitutional form of government is the *sine qua non* of peace, why is the principle to be limited to belligerent nations? Why is its application not equally valid, or even necessary, to nations that maintained a difficult or doubtful neutrality? And what is there in the nature of the case to limit such intervention to any particular period of time? Is there any logical reason, for example, why such guidance and control as the United States has supplied to Latin America should terminate on the cessation of hostilities?

§ 5

AT THIS point certain doubts as to the wisdom of the policy obtrude themselves. There may be a question as to the long-run stability of any regime established or maintained under external coercion. The constitutional revolution of Germany in 1918–19 might perhaps have taken a different course, possibly even a more stable course, without the doctrinaire intervention of Woodrow Wilson; for paradoxical as it may seem, a policy may be doctrinaire even though its particular doctrine is admirable. The lack of the historical sense in Wilson was most conspicuous in that it permitted him to be an idealist most of the time and to appeal to history when it suited him. It is more logical, as does Professor Loewenstein, to throw history overboard altogether and ride the wave of the future on a fountain pen. But how far will it go?

Undoubtedly, it will go as far as the physical force will take it; but force of this sort very seldom outlasts a generation—except in cases where the controlled territory is reduced to *de facto* colonial status, and the interests involved have produced an orderly and quasi-permanent system of control. (Witness the mandated territories of the League of Nations.) That is the logical—and factual—outcome of the doctrine of intervention. No doubt, the reduction of a considerable part of the world to a semicolonial status might be justified by the planetary magnitude and universal beneficence of the end in view; many who are now dazzled by that end owe it to realism to follow Professor Loewenstein as to the means. But others may argue that the means would be self-defeating. For what strikes controlled or disfranchised populations most acutely is not the splendor of the end but the immediate impact of the control; and in resenting that they are liable (should it be necessary to breathe the name of Ireland?) to refuse all collaboration to an end in whose benefits they themselves might otherwise have shared.

Further, exponents of the new legitimacy may discover that its guiding principle (whether financial or political) is no more absolute than the old one. Can we for instance really be sure that "only governments are aggressive, not peoples," and that democratic freedom would reveal a controlling preference for peace—even under conditions that, to the best of our judgment, would be objectively just? Perhaps, in time; but in this as in all other cases, peace is not to be conceived in negative terms: it consists in the extension of the sense of community, for which far more than political action is required. Again, can one be sure that a democratic political system of and by itself dissolves—or even diminishes—racial and religious hatreds? Is not something else needed, that no political system can supply? Yet if, as against a religion of democracy, the claims of another religion to the key of peace are reasonably urged, may the case for intervention be invoked by those believers also? They do not invoke it; for the reason that they have learnt by long experience the bitter futility of force. They know, as all true liberals know, that as soon as coercion is exalted from an exceptional remedy for the exceptional case to a general method for attaining no matter what millennium, such violence is done to the true nature of man as blood and sweat and tears must in the end atone for.

That is why it is both dangerous and misleading to couple ethical ideals with the organization of an international authority of which the members and the beneficiaries are to be "peace-loving nations." For what is this "peace" but the purposes of the few great powers who can wield enough force to preserve it? And what are "peace-loving nations" but those whom those powers themselves will select as concurring, actively or passively, in those purposes?

This is not in the least to question those purposes, nor the probability that peace does in fact, for a certain time, lie in that direction—precisely so long as the purposes can be reconciled, or compromised: what we are contesting is the introduction of ethical absolutes into the sphere of political dynamics. If you say that a cardinal aim of your policy is to preserve your frontiers from future invasion by land-hungry and powerful neighbors, or to secure better access to the seaways of the world, or to safeguard

your line of communications to certain mineral resources and markets, you are referring to a plane of action in which the application
of force may be legitimate and even generally beneficial; because
its objects are definable, specific, and understandable, and subject, in case of difficulty, to realistic negotiation. It is probable that
such peace as mankind may achieve will in fact come this way,
and no other; and it is possible that in the course of generations,
with the creation of a wider sense of community, great-power politics may be elastic enough to provide for those changes which
genetic and technological factors will certainly require. But if
you mask this reality with an ideology borrowed from the sphere
of personal absolutes; if you pretend that such ethical values as
peace, freedom, justice are going to be secured by an international
assemblage of bombing planes: then you merely multiply the occasions on which physical force may be plausibly invoked, and invite a perpetuation of that political chicanery of which, this past
quarter century, all decent men have had a bellyful. The relation
of political realities to ethical values is not one of means to ends.
To suppose that the tangible aims and purposes of the great
powers will be subordinated to ideal ends by the creation of an
international assembly that they themselves will convoke and control is naïve in the extreme.

In a world of limited resources inhabited by closed societies
with material aims, it is inevitable that those societies come into
conflict with one another. Even on a material plane, the attempt
to argue that all would be better off under an agreement to compromise is frustrated by the brute fact—well known in foreign offices, but never publicized—that the contention is false. The
average of welfare might be higher; but the most powerful states
may be materially better off as the result of a victorious conflict
than they would be as partners in a peaceful compromise: and
they know it. Many individuals in those states may be willing,
nonetheless, to say that international community is worth the
sacrifice of gains achieved at the present price; but that is what
states as such can never say, because they are not organized and
supported for any such altruistic purpose. A state that appropriates
the greater part of the national income, and a year or two of the
life of every male citizen, to keep itself powerful, is not going to
sacrifice or forego any material advantage it may hold or acquire;
and it would be overthrown if it did. Externally regarded, the ter-

ritorial state is nothing whatever but a physical-force machine, maintained to guard and promote the material interests of those who put up the money. It is neither equipped nor intended to promote the interests of outsiders, and their welfare is necessarily incidental and secondary to the purposes for which it is held accountable to its constituents. An assemblage of states will no more produce a universal moral order than a lot of lobsters thrown into a pound will produce a republic of lobsters. This is not because states or lobsters are "bad," but because their nature falls short of personality. To talk of states as if they were persons, endowed with the spiritual impulses and aspirations of human beings, and therefore morally accountable, is a piece of pure abstraction for which not even Hegel can be held responsible. It is a habit of modern journalism, catering to that mixture of vulgar passion and dominant materialism which renders unto Caesar the things that are God's because Caesar can be bribed.

To treat states as if they were, or could be, moral agents, was a policy tried for centuries. Everywhere the attempt led to disappointment and disaster. Nations in which personal liberty was safest grew up under systems established by men—like the Whigs of the English Revolution and the American founding fathers—who had no illusions about the nature of mass action, and took particular pains to keep the state in its place. The glorification of the state by French doctrinaires and German idealists produced a situation in which both the liberty of the subject and the safety of outsiders were perpetually imperiled. The state cannot attain a higher plane of action than that of the people who run it; and as the sphere of its domestic operations becomes wider, while its purposes become almost exclusively economic, it tends to strike a lower and lower average. Those who dream of universal peace arising from the interactions of a congeries of states are likely to be awakened by the nightmare of universal war.

§ 6

No FALLACY has done as much to sidetrack American idealism as the notion of a "world police force." As every citizen knows when he is sober (and sometimes discovers when he is drunk) the policeman is merely the symbol and agent of community. He can be effective as a policeman only because there is general agreement in the community as to what the rules of conduct shall be, so that infractions are universally recognized as exceptional, and rarely occur. The function of the policeman presupposes the community; he does not create the community. If no community exists the policeman is no longer a policeman but an armed force; and as Americans are never tired of telling the British in India, an armed force, though it may preserve order within the limits of its power, does not create a free community.

It is worth while to ask just how much work, in the present world of armed states, a world police force would actually find to do. In striking contrast to the situation in the closing months of the previous war, when at least important principles were under discussion, American attention has been deliberately focused on the mere machinery of force, to be applied to nobody quite knows whom in support of nobody quite knows what. It is possible that the statesmen of the other two great powers found it expedient to indulge the American passion for scheme making while the really serious business was privately attended to elsewhere. But the discussion of future force has brought out one fact of significance: the crux of the entire problem lies in the relations of the three dominant powers with one another—with which the proposed international machinery will have nothing whatever to do.

It may well turn out that the whole apparatus of international sanctions and a resuscitated League of Nations will find very little work: not because of the coming of the millennium, but because of the radically different political situation. Wilson's policy was the multiplication of sovereign states: there were six more after Versailles than in 1914, some of them very jealous of their autonomy, others kept apart by force. Wilson also promulgated the fiction of the equality of states, which is now effectively abandoned; in no future international organization will small states be allowed a veto power, by the rule of unanimity or otherwise, over policies on which the big ones are agreed. But it was an essential part of the Wilsonian scheme that the disintegrative tendency of self-determination should be countered by an effective interstate organization; and the very nature of the one part of his program provided plenty of work for the other.

All that is changed—mainly by the enormous advance in the technology of war, to which international realities are bound to conform. Assuming that the announced intentions of the Anglo-

American allies toward Germany and Japan are carried out, there will be, for the next few decades, only three powers in the world that can produce or control enough machinery, chemicals, and expert personnel to wage modern war. Even among these the position of Britain is highly contingent, and the influence of the dominions in regard to foreign commitments will be increasingly conservative. China can be considered an international power only insofar as some other economy is brought in to arm and equip her undernourished millions; and it may be that the Chinese people will eventually prefer to take their chance without all this expensive apparatus.

Considerable areas of the planet must be regarded for the foreseeable future, as beyond the action of any international organization based on the counteraggression theory. First among these, of course, is the British Empire and Commonwealth of Nations, comprising one fourth of the world's land surface and about the same proportion of its population; to which may be added, for all practical purposes, the extensive territories mandated to Britain and the dominions after the first World War, with whatever else may be picked up after this one. It is a safe guess, backed by ample evidence, that the internal relationships of this vast system will in no circumstances be placed under the control of any external organization.

Second, the Russian empire, already two thirds the size of the British in 1939, and the largest integrated land mass in the world, similarly removes most of the Euro-Asian continent. And here again, it is reasonable to include in that system certain affiliated territories on both its eastern and western borders, whatever may be the political form of the affiliation. From the western Baltic to the Adriatic, the influence of Russia will be effectively exerted to forestall any situation that might tempt the intervention of an alien authority.

In the Far East, whatever may be the political situation south of the Amur River, Russia will probably object to the establishment of American bases on the Asiatic mainland or the Japanese islands; and that will settle the question of hegemony. It is to be noted that air power is the one weapon advocated by Russia as the arm of any international force.

On its southern border, most of which is accessible only by air, a situation of the utmost delicacy prevails as between Russia and

Britain in the Middle East. Fundamentally, it is a continuance of the problem created by the convergent expansion of the two systems in the latter part of the last century. The present situation is unlikely to prove permanent; it dates only from the expulsion of Riza Shah in September, 1941, and the treaty with Russia and Britain accepted by his successor a few months later. But however the present partition of Persia, and other arrangements in the Middle East, may develop in future, neither government is likely to invite or to welcome the intervention of any third power.

Americans have never fully appreciated the permanent concern of the British Foreign Office with the Moslem world. That is no doubt because Moslem interests have no very vocal or highly organized representatives in the Western hemisphere; nor, most of the time, do Moslems act, feel, or even exist as a unit. But there is always the possibility that they may; and there are over two hundred and twenty millions of them—by far the largest community outside the Church of Rome. Their world stretches all the way from Dakar and Casablanca to Kabul and Calcutta; most of it is under British control, the rest mainly French; and it has called forth the services of generations of Scotsmen, Englishmen, and Frenchmen of such courage, character, and scholarship as the more circumscribed diplomacy of the United States has seldom had occasion to require. Never have the relations of Britain with Islam been as critical as now. They are a dominant concern of British policy. Yet they are not of a kind that leagues of states or stop-the-aggressor schemes of American theorists can—or ever could—take care of. They involve the future of India and Egypt, the oil of the Middle East, the status of Levantine Christians and Palestinian Jews, the development of the Sudan, the control of the Suez Canal, the exploitation of North Africa, and a multitude of immediate and specific problems. Neither Britain nor France will readily assent to the entry into this vast diplomatic field of any third parties. While the interests of those two states are far from coincident, they are in each case too serious to admit of appeal to any abstract criteria or outside agencies; both states are traditionally reluctant to court the intervention of other powers which might be willing to enlarge their responsibilities in the Near East. It further appears beyond question that the present obscurity of status of mandated territories will be settled de facto rather than de jure. The continued French effort to subdue the Syrian

Arabs by the arms of Central African Negroes furnishes a further example of the gap between American ideals and imperial realities. On the assumption that the San Francisco scheme were in operation, it would lie within the competence of France, as one of the "big five," to veto any international action in Syria; nor is this the only critical case. It would be equally within the competence of either contestant to veto any outside concern with whatever may be left of Iran; and there are several other areas which will in their turn reveal to "Americans United for World Organization" the true nature of the instrument whose virtues they have been so loudly proclaiming.

Across the south Atlantic—much closer than New York is to London—lies the most carefully circumscribed diplomatic enclave in the world. The attempt of an Oriental power to assert a Monroe Doctrine for east Asia has been spurned and denounced by the United States; but the Monroe Doctrine of the Western hemisphere was explicitly recognized in the Covenant of the League of Nations, and has been reaffirmed and conspicuously extended in recent years. Twelve months before the opening of the second World War President Roosevelt, speaking in Ontario, announced that "the people of the United States will not stand idly by if domination of Canadian soil is threatened." After the outbreak of hostilities, the United States informed the European belligerents that it would not recognize any transfer of territory in the Western hemisphere from one non-American power to another; the Senate concurring on June 17, 1940. The policy was endorsed the following month by the foreign ministers of the American republics meeting at Havana; and they further recognized, in the words of Mr. Cordell Hull, that "the use of these possessions to promote systems alien to the inter-American system [whatever that may mean] could not be countenanced." A few weeks later, Mr. Roosevelt, announcing to Congress his acquisition of naval bases from Britain, explained that they were "essential to the protection of the Panama Canal, Central America, the northern portion of South America, the Antilles, Canada, Mexico, and our own eastern and gulf seaboards" (September 3, 1940); on October 12, 1940, he informed the nation that "they were acquired for the protection of the whole Western hemisphere."

Following the commencement of overt hostilities, it speedily became evident that the foreign relations, both political and eco-

nomic, of the Latin American states were not a matter of indiffer-
ence to the Washington administration; and the activities both
of their own subjects and of foreign firms and agencies within
their borders were subjected to increasing scrutiny and, where
necessary, economic coercion. In the case of Argentina, which
strove to maintain an independent foreign policy and an interpretation of neutrality different from that of Mr. Roosevelt in
1939–41, the economic coercion included an almost complete embargo on American exports and the freezing of Argentine gold
holdings within the territory of the United States. It is relevant
to observe in this connection that both the American President
and the then Secretary of State permitted themselves a liberty of
public expression concerning their opponents, both foreign and
domestic, that has rarely been equaled by the responsible leaders
of any nation except Germany.

It is further noteworthy that the attempt of Argentina to lay its
case before a meeting of the Pan-American Union, of which that
state was a member, was carefully frustrated by the calling of a
meeting of Latin American states under another title, from which
the Argentine was excluded. In addition to these negative policies,
the enormous expenditure and investment of public funds of the
United States in friendly or allied countries of South America must
be borne in mind; and it is therefore legitimate to ask how much
of a welcome the world policeman would find in the event of
trouble south of the Rio Grande. Would the State Department be
willing to waive the special exemption accorded the Monroe Doctrine in the original League of Nations Covenant? Would it stand
on Secretary Olney's declaration that "the United States is practically sovereign on this continent"—a contention obviously
strengthened by its assumption of the burden of hemisphere defense? And how far would Britain be willing to go in implement-
ing a decision adverse to America? It is more than likely that the
exclusion of the interrelations of the "big three" from general
scrutiny would also, for obvious practical reasons, extend to their
satellites and spheres of influence.

If, in this rapid glance over world power-alignments, we finally
return to Europe, how much scope for autonomous foreign policy
and third-party intervention can we discern? Whatever discre-
tion may be left to whatever sort of Germany, there will be no
possibility of independent external action for a generation. Small

states, whatever constitutions and boundaries may be assigned them, will exist only by and with the consent of the extra-European powers; they will not again be put in a position to become the objects of a major international contest. Major conflicts of external policy are hardly likely to arise because no minor state will have enough actual autonomy to create them: but if they do, they will come immediately under the cognizance of one or more of the great powers, whose interest it will be at all costs to localize rather than to generalize them. The notion of the sovereign equality of all states has fortunately been abandoned; and with a return to realism it may be expected, and hoped, that frontier guarantees and frontier disputes will be neither encouraged nor allowed to attain world-wide importance. The juridical and quasi-ethical handling of interstate relations is indeed already superseded by the political and diplomatic methods which alone are suited to that sphere of operations. Any uncertainty is surely dispelled by the fact that small powers desiring to attend the San Francisco Conference on World Security had first to declare war on the enemies of the great powers in order to get a ticket. Countries that declined to do so were ipso facto not "peace-loving nations"—a curious and highly significant paradox.

Thus we find ourselves once again in a world of great powers, satellite powers, and spheres of influence; and the road back to reality has been hard on the corps of idealists who shaped the popular version of American foreign policy. But the result is salutary. It is better to realize that that is the only sort of world in which nation-states live, move, and have their being. All international politics is power politics. Sometimes it permits a measure of peace, sometimes it calls for war; but in neither case has it much to do with the hopes and aspirations of those who long for broader brotherhood. International community lies on a different plane from international politics; and those who seek the road to it must carry not a gun, but a cross.

XIII

The Peace-by-Force Illusion

*1. The static tendency. — 2. Total war and total peace.
— 3. The functional basis of community. — 4. International
big business. — 5. State versus cartel. — 6. The
foreign-trade outlook. — 7. The role of competition.*

§ 1

IN its approach to the problems of world policy, modern rationalism inevitably puts police ahead of politics. Its idea of law is Austinian rather than social. It substitutes the conception of peace as a state for that of peace as a process. It is static, not dynamic. It tends toward legalism, ideologies, and formulas; and however logical these may seem from its own standpoint, in application they are bound to be reactionary and productive of further conflict. It goes to work on the map with a knife and an eraser, and offers two-dimensional solutions to three-dimensional problems so persistently as to make one wonder whether peace is in fact its primary purpose. Elasticity and adaptability, though they are the essence of living process, play so small a part in its schemes that this changing world would be a safer place without such instruments. The Covenant of the League of Nations was an example as startling as it was futile. There we had an elaborate and peremptory machinery set up to preserve a status quo in which occasions for future war were admittedly embodied, yet the sole dynamic outlet was the feeble and abortive Article 19:

The Assembly *may* from time to time *advise* the reconsideration by Members of the League of *treaties* which *have become* inapplicable, and the consideration of international conditions whose continuance might endanger the peace *of the world*.[1]

That was all: with power in the Council, by the unanimity rule, to block any proposed change, and no means whatever to enforce

1. Italics supplied.

one. The Dumbarton Oaks proposals of October, 1944, show an even greater rigidity. Any state "may bring to the attention" of the Assembly or Council a dispute or threatening situation; but the Council alone will "determine the existence of any threat to the peace," investigate, make recommendations, call out the forces, and "*take* such action by air, naval or land forces as may be necessary," while "the General Assembly should not on its own initiative make recommendations on any matter relating to the maintenance of international peace and security which is being dealt with by the Security Council." Amendments to the scheme require a two-thirds vote of the Assembly and *unanimity* of the permanent members of the Council.[2]

The confidence in their own impartiality displayed by the three non-European powers that wrote the scheme is reassuring or alarming according to one's understanding of great power politics; what is more remarkable is the casual cynicism with which the League of Nations, still in existence, is thrown overboard. The immediate reason for this decision, plain on the record, is that in December, 1939, the League, acting on the appeal of Finland, had the temerity to expel Russia as an aggressor nation; the Russian Government having refused to submit the case for settlement. Since that date the Russian Government has made no secret of its hostility to the League and its methods of procedure. That attitude did not stand in the way of the Anglo-Russian Treaty (good for twenty years) of 1942, nor the alliances with Czechoslovakia and France; but it throws a curious light on the complaints of Mr. Roosevelt, Mr. Wallace, and other Americans that the trouble with the League was that it lacked enough force.

The initiative for the Dumbarton Oaks meeting came, we are officially informed,[3] from Mr. Molotov. It is perhaps not surprising that the scheme there propounded has very little to say about justice or democratic procedure. From the point of view of the dominant powers force in the supreme desideratum, with as much support from the small states as it can get since the use of their territory and possessions is envisaged as and when necessary. By the same logic, the "peace-loving nations" whose support is invited are by definition those that are willing to declare war on the

2. Chap. viii, A 1, 2, 4, B 1, 2, 4; chap. v, B 1; chap. xi. Italics supplied.
3. Sir Alexander Cadogan at the opening session, August 21, 1944.

enemies of the big three. The one thing that can be said for the scheme is that it affords to all men a demonstration of the kind of society they have created; what cannot be said is that it points the way toward a better kind.

Peace-by-force schemes of this sort are familiar historical phenomena. Indeed history textbooks of the older type are largely concerned with their formation at the end of one war and their disintegration at the beginning of the next. Their reactionary quality, we have suggested, arises partly from the quantitative obsession of the post-Reformation era. It arises also from the atrophy of the historical sense in secular idealism. This is conspicuous in the American approach to Europe. One would not, of course, for a moment suggest that Americans are not abundantly informed. On the contrary, they are so abundantly informed that the ideal of American education is almost that of a talking encyclopaedia. Such knowledge, however, is of facts and events as set forth in books and documents (Woodrow Wilson was a conspicuous example) wherein certain selected results of a continuous process are more or less dried out and displayed, but in which the process itself can never be contained, nor its essential nature depicted. West of the Vistula and the middle Danube, Europe is, at a very profound level, a spiritual being, writhing in the grip of a tragic destiny that is simply inaccessible to the American mind, and only slightly less so to the British. It may be that peace is no part of that destiny, but only death: a certain reverence in any case is indicated. It is surely significant that while Europe has contributed so much to the culture of America, America has contributed so little to the culture of Europe. Not that it has nothing to contribute; what it has to offer is radically inassimilable. It is no less significant that between Europeans in other parts of the world —again, at a profound level—there exists a curious empathy, into which non-Europeans cannot enter. They will fight their European battles over again on foreign soil, all the more keenly when they are soliciting American support for rival causes; but the rivalry rarely goes so deep as to dispel a tacit community of feeling— manifest in the unspoken assumptions of ordinary conversation— between people who have wrought so much, and suffered so much, in common. Only in very recent times was the Western peninsula so deeply riven. It may be that even now, as the walls of the ancient capital lie shattered, its spirit rises above the ashes of a material civilization, free of the alien forces of both East and West. EUROPE shall live again.

It is historically necessary. Europeans have listened too much to talk of decadence, to theories of the inevitable westward march of culture. The progress of the spirit is not a geographical affair. While the technical and financial center has been moving westward, the biological center has been moving eastward; and the material potency of the new world may prove less significant for Europe than the amazing fecundity of the Slavs. With Europe in pieces, the world pattern will make no sense. The reintegration of Europe is the key to the whole puzzle, and talk of a world order is futile until that necessity is complied with. It follows that national policies should be shaped with this cardinal aim in view, and modified where necessary in order to promote it, or at the least, not to obstruct it. Surely, statesmen who would refuse to coöperate in the unification of Europe, from which so much material as well as immaterial benefit to all would come, are hardly likely to coöperate sincerely in the construction of a still wider community.[4] And any outside forces that fan the flames of political and ideological hatred inside Europe perform a disservice so serious that drastic measures might be justified in order to give Europe a fair chance.

§ 2

IT MUST not be casually taken for granted that there exists anywhere as yet, on any considerable scale, a positive will to peace. War, even today, has much about it that is very attractive, especially to those who take no active part. It heightens the emotions, gratifies the gregarious instinct, offers a primitive outlet to impulses of genuine idealism. It furnishes an illusion of power and superiority in much the same way as certain neurotics are reassured by the sensation of driving an automobile. It loosens many conventional restraints, and compensates periodically for the psychological cost of urban civilization. It provides the mass catharsis of hate as a perverse but socially sanctioned form of the instinct to love; and since the exercise of the latter is more expensive in

4. Lord Cranborne, speaking for the British Government on February 6, 1945, dismissed the notion of European unity as "only academic and no more." See *The New York Times*, February 7, 1945.

proportion as its results are more valuable, the need to hate becomes an autonomous motivation with which it is difficult for any
rational procedure to cope. On the whole, the notion of international peace is still an aristocratic conception, and successful
politicians are hardly ever to be trusted as its wholehearted exponents.

The root of the problem is that peace is commonly conceived
in static and negative terms; and the best argument that can be
advanced from such premises is that war is very expensive and
does not always bring commensurate gains even to the victors.
Such an argument is quite inadequate, and largely irrelevant. The
negative ideal of the prevention of war has no practical force until it is absorbed in the positive ideal of expanding community.
Down to the smallest details, therefore, the positive creation of
community must take precedence over the historic futilities of
the negative policy; and those who are not interested in the extension of coöperative community must stop talking about peace,
since all they really stand for is the status quo.

The great communities called nations did not develop through
a coming together of gilds, corporations, domains, or other closed
units; they arose from a partial dissolution of such units, a general opening up. Where such units were allowed—as in eighteenth-
century France—to form a sort of association for mutual protection, the result was not a wider type of community but an explosion. In the more fortunate cases, the active life of a growing
society passed them by, flowed all around them, and as it were dissolved what stood in the way; though, as in England, a good deal
that was decorative, traditional, and useful survived. So we may
not expect very much in the way of expanding community from
an association of nations and representatives of nations: least of
all when they are responsible to, and sometimes dismissible by, a
public opinion manipulated by a yellow press. At best, the national
interests as such are amenable only to a glorified kind of horse
trading, because their spokesmen are forbidden, by the very nature of the case, to treat the interests of alien groups as on an
absolute equality with their own; that is not what they are there
for, and it is emphatically not what they are trained for. That is
no reproach to the national constituencies or their representatives;
it merely indicates that the creation of a wider community must
rely, in the main, on other than politico-national agencies. Such

agencies have, for all liberal purposes, passed the zenith of their usefulness, and the mentality they engender now stands in the way. Americans have recognized this in the case of certain South American states; but the truth of it is not limited to the Chaco.

Few things were intrinsically funnier, in recent months, than the abortive effort to organize planetary aviation by means of a congeries of jealous territorial units. Even the notion of the sovereign equality of states put in an appearance, as the delegates sought to project the earth-bound limits of their national constituencies into the stratosphere. What was most pathetic, and most alarming, was the lack of any realism bold enough to affirm that the entire basis of the approach was anachronistic in regard to the technical problem.[5] But it is not only in regard to aviation that the territorial nation-state has revealed its inadequacy. In ocean transport also the overriding national interests have for decades perpetuated an incredible amount of wastage, duplication, and confusion; in radio a semblance of order has been achieved and preserved only with the utmost difficulty; and in the entire field of applied science the provincialism of existing institutions cries out for a bolder and broader conception of copyright, patent law, and scientific interchange.

The modern tendency however has been all the other way. Nineteenth-century wars were kept within bounds by the tradition, well recognized in international law, that civilian property and business were outside the sphere of combat. Civilian assets were not exposed to arbitrary distraint or permanent seizure, and apart from such territorial and financial stipulations as one state might impose on another, the economic and cultural life of the belligerents was generally allowed to continue pretty much as it had been. Twentieth-century practice has changed all that. During both World Wars limitless lists of contraband coupled with unilateral declarations of maritime law put every sort of commerce in jeopardy, and made waste paper of all precedents. The close of the first war was marked by a determined and successful effort to impair the economic recovery of the principal losers, and to retain certain civilian properties. The second war has seen the extension of that policy to a point at which international law in war has ceased to exist. For years the Government of Germany, so

5. The proposals of the Australian and New Zealand Governments did imply this recognition; and for that reason got nowhere.

far as its arm could reach, had based a policy of confiscation on a racial theory that had no standing in civil law, international law, nor Christian ethics; and when the war began, that violation of the comity of nations proved contagious. Anglo-American leadership, in both speech and action, launched a crusade that admitted of neither legal nor territorial limits to the exercise of coercion. The concept of neutrality was denounced in both theory and practice. Not only enemy assets and interests, but the assets and interests of any parties whatsoever, even in neutral countries, were exposed to every constraint the belligerent powers could make effective; and the assets and interests of neutral states and their civilians, lodged in belligerent territory or under belligerent control, were subjected to practically the same sort of coercion as those of enemy nationals. Thus "total war" became a sort of war that no civilian community could hope to escape; and "peace-loving nations" will draw the obvious inference. Balkan and Latin American concerns trading with Germany since 1934 discovered that their assets and accounts in Germany were subject to the dictates of German national policy. That situation has now become general; and one of its results will be that states whose economy is mainly genetic, and their nationals, will endeavor to avoid exposing their assets to the control of the great powers. Thus a further factor (there are several others) comes into operation toward the disintegration of world economy and the permanent contraction of the volume of world trade. This in turn discourages private foreign investment, and would discourage the export of public funds also if business considerations had anything to do with it.

The idea of peace by force is a dangerous and costly illusion; but it owes its popularity to a very natural disposition. The common idea of peace is that of a system into which you fit on our terms, never a system into which we fit on your terms. Freedom means our liberty to do what we think proper, not what you think proper. In proportion as our autonomy is to be limited by the assertion of will or purpose that is not ours, we decline to recognize such a state of affairs as peace or freedom: we fight for "liberty." Unfortunately, we have to admit that while we are right from our point of view, you also may be right from your point of view. We are clearheaded enough to see that; consequently we get nowhere. But to organize a system of which the rules are yours-and-ours: to define a set of mores that rests on a consciousness of we-and-you: that is a long and arduous enterprise, demanding an actual experience of common intention and endeavor. The other way is easier. Force can accomplish considerable results—provided, of course, that it is superior force (inferior force is no good). It can encompass punishment, revenge, conquest, control, and the kind of peace that is called imperialism. It appears likely that the elimination of national conflict will in fact depend (for a certain time) on the two centers which alone can amass such overwhelming force—America and Russia. That was how Persia did it, that was how Rome did it. Russia to rule the old world, the United States the new: that is very possibly the shape of things to come. All we suggest is that that is not the sort of order for which liberalism stands; though we have frankly stated that there is no predestination for the liberal ideal. That ideal remains a hope and a possibility. Those who serve it will therefore seek to create, even within the harsh rigidity of a quite different order, the conditions of expanding freedom within expanding community.

The liberal tradition has for centuries tended to limit the scope of state action and to keep the state as such outside the conduct of ordinary communal activities. Never was that tradition more relevant than now, when the dominant aim of all major states has become the organization of the force that makes war the continuation of diplomacy. The state comes into the conference room jingling a pocketful of coin on one hip with a gun strapped on the other; and it usually forgets to take its hat off. People who seek to get something constructive peaceably accomplished have found they get along better without that sort of kibitzer. Even when they fail to agree, they fail more safely. It is a curious fact that when state activity is invoked in any considerable degree for the promotion of even the most desirable services, it generally ends by dominating or even monopolizing the field. Our fathers knew this, and warned us. They knew too that such invocation of the state invariably magnifies the executive at the expense of both the legislature and the judiciary. The history of the United States since 1933 has been an amazing demonstration of this fact. It is evident not only in the degree to which executive orders have been used to circumvent the Congress, executive agreements to circumvent the Senate, and executive power applied to influence the courts; it is evident in the attitude of executive officers toward the people, their representatives, and the press. Some of the most powerful officials in the land disdainfully refuse all communication or explanation, in a fashion that not even the most popular of British premiers could dream of following. Other officials expound their policies at their own convenience in articles and statements for the magazines which Congressmen are graciously permitted to read after publication. "At his press conferences," says an experienced and judicious observer,[6] "the President, in an affable manner, succeeds in telling very little news on international matters. It is almost fair to say that he regards these meetings as mental contests with the White House correspondents." Following his lead, there arose a perceptible disposition to treat the institutions, powers, and practices of representative government in America as necessary nuisances in the application of the higher wisdom; but if in truth state policies are beyond the understanding or the sympathy of the common people, would not democracy be better served, in the long run, by modifying the policies than by short-circuiting the procedure?

Much of the difficulty arises from the fact that the realities of power politics stand in sorry contrast to the ends for which the American people have supposed themselves to be fighting; and it must be said in fairness that this contrast is inherent in the situation. The Roosevelt administration was more afraid of disillusion than it was of disunity; but both are on the way; the part of wisdom is to seek for the most tolerable settlement compatible with strict realism in the given circumstances, without any pretense that the settlement can, or should, be more than tentative; then, in such breathing space as may be gained, to work resolutely and patiently at the foundations of a more genuine community. We must at length accept the task laid down by General Smuts when he signed the Covenant in 1919, namely, to transform the League of Nations into a league of peoples. In that enterprise the militant nation-states and their international force machine can be at best of only minor assistance. We must look elsewhere. Where shall we look?

§ 3

IN ATTEMPTING an answer to this question, both writer and reader must be on guard against the conventional assumptions. We are

6. Edwin L. James, in *The New York Times*, February 4, 1945.

tempted and encouraged to suppose that some merely external readjustment in our ways of acting, some realignment of our collective policies, practices, and lethal apparatus, will lead us into a new society; despite the unanimous testimony of history that the hope is vain. Broadly speaking, international (or better, supernational) ways of thinking, feeling, and acting cannot be simply superimposed on national ways. The larger mode will not embrace the smaller; it must replace it by means of a thorough permeation. Nor will it suffice to act on the assumption (even though it may be true) that this national way is superior to that national way. Perhaps only the immigrant knows both the truth and the fallacy of that assumption. The sense of superiority, the drive toward ego-maximation, are so deeply involved in the totemism of nationality that a forthright emancipation from it must be the cardinal aim of liberal policy. That aim, in the circumstances of today, is revolutionary; and in pursuing it the liberal, like Pilgrim, advances into uncharted and dangerous ground. He can point to no broad highway. He must instead seek out all possible paths of escape, trusting that the advance of many feet will widen some of them.

But the geographical analogy is inadequate. The type of thinking and feeling that our age demands is not simply or mainly directed to a wider geographical area. People of distant lands will remain strange and remote to most of us, however much we may learn about them; even foreign travel is apt to endorse the conclusion that there's no place like home. The prime necessity is a more catholic conception of human nature, our own included, for which the absolutes of nationalism and racism will be too petty and provincial. Such a conception can be fostered by life in the small community no less than in the large one, since it is depth rather than breadth that matters, and the concrete is more salutary than the abstract. To this end the agencies of religion and education are obviously essential, with the former fundamental to the latter. It is of paramount practical importance to all men that they should cultivate the consciousness of that which is so far above them as to flatten out their local prides and particularities; for oddly enough it is only through the practice of spiritual humility that man attains his full stature. This means the universal extension of a common religious discipline, the same in all essentials for all people. As we have seen, both Comte and Wells, with many other observers, arrive at the same conclusion as the apostles of Christianity; the point at issue being not the necessity, but the nature, of the common religion. Man cannot redeem himself by any process of self-glorification; nor can religions be invented to serve a temporal purpose.

The ideology of the peace-by-force school sits like a nightmare on the American mind. Its exponents find it necessary to be increasingly apologetic. The war administration, having played on the fear-motif in the period of undeclared warfare, logically plays on the force-motif as the clue to "security"; but it has signally failed to arouse any enthusiasm, and its refusal to make public the terms of settlement creates a profound distrust. The American people, both individually and collectively, are incredibly generous and altruistic; their conception of their part in world affairs is marked by a unique and almost passionate disinterestedness; they aspire to a role of constructive benevolence that is poles apart from the power politics of the old world; and if their childlike confidence is betrayed they will turn on the betrayer. The words of Vera Brittain, written in 1943, find a spontaneous echo in American hearts: "The vicious circle of recurrent war will be broken for the first time when one side foregoes its 'right' to demand retribution, and instead offers hope, comfort, support." The instinctive American attitude is far more deeply rooted in Christian idealism than is generally realized, and the proposals of Mr. Morgenthau and his backers, whatever their political pretext, do violence to something fundamental and indomitable. American Christianity, both Protestant and Catholic, may well rejoice that in the two reports recently presented to the Federal Council of Churches, so clear and realistic a statement of the common Christian tradition received so powerful an expression.[7] We quote from the message of the Cleveland Conference:

The settlement following the war should be inspired by the desire to secure the maximum of collaboration among the peoples of Europe and encourage the economic development of Europe as a whole including Germany. . . . The settlement should make possible the reconciliation of victors and vanquished. . . . The treatment of Germany should be calculated to strengthen the forces within that country committed to

7. *The War in the Light of the Christian Faith* (25 cents), *The Churches and World Order* (10 cents), Federal Council of Churches, 297 Fourth Ave., New York, 10, N. Y.

liberal civil policies and to international coöperation. . . . Treatment of Japan by the United Nations should be favorable to constructive forces within Japanese society, and should aim to bring Japan at an early date into normal relations with the world community.

That is both genuine liberalism and genuine Americanism, because it dares to put its trust in the forward-looking, community-building factors, rather than in the negative policies of repression, punitive action, and the kind of security that rests on force. In the long run, as history very clearly shows, it is the only realistic and practical approach to peace.

But what power politics has actually required of the American people is something totally different in spirit, in method, and in effect. The reality was very courageously depicted in one of the leading Christian periodicals:

We shall leave behind us after victory nothing of the acclaim for knight-errantry which greeted our participation in World War I and remained as a universal reservoir of good feeling. We shall find that our reputation has been transformed by the hideous character of one of our military operations. Upon the armies of the United States there devolved the unhappy responsibility of manning the mighty air force which this nation alone was able to provide. Our obliteration bombing will rest like a curse upon the fair name of our country for generations. The very stones in the debris of what once were noble cities will cry out against us long after peace has settled down. As men labor to restore their homes and public buildings they will say, "The Americans did this." And the story will be told with endless repetition of the women and children, the aged and the sick, who were caught in the flame and crushed in the ruin rained down from American planes. It is a fact not to be disregarded that the Russian advance was accompanied by no such obliteration bombing. . . . We are not coming out of this war bringing with us our traditional reputation as a noble and disinterested friend of civilization. We are coming out as a Great Power, and any acclaim we shall receive henceforth will be a cool but respectful tribute to our power rather than a spontaneous and hearty expression of trust and affection. This will hold no less for our allies than for our enemies.[8]

That is the sober truth of the American world position which the American people themselves must face as frankly as all other people are now facing it; and when the full story is told there will be

8. *The Christian Century*, May 30, 1945.

even darker aspects. The spiritual and psychological bases of international community are now more tenuous than they have been for over three centuries; and it is idle to imagine that fair words or pacts on paper can restore them.

The scheme of world order proffered by the "big three" at San Francisco (how nauseating becomes this ceaseless talk of bigness!) is the logical conclusion of a strictly materialistic philosophy. What is offered is an undisguised sphere-of-influence partitioning of the planet, of which the conspicuous feature is the determination of the big powers to exclude each other, and a fortiori any third parties, from any area or situation in which any one of them has or asserts a major interest. The intent of the whole procedure is to secure advance assent to this policy of exclusion, notwithstanding that in the most critical areas the spheres of influence are not yet defined. How they are to be defined we are not informed; but obviously no general ethical or juridical principles can be laid down, since their formulation would constitute a valid ground for third party intervention; and it is argued with brutal candor that outside the big three-plus-two the requisite physical force would not be available to make any general principles effective. It is for this that the American people will be asked to sacrifice, through an unlimited future, a major part of their productive resources, and possibly a year or so of the life of every male citizen; yet history gives no assurance that this sort of bigness has ever brought peace one step nearer, nor ever been big enough to overcome the defiance of even unarmed people.

When events are moving in an atavistic direction, anachronistic minds appear advanced; and in proportion as men abandon their whole tradition of spiritual enlightenment, their tendency is inevitably atavistic. The Atlantic civilization finds itself headed no longer west, but back toward the cradle of the race; and Britain, having led the destruction of Western Europe, now has to barter its own traditions to buy a new balance of power. The prospect is one with which liberalism cannot compromise and remain liberal. Even at the risk of total extinction, liberalism must proclaim a different road to community: a road that has nothing to do with "bigness" and its concomitants of bribery, bombs and ballyhoo. That road lies in stimulating functional coöperation, regardless of nationality, in every quarter where it exists already, or can be brought into existence.

Common work is the normal basis of community. The policy that aims at expanding liberty within expanding community therefore seeks to put the processes of resettlement and reconstruction, to the utmost extent possible, on a functional basis. Whether it be the administration of relief, the control of disease, the restoration of power and water supply, the reclamation of flooded areas, the control of rivers and harbors, the organization of essential transport, the distribution of imports, the stabilization of currencies, the direction of industrial policy, the reëstablishment of genetic industry, the pooling of resources, the reëquipment of scholarship, research, music, and other arts—in all these, and a hundred more unpredictable fields, the aim must be the establishment of mixed commissions of qualified people, on an ad hoc basis, wherever opportunity offers a suitable field for common enterprise. It is neither necessary nor advisable that large numbers of strangers be put to work together. It is both possible and desirable that leadership, technique, and resources be put on a nonnational basis, wide or narrow according to the task in hand, for specific purposes. The leaders of such functional enterprise would constitute a group of master-architects, consciously and singleheartedly devoted to rebuilding the city of man brick by brick and stone by stone. They would be doctors, scientists, engineers, geneticists, businessmen, bankers, traffic managers, architects, scholars, artists; and it is at least conceivable that out of their association for specific tasks, backed by the encouragement and resources of genuinely peace-loving nations, some elements of a permanent functional internationalism would arise.

This line of endeavor is not as novel as it sounds. Economists will recall how in 1924, 1929, 1930–31, the hopeless muddle that political rivalries had made of European affairs was handed over, on American initiative, to technical commissions, whose partial success was avowedly and directly due to the fact that they were nonpolitical in character: why should not the same method be invoked this time before, instead of after, the disaster? It is also worth while to remember that in the famine-haunted Europe of 1919 the best-known American name was that of Herbert Hoover, whose work bore spiritual as well as physical fruit precisely because it was nonpolitical. These were far from being the only cases; and it is not unreasonable to urge that the functional basis of action offers a so much better approach to international community that it has a valid claim to priority over the political basis.

There can obviously be no such thing in concrete visible form as a league of peoples. But there can be leagues, both implicit and explicit, of people who are trying to do the same sort of thing, to solve the same or complementary problems; in fact, there is a strong human tendency to form such leagues, which resists and survives the nihilistic onslaught of militant nationalism. Take a minute example: the help of the Nisei girls in running American homes and caring for American children during the dispersion has evoked feelings of grateful affection that will follow them as they now return, in loyalty to their families, to attempt a resettlement in circumstances of the utmost difficulty and even danger. That fact, coupled with the vindication of justice by the Supreme Court, constitutes an achievement in community that will bring lasting benefit not only to them, but to their nation; nor will America forget those of Japanese ancestry who gave their lives for the fulfilment of a common purpose.

Take another example—still, alas, on the small scale. One of the tragedies of this, as of every war, lies in the persistent effort of doctors, mathematicians, workers in disinterested research, artists, and scholars, to keep in touch with what their colleagues in neutral and enemy countries are doing. In recent years fine men have killed themselves in despair over the difficulty, and there is reason to suppose that some have been killed for making the attempt. If this seems but a minor matter, let the reader reflect that never was the mood of Western man as pessimistic as now. Neither in private nor in public utterances is there the slightest sign of belief or confidence in a peaceful future. A strong effort of recollection is necessary to recapture even such hopes as arose in the autumn months of 1919 or 1926. Everywhere, most especially in responsible quarters, all the talk is of the third World War, of the amassing of resources and the stimulation of technique that will be required for it. Nowhere is there the least willingness to entertain the assumption that it need not take place. American statesmen who were loudest in their optimism and most lavish in their promises of brave new worlds now hardly even bother to pretend; and while occasionally, in half-hearted tones, they repeat the old incantations, the ring of conviction returns only when they demand bigger and better armaments and peacetime military conscription. The average American, to whom the most brutal war in history is still a remote and abstract affair, has no conception of the horror for which he is being preconditioned. If he had, he would give heed to the biblical maxim, Despise not the day of small things. And if he could still find hope in his heart, he might reach out, in passionate scorn and indignation, after things that were not so small.

A significant proposal was recently brought before the Royal Empire Society in London.

Professor A. V. Hill, secretary of the society, suggested that the next war would be, not a conflict between armed forces, but a deliberate attempt by scientific methods to destroy cities, massacre populations and make whole countries uninhabitable.

"The only hope of averting disaster which science misapplied could inflict on humanity," he said, "is an international brotherhood of scientific men with a common ethical standard by which potential crimes of this character would be exposed and prevented." [9]

Many people have wondered how long the scientists—the advance guard of civilization—would consent to be passive tools of the forces of destruction, alike in the armaments and chemical industries and in the service of the national war machines. But the situation is not as simple as the opponents of war might suppose. Scientists, in their leisure hours, are also human beings, no more immune to patriotic appeals and alarms than the rest of us; only insofar as their international solidarity can be realized, in conscious devotion to humane and constructive purposes, can they be called on for a stand that would be both costly and dangerous. It is to be noted that the American Government, like that of Russia— and possibly with some such contingency in mind—has not only created a vast research organization in wartime, but is seeking to expand technical research under its direct auspices in peacetime. Scientists in private industry who presumed to act on their individual valuation of purposes would of course face unemployment; scientists in government service who rebelled, especially if they refused to maintain secrecy, would risk imprisonment and execution. National force will not surrender without a struggle, and is always prompt to attack its internal enemies. Nonetheless, the project of an international pressure group composed of scientists and research workers may be counted on among the future agents of community. Nor will such a group lack allies.

9. AP dispatch, London, January 31, 1945. *New York Herald Tribune*, February 1.

Among its allies will be the writers and reporters of the various nations who prefer to call their souls their own. It is safe to say that among such men and women—a high proportion of the profession—there exists a truer conception of the common good than that of the political officials who constitute their chief problem. The reporter hates censorship and distortion, not because of a dispute about ends but because truth is his métier: he risks his life to get it, racks his brain to tell it, and wants it delivered clean. Sanity in national and international affairs depends on the fulfilment of that purpose; and if there is one function above all that can never be entrusted to governments, this is it. There exists already an organized movement to establish, as part of the postwar settlement, the right to tell the truth. Insofar as it succeeds it will be a powerful agent of community. Not—which heaven forfend— that the associated writers and agencies will constitute a peace society; they will constitute something much more novel in international affairs: a truth society. The full story of what disinterested reporters, commentators, authors, and publishers have been up against in the past six years cannot be told, nor does the public realize the extent of its obligation to their courage and persistence. With few exceptions, modern governments do their utmost to control not only the actions but the thoughts, emotions, and sources of information both of their subjects and of people in other countries; and the intensity of the political struggle has on certain important occasions undermined the probity of respected public officials.

To survey all the agencies of international functional coöperation that may be organized or resuscitated would require another volume. It is essential, however, to grasp the main issue involved. The extent to which constructive international work can be undertaken will depend on the broad policies of the victorious powers. By the control of passports, visas, and travel facilities they can either encourage or thwart the resumption of international intercourse; they can, if they wish, apply a discriminatory treatment so as to carry the political and military antagonisms of the past into private as well as public efforts at reconstruction; discriminatory economic policies can be implemented by restrictions on communications and the movements of private citizens. If the policy of the Carthaginian peace advocated by Messrs. Morgenthau, Berge, Baruch, and others is adhered to, that is what will happen. By such means the pattern of international life can be held for a limited time under the domination of the big three and their satellites. It is here contended, however, that a durable international order cannot be founded on the force relations obtaining between a particular set of states at a particular time; that the growth of such an order depends on the free and voluntary coöperation of all agencies serving a humane and constructive purpose; that such coöperation should be liberally encouraged by all peace-loving nations; and that the risks involved in this course are far smaller than those attendant on the peace-by-force illusion.

§ 4

IN THE development of functional internationalism, the leading economic organizations will obviously play a role of the utmost importance; and the hostility of the American Department of Justice to international business agreements is so notorious as to call for special notice. A glance at what is just now the most critical area will serve to introduce the problem.

In the forty years following the Franco-Prussian War, Germany built up the most highly integrated steel industry in the world. Its output far surpassed that of any national territory except the United States in the opening years of the twentieth century. Nobody could have foreseen that result when Bismarck took Lorraine, for the technique was not then in existence. It was English research that really founded the prosperity of the west European steel industry, and the Thomas-Gilchrist process did not come into general use until about a decade after the Peace of Frankfort. Then Lorraine went ahead—with Belgium, Luxembourg, and France also getting the benefit. The railroad system that conveyed the coking coal of the Ruhr to the ore of Lorraine was keyed into the fabric, and the mixed mills of the Saar Valley were fed by both. One of the principal products was cheap steel rails, and one of the principal families concerned was the Franco-German house of De Wendel. A sane world would have rejoiced over the expansion of its resources; and there were in fact certain leading men in both Germany, France, and Britain big enough to see it that way. But on the whole, the appeal of territorial nationalism to the mass mind was more influential.

So the Versailles Treaty cut political and economic frontiers across the whole technological integration, just as the Silesian struggle did farther east. The Ruhr remained German. The Lorraine mills, with their insatiable appetite for Ruhr coal, became French. The Saar territory was placed under the absentee government of the League of Nations, but the French got the mines for fifteen years. It was not enough. French nationalism and high finance, which had taken a very active interest in the construction of Russian strategic railroads, and were now arranging a similar service to Poland, desired that the entire west European steel industry be brought under French control. French realists, then as now, considered that the only way to disarm Germany. The Anglo-American blend of empiricism and idealism frustrated the attempt in 1919; it was renewed by Poincaré and the French Army in 1921 and 1923. By 1924 the failure of that method was apparent; bayonets had produced neither coal, reparations, nor stock participation in German heavy industry. The following year Germany was to recover most of her tariff autonomy, and there was every prospect of a vigorous trade war.

Thanks very largely to American initiative and assistance, pacific counsels prevailed. The reparations incubus was lifted out of politics with the aid of substantial loans to both France and Germany. The Herriot-MacDonald-Stresemann teamwork prepared the way for the Locarno treaties; and the big industries drew up their own peace pacts across the frontiers. The most famous of these pacts was the International Steel Cartel. Many others were created, extended, or revived at about this time; and current opinion—so far as it noticed anything deeper than the political façade of things—was distinctly favorable. Much of it has remained so, seeing in voluntary economic agreements the only alternative to a chaotic free-for-all in international affairs, with every foreign office backing its local team of bankers, promoters, and producers.

These working agreements between national industrial groups have been developing steadily for three quarters of a century; they represent a permanent trend in economic organization running, in America, about a generation ahead of current political ideology. Thus, for example, American railroads were establishing uniform rates in the 'eighties, and the courts in the 'nineties admitted that neither the policy nor the rates themselves were ipso facto unreasonable; nonetheless, it was 1920 before the politicians officially recognized that the relations of rival hucksters on a village street were not necessarily the most suitable model for a transcontinental transport system. That same period witnessed the second technological revolution, compared to which the so-called industrial revolution was a small and local affair. The age of little business passed rapidly into the age of big business, just as, in our time, for every basic industry without exception, the age of national big business has passed into the age of international big business. As usual, work organization, which is concrete, has outrun talk organization, which is abstract; so all the time popular politicians have been fighting a negative rearguard action in the name of "progress."

International big business, as is now fairly well known, proceeds on the principle of private planning of certain spheres of operation. It is an odd fact that most of its American opponents wish to endow political authority with a far more inclusive power of "planning" over a far wider area of economic life; but many of them, in their outlook, are aggressive economic isolationists. The cartels, as a rule, allocate foreign markets by agreement between their member groups, so that international competition in export trade is eliminated. They usually give each member group a monopoly of its domestic and colonial market. Many of them also allocate relative proportions of total exports, or more rarely, total output. Some fix prices; the prices, for example, on electric lamps, are not always high; but they are generally higher than those which would result, in the short run, from competitive price cutting. The long-run effects of competitive price cutting would however, in many cases, be much less favorable to the consumer and the wage earner; especially if such price cutting involved the competition of foreign groups whose export business was subsidized by their governments or their domestic consumers.

International arrangements of the type under discussion are facilitated, in many industries, by the practice of granting monopolies on technical innovations. The patent license is ipso facto a grant of monopoly powers. The American patent law grants much looser and wider powers than that of other countries; consequently an American, or pseudo-American, concern licensed by a foreign owner of a device covered by an American patent is in a stronger monopoly position than a British or a German concern licensed by the American owners of a device patented under British or

German law. An obvious remedy is to tighten American patent law with a view of restricting its monopoly potential. It is remarkable that Mr. Wendell Berge, Assistant Attorney General of the United States, in his recent book on cartels,[10] avoids discussion of this question, on which members of Congress and others have expended so much study in recent years. Revision of the patent law is admittedly necessary, and the only excuse for its further postponement would be the assurance that the matter would be referred to an international commission seeking more uniformity and equality of treatment among the nations so intimately related in this question. The attitude of the United States on copyright law gives little encouragement to any such hope. Meanwhile, all that Mr. Berge has to propose is that the American Government itself should conduct technical research on a scale which "could become one of the principal means of stimulating and encouraging new industry and at the same time overcoming the effects of the business cycle." Apparently neither the research facilities of American industry, nor the very fruitful work of American universities and institutes of technology, deserve mention in this connection; nor is the matter of cost allowed a hearing. The prospect of making the American Government itself a party to infringement suits under existing law offers interesting possibilities.

That enterprising guild of journalists popularly known as the Department of Justice has on various occasions essayed to evaluate, on a priori grounds, just how much was given and received by American concerns under international cross-licensing agreements. In so doing it has had to impose its own criteria, which have been markedly at variance from those of the scientists and corporations directly concerned. But any such *post hoc* evaluation misses the point. The uses and benefits of any patent are never wholly predictable. Cross-licensing agreements represent, in the first place, an effort at mutual protection of intangible assets within foreign jurisdiction; and in the second, a framework within which scientific teamwork between the parties can be carried on to mutual advantage. It is a legitimate criticism that the advantage is often too narrowly restricted, and too harshly exploited; ways and means of meeting that criticism can be devised; but the internationality of the arrangement is in itself a feature that should be commended and encouraged. International coöperation in ap-

10. Berge, W., *Cartels*, chap. iv.

plied science is no less desirable than in medicine, scholarship, and the arts; and it is more practical to develop it, and guide it, on the existing basis than to destroy it and then sit waiting for the ideal medium to turn up. That ideal medium is not likely, in any case, to be the national political state. It might conceivably be an international version of something like the Automobile Chamber of Commerce; but to be effective it would need to be autonomous.

§ 5

THE political aims of the Department of Justice are not easy to discern. In the course of its investigations it has discovered that certain American and foreign corporations in associated lines of business had made arrangements, or at least expressed a wish, to preserve their basis of association during the period of national war with a view to its resumption afterward.[11] The task was difficult. As one member of an international group expressed it in 1939: "How we are going to make these belligerent parties lie down in the same bed isn't quite clear as yet. . . . I hope we will find some solution. Technology has to carry on, war or no war." That attempt of businessmen to protect the structure of international business from annihilation by political and military hostilities was, according to the Department of Justice, very wicked of them; to any who refuse to accept war as a permanent and inevitable form of international relations, it was very sensible of them. What else were they expected to do? Smash all their economic and technical affiliations because the state in which they were located was at war with the state in which their partners were located? Apparently they were expected to do just that; but in the absence of proved criminal intent in the original arrangement, the attempt to preserve it in suspension was neither criminal nor unpatriotic [12]—save on the assumption that the waging of war, the preparation for war, and the total regimentation of life to that end, are to be permanent features of national policy. In that case there will be not only no international business, but no business at all except war business.

It is part of Mr. Berge's case against the businessmen that "they

11. See e.g. Berge, *op. cit.*, pp. 27–28.
12. On the legal aspect see Evans, J. B., *Leading Cases in International Law*, chap. xiii, sec. 2, 477–497.

never thought in political terms." He quotes with evident disapproval the following statement by an executive of General Motors:
"An international business operating throughout the world should
conduct its operations in strictly business terms, without regard to
the political beliefs of its management, or the political beliefs of
the country in which it is operating." [13] It is Mr. Berge's contention, and that of the Department of Justice for which he must be
presumed to speak, that national political aims are ipso facto superior to business policy and must override it whenever and wherever there is a possibility of divergence. From this point of view
the policy of the German cartels, so far as it was keyed into German
political action, was all right, and the policy of independent business enterprise was all wrong.

We have here an example of the monistic tendency of the
national state, and its inherent antagonism to active internationality of a kind that it cannot dominate. The conviction that the state
—that is, for practical purposes, the particular collection of people
wielding coercive power for a limited time in a particular administration—is necessarily and supremely right, gives its officers an
amazing assurance both as to what they do and how they do it.
We have spoken already of the magnification of the executive at
the expense of the legislature in other spheres: here now is Justice.
Its officers formulate a policy as to the interpretation and application of a fifty-year-old law which is in effect, as Mr. Berge emphasizes, a "political question . . . of national concern" and is,
in certain of its aspects, highly debatable: is, in fact, under very
serious debate by responsible authorities both at home and abroad.
They implement that policy by ransacking the files of scores of
corporations and amassing such information as they can get from
leading foreign corporations also, such as the Imperial Chemical
Industries of Great Britain. From this material they make their
own ex parte selection, which is then presented simultaneously
to the courts and to the public by means of newspaper releases,
speeches, interviews, books, and popular magazine articles, backed
by a sensational campaign in the propaganda press. In scores of
cases the matter is left at that, with hearings and cross-examination
indefinitely postponed. Thus on the same day (January 18, 1945)
on which the latest government suit against General Electric was
filed, Mr. Berge is reported as issuing a press release, holding a

13. Berge, *op. cit.*, pp. 231–232.

press conference, and giving a lecture in Washington on cartels, of which the sum and substance as appearing in the newspaper headline is that the company's arrangements "SLOWED WAR." [14] "Mr. Berge did not know whether the suit would proceed or be postponed." Against all this the company can merely issue a statement which the public has been elaborately prepared, by official as well as unofficial action, to discount. In other cases the lodging of an indictment has been promptly followed by injunctive procedure under which hundreds of thousands of dollars worth of both domestic and foreign-owned properties have been seized or frozen.

There can be no doubt that in many cases the Department's accusations rest on grounds that the courts will sustain; there is equally no doubt that in the leading international cases it is the Department's selection and interpretation of the facts, and its interpretation of the law, that is the issue. Whether, and when, and under what circumstances, anything that can be accepted as a verdict of impartial justice can issue is a question on which the Department's mode of procedure throws little light. The Department, by its own frank statements, has raised issues of general policy and national concern. It has stepped into the arena of political and economic controversy where plain citizens may freely make rejoinder; and one would suppose that Congressional investigation and debate would play a decisive role.

§ 6

CERTAIN main lines of official policy can however be now discerned; and they are such as to call for thoughtful and dispassionate consideration. The claim that national policies must in all circumstances override economic interest, domestic or international, is a very old one: it is the basis of all economic nationalism. We may wonder where civilization would have been had it always succeeded; but it has always a certain short-run popularity and plausibility. In application to the present international situation, here is what it leads to in the official hands of Mr. Berge:

There is a further step we can take. The research which has been developed in Germany during the past ten years under the Nazi regime is research which in right belongs to the people of the United Nations.

14. *The New York Times,* January 19, 1945.

. . . It should not be considered as belonging to private hands either in Germany or elsewhere. The United Nations should make sure that steps are taken to make available this research so that it can be used generally.[15]

The policy of retroactive confiscation and the spirit that under-lies it may or may not find warrant when, in succeeding decades, historians examine the evidence on the responsibility for this war as they did in the case of the former one. Without exception, in that case, they discovered no monopoly of responsibility. But what-ever warrant they may find, retroactive confiscation, like current confiscation of sequestrated property, is exposed to certain prac-tical objections. It is deadly to all foreign investment, and rep-resents a destructive line of action without adequate constructive compensation. It is of the same order of thinking as Mr. Baruch's desire "to de-industrialize Germany and Japan, at least for a gen-eration, so they won't resort to war again. Also we've got to see that those subsidized slave-labor countries do not again flood the world with their cheap products, lowering the standard of living in the United States." [16] To encourage people to believe that de-structive action on such a scale can be taken without vital injury to the entire world economy is beyond excuse of either age or passion; it recalls the worst moments of Tardieu and Poincaré. Consider the outlook for a defeated Germany, a defeated Japan. Are the people of those countries to be allowed the opportunity of a rising standard of living, or are they to be isolated from all the rest in a condition of hopeless helotry? If the former, they must make a speedy reëntry into foreign trade. They must at once obtain certain minimal imports to sustain life and industry, and they must endeavor to sell the results of their work abroad. Where and how will they find markets? Even though the whole of mining and heavy industry be taken away from the Germans, that will provide no new markets for coal and steel; and if the Germans are to have any, someone must buy German goods—the problem can-not be solved on an everlasting loan basis. Even though Japan be stripped of her whole empire, the Japanese will still need wool and coal and cotton, and someone must buy Japanese textiles. Will India, or South and West Africa, or the United States? If inter-

15. Berge, *op. cit.*, p. 247.
16. Press release from London, April 4, 1945.

national community is the aim it must start from reality; and one of the realities of the twentieth century has been the increasing effort of the Western industrial nations to keep Japanese goods out of their domestic and colonial markets. Well-meaning persons have lectured the Japanese on the low level of Japanese real wages (forty years ago the Germans were similarly admonished); but to raise that level without an expanding foreign trade is utterly impossible, and to impose penalties on Japanese goods merely makes the Japanese work harder at still lower remuneration.

The vicious circle is tightened by two elements in the prospective world situation. First, it is very possible that there are factors tending permanently to diminish the total of world trade, which may never again reach the volume of the late 1920's. Among these must be reckoned the strongly autarchical tendencies manifest in such important areas as the United States, Russia, India, Great Britain, and the Dominions; the effect of synthetics in reducing the interdependence of genetic and industrial countries; the artificially stimulated industrialization of the former; the dead weight of frozen international debt; the extremely precarious nature of international means of payment; the consequent hesitancy of private investors to resume the large-scale export of capital; the instability of tariff and trade regulations; and the general lack of any long-run sense of economic security. The contracting influences may be to some extent offset by the closer integration of such regions as Western Europe, Latin America, and North America; but the probability is that if Germany and Japan are left merely to fight their way back into a shrinking world market, the struggle will be increasingly arduous and bitter. And what is true of those countries will be true in considerable measure of Great Britain also.

Second, there is considerable evidence to suggest that the opposition of the United States administration to international economic agreements springs not merely from an abstract devotion to the principle of free competition (plus tariff protection) but from a determination to back an aggressive trade drive on behalf of American business. If American declarations about free enterprise and the opening up of foreign markets presaged an intention to begin at home by opening up the American market, the British would be more impressed. In an important statement on economic policy by the then Attorney General of the United States on February 23, 1944,[17] Mr. Biddle said: "If we recognize that consumers may have a just complaint when they are forced to pay monopoly prices for goods or products sold them by a foreign producer, we should"—remember that the tariff is the mother of the trusts? Not at all—"create some forum in which these complaints could be heard." Foreign firms, as well as domestic consumers, have been complaining for a long time; but without much effect. In the same statement Mr. Biddle declared that "this Government should stand ready to assist American producers, if necessary, to gain access to foreign markets." If the public were permitted to know more about the activities of the Export-Import Bank and its affiliated agencies operating with public funds, and of the nature of economic warfare as waged in Latin America, it would gain a vivid insight into Mr. Biddle's meaning. It was certainly interested, in April, 1944, to learn of the journey of the president of that bank to the almost unexplored Doce River Valley of Brazil in connection with a fourteen-million-dollar loan to a local corporation.[18] If the prospects are as sound as Mr. Pierson reported, it is not altogether clear why a government agency should be needed.

In putting all the resources of a great power behind the expansion of its foreign trade, America is following a well-trodden though not necessarily a safe road. It may be pointed out, however, that during the most active phase of British economic imperialism, the British Government did not aspire to become a direct investor or to any great extent a direct creditor; and that Britain itself adhered to the principle of free trade. That situation is changed for the worse in both respects. The British Government is now a direct debtor on trade account, on a very large scale; and it has clearly stated that the principle of empire preference will continue to govern its trade policies after the war.

Taken together, the foregoing considerations presage a difficult, and perhaps dangerous, trade situation, emphasized by the superfluity of both shipping and air transport. Even if the trend toward total shrinkage is somehow reversed, the trend toward partially or wholly closed systems is likely to continue. So, in all probability, is the trend toward direct intergovernmental debtor-

17. Complete text in *United Nations Review*, Vol. IV, No. 3, pp. 124–127. See also press of February 24, 1944.
18. *The New York Times*, April 28, 1944.

creditor relations. It is worth noting that the American National Association of Manufacturers takes a decidedly unfavorable view of intergovernmental loans as trade-promoting agencies. In a report made public on February 7, 1945, the Association says:

There are few instances, except in attempting to prevent war or when conducting war, that loans to governments are appropriate, as in most instances governments contract loans for political rather than economic purposes, or else employ loan funds for economic purposes in an inefficient manner.

The principle that governments are not, as a rule, desirable borrowing entities, applies to central governments and also to political subdivisions. Loans by governments to governments are ordinarily made for purposes of high state policy and should be considered as costs of war prevention or else as costs of actual war. Governments are not primarily economic enterprises. They do not feel compelled to balance income against expenditure. Their record in the faithful observance of contractual obligations is not favorable.

Under these circumstances, voluntary international agreements for the sharing of export business may be less undesirable than a return to all-out state-aided competition in the few remaining open markets. The position of the present administration is not strengthened by the fact that it is now (February, 1945) paying a four-cent subsidy on cotton exports, and being undersold at that. No sane person would wish to see foreign trade revived on a dumping basis, and most countries will not permit it. The British Government is planning a national campaign to stimulate the export business on which, according to its advisers, British prosperity will continue to depend; but British industry, while willing to fight if fighting is to be the order of the day, is apprehensive of the unsound and perhaps dangerous situation that might result. Lord McGowan, chairman of Imperial Chemical Industries, which together with other foreign concerns has been brought to suit by the American Department of Justice, maintains that "unrestricted competition is no longer a method which generally commends itself: the alternative road is by coöperation and agreement." [19] He is willing, as are most of his compatriots, to accept a considerable degree of public supervision of international business agreements; either by compulsory registration, or by the appointment of gov-

19. See Benton, W. B., "Business in Britain," *Life,* October 25, 1943.

ernment directors to the boards of the controlling enterprises. Their general point of view is thus expressed by a British exponent: "It is arguable that commercial competition is the starting-point of international political competition which has so far only been resolved by war. National industrial combination leads inevitably to international industrial combination, which may be a thread on which to crystallize international political combination." [20]

The National Foreign Trade Council of the United States, through its board of directors, has recently endorsed the legalization and registration of agreements; though with stringent reservations as to secrecy that embody the prospecting spirit of the American frontier.[21] A considerable element of British opinion, in agreement with leading German businessmen of 1939, looks forward to a coördinated organization of the whole field of world supply in basic materials by means of international product committees, which might even exert some influence toward a supernational allocation of production itself. This is the general aim of the World Trade Alliance Association sponsored by Sir Edgar Jones and other British industrialists.

International business organizations accepting such an aim would of course have to accept public responsibility for their arrangements; but there is at present no central authority for them to be responsible to. The conflicting policies of national states do not resolve in a positive synthesis, and are hardly likely to do so. No group or sum of national states adds up to a genuine economic community; the power politics of the territorial units has repeatedly proved hostile to the functional integration toward which the actual work of the world is tending. The very nature of territorial states as revealed in their mutual relations seems to call for some superstate of the same order of being, exercising more of the same kind of authority backed by the same kind of force. The functional basis of regional and world community does not belong to that order, does not talk the same language, does not invoke that kind of authority; it operates, so to speak, in an engineer's or scientist's world, where the problems are those of continuous ad-

20. *The Outlook*, No. 47, March, 1944. See for further argument in this sense, De Haas, A., "Economic Peace through Private Agreements," *Harvard Business Review*, XXII, 139–154.
21. See *The New York Times*, February 7, 1945.

justment and dynamic equilibrium—the sort of problems any economic system has to deal with. Those problems are not solved by the intervention of superforce, but by the conscious coöperation of working people—bankers, business managers, technicians, agriculturists, trade-unionists—who for their own sake desire the extension of active economic community. There is just one essential stipulation, resting on an old liberal principle: as the component organizations should be free of political coercion, so they must consent to decline political assistance.

There is evidence that they would be willing, on the whole, to do this; but would American opinion let them? It must be frankly recognized that in the eyes of the rest of the world, American policy is now directed toward an aggressive trade drive backed by state aid and state subsidy; and official insistence on the sanctity of free competition is the conventional overture. Well, other nations have done it, and now is America's opportunity: fair enough. But in view of the fact that foreign trade is more of a life-and-death matter to several other countries than it is to America, competition on a national basis will be bitter and governments will not be able to stay out of it. Under such conditions it does not follow that a competitive price is ipso facto a fair price; it may be less fair than an agreed price, and a great deal more destructive. When the giants fight, small men have to run for cover, and a great deal of sound local business is trampled down; when the giants agree, small men may have their chance.

There are certain widely held objections. The giants are bad giants. To one section of American opinion backed by a subsidized press, the mere fact that a man has achieved outstanding success in financial or business management disqualifies him for any position of further public responsibility. This type of opinion affects to discern an altruism in labor organizations and their leaders that is superior to anything found among those responsible for major economic operations.

It is best not to argue about the degrees of altruism that adorn economic self-interest; and for the immediate issue the question is irrelevant. Whatever changes in the internal structure and control of business the future may bring, the international issue will be the same: increasing coöperation of the major functional agencies regardless of nationality, or foreign competition on a political basis with political support. Russian economic policy faces this issue just as much as British or American. It is best not to argue about altruism.

The more serious objection refers to the restraint of competition which international—or any other—economic agreements involve. The popular notion of competition contains various elements. It has a strong "frontier" association in the idea of a man being a law unto himself, prepared to defend himself and his interests against all comers. This ideal has certainly played a great role in American history, and still has its uses; but when it is applied to national policy as a whole—as, for example, Mussolini presumed to apply it—it has an unmistakably primitive coloring. Independence is not diminished by the act of entering into an agreement provided the act is voluntary; and the course of social development, as the contract theorists noticed, proceeds along just such lines. Independence is menaced only when people are coerced into coming to terms.

The notion of competition as struggle gained a specious support from the misapplication of Darwinian theory to the life of civilized communities [22] (again, Mussolini favored this analogy). We have already criticized this line of argument, and it is not necessary further to insist that human community consists essentially in lifting human relations out of the Hobbesian jungle. Moreover, under conditions of unregulated economic struggle there is no assurance whatever that it is the fittest who survive; nor are the qualities inculcated by that struggle such as to command unqualified esteem. The best that can be said for some of the practices involved in international economic competition is that they are not quite so bad as those involved in international political competition.

Liberalism is not indissolubly wedded to the concept of price competition. There is nothing surprising in the fact that in economic as in political life, freedom leads to an increasing amount of voluntary agreement. Further, as Sir Richard Acland once remarked, the important thing about competition is that somebody wins, and then the competition is over. Again, where trade-unions are officially encouraged to eliminate competition between employees, and groups of employees, employers may be expected to follow suit. Over a very large part of the domestic economy the role of competition in price determination is rapidly declining,

22. Cf. Hofstadter, R., *Social Darwinism in American Thought, 1860–1915.*

and the American Government itself for more than a decade has been upholding (for better or worse) a very wide area of administered prices. In the foreign field, American exporters have for the past quarter century had freedom to combine; and governments themselves, including the American Government, have entered into agreements to control output or markets in such important commodities as wheat, sugar, coffee, rubber, tin, and oil.

A large part of the economy, both domestic and international, is in fact in a transition stage; and it is useful to remember with Kropotkin that if the appeal is to "nature," coöperation is just as "natural" as competition. But under nearly all types of controlled price or marketing systems, the incentive to lower costs remains, and in time affects the general technological level. Moreover, an arbitrary policy puts a premium on substitutes and new sources, and a good deal of the American fear of monopoly would be disposed of were tariffs generally reduced, or at least reduction resorted to as the most obvious of corrective measures. While there is truth in the contention that the allocation of markets and the cross-licensing of patents under cartel agreements can themselves act as a prohibitive tariff, restrictive policies have very seldom been able to stand for long—never permanently—against increased sales opportunities.

These considerations do not, of course, dispose of the case for some supervision of controlled systems; but such supervision should be constructive, not destructive. The growing internationalism of modern business organization is in itself a natural, logical, and salutary development; and while it gives rise to new problems, the wholesale attack of the Department of Justice seems deliberately designed to empty out the baby with the bath water. The contention that business operations must be subordinated to the power politics of a particular setup is reactionary and dangerous. As between political and economic modes of action, the latter have for the past twenty-five years proved themselves the better way to international community, most clearly when ignored or overridden. The nature, therefore, of the supervision of international business must in no case be such as to refurbish the rivalries and animosities of the political world. A demand for the representation of consumer interests—as for example in the second rubber cartel or the international coffee agreement of 1940—is legitimate and will encounter no serious opposition; but it may be hoped and expected that the operation of that or any other mode of control will be increasingly collaborative rather than coercive, as it is in the public controls of the domestic exchanges and utilities.

Ultimate reliance must be placed, not on the coercive power of a supposedly superior state machine, but on the increasing sense of fairness and responsibility among the people actually in charge of operations. While there is always room for improvement, there has in fact been very marked improvement in this respect during the present century; and the shortcomings of economic strategy have been far less onerous to mankind than the total débâcle of international politics. The integrative organs of a world economy cannot be designed in advance; they will grow out of experience and assume forms and methods different from anything we have now. Our era, especially in America, has produced a luxuriant and chaotic growth of forms of competition; its forms of coöperation even in the domestic economy are as yet rudimentary. The will to peace, so far as it exists, will bring new and wider forms; and those forms in turn will foster the will to peace.

XIV

Liberalism in Crisis

*1. The foundation of law. — 2. Justice versus opinion. —
3. The state in business. — 4. Special problems: the small
man. — 5. Agriculture. — 6. Conservation. — 7. The full
employment policy. — 8. The welfare state. — 9. Beveridge in excelsis.*

§ 1

IN ordinary political discussion what we generally mean by the
word "state" is the agency, or collection of agencies, that
formulates and enforces law—or as we sometimes say, "the"
law. And what we generally mean by the word "law" is a set of
rules and principles that embodies our sense of right and wrong,
and carries out that control of our mutual relations which the
preservation of freedom demands. The liberal tradition has always
sought to hold this control to a minimum; and until very recently
men in English-speaking lands have rather prided themselves on
the fact that they could maintain a tolerably harmonious society
under increasingly complex conditions without greatly extending
or tightening this sort of control. Surely that was something to be
proud of? It was no merely negative achievement; it arose from
long experience of purposeful endeavor and deserved the name of
progress if anything did. Before it is finally abandoned, it is reasonable to ask that people consider very seriously what they are
doing, and why they are doing it.

We respect the state, not because it is big and powerful, not
because it can coerce, but because it embodies a purpose that we
respect in ourselves. It stands for order and fairness; it is charged
with the maintenance of the conditions of freedom; it makes effective that will to community which is bred into the vast majority
of us. We respect the rules because we respect in ourselves the
purpose they are intended to serve; so when and where coercion
has to be exercised, we support it and submit to it. If some of us

get involved in an irreconcilable dispute, we "go to law," and accept the decision of the judge. Even if we are dissatisfied with the verdict, we endorse the intent of the procedure, so we generally comply. In the same way, a very few policemen can usually "keep order" because it is really the community that keeps itself in order. When a community splits into factions, the police may be very quickly overpowered; anyone who has seen that happen knows how fragile civilization proves under such circumstances.

Men were able to make a success of their revolt against external authority because, and insofar as, there developed within them an internal authority, a sense of right, that permitted an increasing spontaneity in communal existence. This sense of right (*Rechtsbewusstsein*) is the living source of all explicit law. It is not a static or finally formulated attribute any more than is the sense of beauty or the sense of courtesy. It embodies tradition, responds to education, and grows in freedom. While it refers to, and in some measure springs from, social experience, it inheres in the minds of living persons as persons, not in groups as such. This fact has always inspired the great exponents of American democracy; and it is depressing to hear contemporary politicians, in the name of progress, pouring scorn on this conviction as it appears, for instance, in the speeches and writings of Herbert Hoover.

In this book we have argued that the sense of right for its final orientation needs the religious apprehension; but we do not intend to identify it with that, nor to suggest that it is by any means confined to "religious people." Such people are prone to read Jesus' statement to the disciples that they were "the salt of the earth" as if he had said that they were the cream of the crop; which is not in the least the meaning. The idea is that of the leaven, not that of the elite. Society needs at all times the existence of people who will stretch their lives forward, as it were, as far as the soul can reach, so as never to lose the light that shineth in darkness. For we must recognize that while the sense of right, on which all freedom in community depends, may widen and deepen without limit, so also, in adverse circumstances, it may wither or be perverted. Such perversion infecting the minds of a great people is a spectacle even more horrible than war itself.

§ 2

So LONG as law is the practical expression of a general sense of right, the amount of coercion actually required will stay at a minimum. But in proportion as law gets away from that basis, the amount of coercion required automatically increases. The attempt to enforce prohibition on the United States was doomed from the start because it made a legal crime out of action that was not generally regarded as a moral offense. In the resulting failure not only law but social cohesion suffered deep and lasting damage. Such damage must always ensue when the power of coercion rests on an inadequate basis of moral conviction.

In recent times the state in America as well as in certain other countries has fallen into the hands of men who proposed to use it as the spearhead of fundamental economic change. For the moment we are not considering the ends in view, though we may say at once that some of them are consistent with the liberal tradition, and from that standpoint desirable. The question is one of means. New deals like that of M. Blum or Mr. Roosevelt are designed to advance certain social and economic programs that are, in the main, matters of opinion—of highly debatable opinion. Opinion in all such cases is a matter of propaganda and pressure groups among which the administration recognizes allies and enemies. Now of course all political action is in some degree matter of opinion, and the duty of an opposition is to oppose. But when the end in view is fundamental change resting on a particular body of theory; and when it is proposed to enforce such change by coercive action; then it may be questioned whether such coercion has an adequate foundation in a vote of 50 per cent plus one. Stable law rests on something more than a bare majority in a matter of economic opinion; it rests on a widespread moral consensus as to the end in view. Where such consensus is doubtful, law is in danger.

This is not a matter of mechanics or procedure, but of statesmanship. If legal or military compulsion is to be applied to remove a business owner from his premises, to support a labor monopoly in exacting tribute from all would-be workers, to fix commodity prices at arbitrary levels, to determine what wages (not merely minima) shall be paid, to repudiate national obligations, to secure the employment of public funds in vast economic operations in domestic and foreign fields—in all such cases, however laudable the intent, it is the part of wisdom to wait upon general conviction. Such waiting may impose a severe strain on a limited amount of patience; but in the absence of general conviction, both the quantity and the quality of coercion are affected, and a crisis arises in which liberals and radicals have to part company.

Social planners—as we remarked in the case of Plato—are liable to what is almost an occupational disease: a certain astigmatism that affects the outlook. It is very rarely indeed that anyone conceives of *himself* as needing to be put under restraint: it is always the other fellow. There are always of course good and sufficient grounds for the opinion. The other fellow is constantly doing things in an antisocial or irrational way, in the eyes of the fellow who does not have to do them at all. Very often the indictment has substance; nonetheless, the "back-seat driver" has become as well known a stereotype as the English mother-in-law. American businessmen have manifested a certain antipathy toward "college professors" in Washington. This does not imply any real dislike of college professors; on the contrary, they are among the favorite pets of well-to-do homes; it means only that the businessmen consider that "college professors" do not know what they are talking about. This again is quite a delusion. The college professors do know what they are talking about; but it is frequently a different universe of discourse from that in which businessmen have to shoulder responsibility and make a living. From an other-worldly standpoint, it is no doubt a better world. It is a world of statistical trends and long-run probabilities in which individual businessmen count for no more than college professors do in this one: a very equitable world, in fact. But when policies drawn up in terms of the one world are imposed by force of law on the other, then the businessmen have the right to a hearing. They too have their policies, which are equally open to criticism. Practical wisdom lies not in the compromise, but in the synthesis. If Plato and—shall we say, Atticus? or Trimalchio?—could have agreed on a four-year plan, something would have come of it; but in that event, coercion would hardly have been necessary. When it comes to coercion, there is this to be said: Any plan honestly propounded by those whose decisions and actions will be directly affected by it is entitled to more serious consideration than a plan propounded by those to whose decisions and actions it will make no immediate practical difference. Of course a plan of the former type is as likely to be biased in favor of the interests of the proponents as a plan of the latter type is likely to ignore them; but if, as in the liberal philosophy, the onus is all against coercion, the rule stands. It will not impress those for whom the men that a free economy has brought to the top are ipso facto selfish, while the leaders of all the rest, whatever their record, are ipso facto altruistic.

It must be remembered that the most familiar and ubiquitous form of coercion is taxation; although the burden may be to some extent postponed, in peace as well as war, by the piling up of debt, it comes back to taxation in the end. When people are paying taxes that are not regarded as oppressive for purposes that are generally approved, taxation strengthens the solidarity of the community. But when people are paying heavy taxes for purposes of which a large proportion profoundly disapprove, these feel they are merely buying immunity from further coercion, and the whole community is adversely affected. This aspect of the matter was very clearly realized in the policies of Gladstonian liberalism, and has been dangerously ignored since.

These observations arise ineluctably from the liberal contention that the primary concern of the state is justice; that the source of justice is in the people, not in the bureaucracy; that the claims of free personality determine the limits of political action; and that liberty is itself the highest political end. If therefore the liberal is confronted with a choice—if he is—between more security at the price of more coercion, and liberty, he can only reply that, foolish as he may seem in the eyes of the experts, he still prefers liberty.

§ 3

IN OUR time the view of the state as primarily the agent of justice has been overshadowed by two other conceptions. The first of these is that of the state as a gigantic business enterprise, in which the entire community is organized for the production of goods and services. The Western nations have now had very considerable experience of this system. For thirty years war has been the outstanding economic enterprise of most national communities, dwarfing all other, public and private, on a dollars-and-cents basis; and the present war is remarkable for the high proportion of in-

dustry and trade that is carried on under direct state ownership
and direction. By the autumn of 1944 the American Government
owned about one fifth of the nation's total manufacturing facilities: 90 per cent of aircraft and magnesium, 75 per cent of ship-
building, 80 per cent of synthetic rubber, 70 per cent of aluminum,
50 per cent of machine tool, and so on. Out of total American exports in 1944, 80 per cent were on lend-lease account. War experience has probably not increased the number of people who wish
to see state enterprise carried forward on any such scale into peacetime; but its success in war production has encouraged a more
optimistic view of state-owned industry than the prospects warrant.

In war production cost is not a controlling factor and demand is
practically unlimited. This eliminates at the outset the major problems of economics. Peacetime industry cannot be run that way, no
matter who runs it. Unless cost and demand as determined in an
open market are allowed to resume their normal function, all
decisions as to what and how much to produce become arbitrary.
This is the point to which the criticism of Von Mises is so powerfully directed:

The ultimate basis of economic calculation is the valuation of all consumers' goods on the part of all the people. It is true that these consumers are fallible and that their judgment is sometimes misguided.
. . . However, the only alternative to the determination of market
prices by the choices of all consumers is the determination of values
by the judgment of some small groups of men, no less liable to error
and frustration than the majority, notwithstanding the fact that they
are called "authority." [1]

Mises sees bureaucracy as neither good nor bad in itself; it is a
symptom, and an inevitable consequence, of the growing "statism"
that is in his view deluding democracy everywhere. The core of
his thesis is that the capitalist system of private ownership and the
quest for profits, provides the sole foundation not only for economic but for political freedom. So long as the consumer is king,
there is an objective basis for rational economic activity which excludes despotism precisely because it is anonymous and impersonal. Substitute the "welfare state" or any collectivist utopia, and
all decisions become arbitrary, bringing in their train the inevitable

1. Von Mises, L., *Bureaucracy*, pp. 26–27.

bureaucrat who must sedulously follow orders from higher up because there is nothing else to follow.

In this line of criticism, the danger to freedom is not mitigated by the possibility that the rulers may have a conception of the common good that is genuinely superior to that of the mass of consumers. The state as entrepreneur might decide that liquid capital would be more usefully employed in the production of books or housing than in the production of chewing gum, liquor, cigarettes, or cheap movies; and so order. That is where the strain arises. Many people would be willing to endorse such decisions on their merits and take a chance on the curtailment of economic and political freedom. Unfortunately, the liberal cannot do that. It comes hard: the temptation to command that these stones be made bread is besetting. Only a very profound faith and a very profound love for common people can utter the *apage Satanas*. One has to respect personality very much indeed to reject doing good by force.

The notion of the state itself as entrepreneur gets much of its attraction from the fact that under modern conditions private enterprise guided solely by the prospect of private profits is often a very poor index to social need or desirability. In their simple form, private property and the quest for profit are wholesome and necessary elements of the social order—provided they are properly understood and held to their true function. Property as Locke conceived it—the result of honest work and sacrifice, serving an immediate human purpose—is a beneficent extension of personality in the world of space and time. But abstract ownership is another matter. Property as an intangible power over the activities and aims of vast anonymous masses of men is vested with no such natural beneficence. The legal and financial instruments by which the tangible is made intangible and the personal impersonal may not in themselves be evil; but their operation demands scrutiny at every step lest in the outcome all human meaning be eliminated.

The claim of private ownership to the ultimate direction of large-scale activity is open to question on several grounds. The function of active direction is now almost entirely in professional hands; ownership becomes merely a residual title to all noncontractual income, interested solely in the preservation and expansion of that income; title is bought and sold on a speculative basis like a commodity, so that at any given time the actual owners of a great business are unknown to the management, to one another, or to the community; yet they may hold legal dominion over vast stores of the earth's resources in this and other continents, and enter into contracts, more powerful than political treaties, with similar groups all over the world. Right order surely demands that this system assume a more positive and continuous responsibility to mankind than can be attained by the negative power of government acting merely as policeman.

The notion of the profit motive has undergone a similar process of abstraction. The right of a man to engage in freely chosen enterprise that he thinks will be socially acceptable, to stake his capital and labor on his adventure in a free market, to enter into co-operative association with good fellows of every degree to the same end—these are surely basic elements of decent life and human freedom. But as originally propounded, and as here stated, they rest on tacit moral postulates. They assume that the human fellowship that is involved and the community that is served are concrete facts of personal experience—as they mostly were in the eighteenth century, and still are for small businesses in small communities. It is for this reason much easier for small communities to be Christian communities; and almost impossible for very large ones. In the small community, the quest for profit, like any other impulse, is kept within a human frame of reference. Under modern conditions, the contention that the prospect of pecuniary profits is an adequate index to social needs is extremely debatable; and the more one knows of the ways in which profits are made, the more debatable it appears.

It does not follow that the line of advance is to supersede private ownership and control by public ownership and control of business in general. In the first place, it is unwise to concentrate economic and political power in the same hands; they are too closely mixed up already. If it desired to saddle business or labor with a more direct public responsibility, there must be an independent agency for them to be responsible to. Second, it is important to dispel the popular notion that the state or the government has somewhere a secret store of supermen with a superior knowledge of how business ought to be run. The only people who know how to run the world's business are those who are running it now, and there is a chronic scarcity of them. Third, government is just as likely to make mistakes in both method and motive as is voluntary enterprise. The mistakes of government are on the whole far more costly, more easily covered up, and less promptly liquidated, whereas those of private business are limited in effect and automatically penalized. Fourth, government in business almost inevitably tends to act as its own banker. It pleads a popular mandate against independent standards of financial soundness, and uses public credit to underwrite risks that private credit would not sanction. This is not necessarily a service to the public. The British Liberal Party, for this and other reasons, opposes the transfer of the Bank of England and the Joint Stock banks to the state.[2]

Sir Richard Acland, in his prospectus for the Common Wealth Party,[3] has the government "planning" all production from the top, allocating orders to the various factories, fixing prices, not only fixing but actually paying wages and salaries on a predetermined basis; yet he expects to preserve freedom of consumption and free choice of occupation. It cannot be done. It may perhaps be possible to run production under a fully powered "economic general staff" as an army is run; but the army will not run—or will do nothing but run—if each soldier is free to decide from week to week what he will do, where he will do it, what he will eat and what he will wear.

So far as social need is concerned, while there are certain things of which modern communities rightly desire more, they give no very clear indication of the things of which they would be willing to take less. But resources are limited, including time and energy, and leisure is itself a good superior to many that enter into the price structure. By common consent, there are certain activities best undertaken by public or semipublic organization, and there is no rigid rule as to what these shall be. Very few of them involve the production of physical goods—apart from implements of war. In the extension of such services liberal policy would stimulate and encourage all possibilities of voluntary coöperation on a nonprofit basis before bringing in the state itself as an active agent; and limited subsidy where the case is proved and approved is not excluded as a temporary measure.

In the general direction of industry such assistance as the gov-

2. The endorsement by the 1945 Liberal Party Conference of the second Beveridge report apparently supersedes this tenet; so far at least as the Bank of England is concerned.

3. Acland, R., *What It Will Be Like* (1942).

ernment can give—by means, for example, of a National Investment Board—is to be welcomed on a voluntary basis. The willingness of British industrialists to work out their plans in coöperation with public officials is an excellent thing for both parties. Further, the tendency toward a separation of ownership from active
control opens the way toward fuller representation of third parties;
and liberalism would develop this possibility in preference, as a
rule, to the method of expropriation, which is either very coercive
or very expensive. Liberal policy frankly recognizes that a free
economic system will at any given time contain considerable inequities, which it seeks to correct by regulatory action; but it also
recognizes that the chance of pure profit is precisely what society
offers as a return for that degree of risk bearing, initiative, and enterprise which it demands and expects of its members. The liberal
would rather put up with the inequities and the ceaseless effort
to correct them than take a chance on a more regimented system
involving perhaps more symmetry but certainly more coercion.
In taking this stand the liberal is not thinking solely of the abundance of material goods. Mr. Elliot Dodds, one of the leading
spokesmen of British liberalism, thus states the modern position:

Personality cannot be fully realized except in community. The Liberal
ideal is not a concourse of atoms, each concerned simply with its own
advantage, but the commonwealth of self-respecting, self-directing citizens, in which the stronger accept their responsibility toward the
weaker, and all coöperate for the general good. Coöperation, however,
to be real must be spontaneous. The spirit of fellowship cannot be enforced. Interdependence must be based on independence.[4]

§ 4

THIS statement, and others like it in the official program of British
liberalism, indicate the basic liberal position that the values of free
personality rank ahead of those of economics. But in application
this position raises certain special problems. While these cannot
be fully treated in a general work, we shall endeavor to indicate
what they are.

The first concerns the fate of the "small man." Liberalism, in contrast to collectivism but in common with the Catholic Church, has
a special interest in maintaining the possibility of independent

4. Dodds, E., *Let's Try Liberalism*, p. 98.

proprietorship, enterprise, and risk bearing. The notion that the small business is doomed by the advance of modern technology and mass distribution is fallacious. Obviously there can be no small businessmen in basic steel or chemicals; but even in such fields, a great deal of "big business" is much bigger than it need be for optimum efficiency. That fact is very conspicuous in regard to consumers' goods and retail distribution. The American consumer is still inclined to identify "bigger" with "better," and big-scale advertising gets its living by perpetuating that delusion; but if quality and service are intelligently considered, the small store and the small factory can more than hold their own in many fields. Interesting corroboration comes from the British Institute of Statistics. In a letter to the London *Times* (March 31, 1941) Professor Bowley and Dr. de Neumann report that "in the period 1918–35 no natural trend against the small firm is observable." Worker output is hardly any higher, on the average, in the big firm. "In wiping out the small firm we should not imagine that we are either accelerating the inevitable trend or that we are always eliminating the most inefficient units."

While the preservation of the widest possible field for independent enterprise does not justify discrimination against size as such, it does demand careful scrutiny of marketing and credit conditions to see that the small firm gets at least a fair opportunity. Local governments and utility commissions can do much that is useful, and taxation policies should be directed toward the same objective. The program is economically as well as socially sound. In many areas of the United States, small and medium mills have come through the past decade with a better record than those of the industrial cities; and there is opportunity for many more, provided the requisite initiative is forthcoming. That, unfortunately, is hard to find; for the unwholesome urbanization of economic life has not only drained the countryside, but condemned to a routine existence a high proportion of those who might have been successful entrepreneurs and key men in small communities.

This obviously touches on the whole problem of decentralization, which is one of the specific tasks of liberalism. It calls for determined coöperation on the part of all elements in society, and as a long-range project ranks second to none. For it affects not only production and distribution, but the conditions of both cultural and biological development. It is the one project that promises to salvage the family; and if people could be brought to see the future through the eyes of those who are the future—the children —the policy of decentralization might generate a commanding enthusiasm.

§ 5

A SECOND and closely related problem is the restoration of an independent and sound agriculture. From the liberal standpoint this cannot be solved by making the farmer a tenant or a ward of the state, or by making his livelihood depend on a perpetual pegging of prices, rigging of markets, and subsidizing of exports. Mr. Henry Wallace, in his famous booklet of 1934 entitled *America Must Choose*, frankly offered his program of state control as a second best to the alternative of restoring open international markets. He appears very speedily to have lost faith and hope in the latter— thereby contributing to its abandonment. There was a plausible argument that since urban industry had received so much state protection in the form of the tariff, agriculture should have a *quid pro quo;* and since tariff protection is not of much use to export commodities, subsidies were apparently in order. It was unfortunate that Mr. Wallace did not more vigorously contest the major premise of this argument. American high-tariffism did not really aid American industry. It pampered it, protecting inefficiency and waste, arbitrary prices and practices, reckless overexpansion floated on the export of capital; and the result was disastrous. No single factor contributed as much to prolong and deepen the world depression as did the Hawley-Smoot tariff of 1930. It aroused retaliation and stimulated isolationism the world over, and in the end American industry and American investments were among the principal sufferers. Even yet the American public has not realized that political interventionism and economic isolationism do not mix.

But what Mr. Wallace offered agriculture was an even stronger dose of the same bad medicine. To turn the economic clock back thirty years: to clamp the two hands at the angle at which they then stood: and to present the result as a "progressive" policy—that was a romantic performance at which historians will not cease to marvel. The money expended on it is water under the bridge. The unsalable surpluses will either rot or be given away; but other nations will not give back the export markets with which American price pegging presented them. It is pathetic to see export subsidies again resorted to, as a desperate final endeavor, in despite of the antidumping laws of this and other nations: 34 cents a bushel on wheat at this writing, 4 cents a pound on cotton—with Brazil still underselling the American South. The longer this business is persisted in the higher will be the costs of it and the more permanent the loss of markets.

There is always a farm problem. The primary producer has to bear the brunt not only of fluctuations in general demand but of uncontrollable fluctuations in his particular field of supply. Those long-term shifts in the world balance caused by biological and technological changes also come home to him; and so do the more avoidable shifts of national trade and tariff policy. His toughest problems have always arisen as the sequel to wars. There is therefore a strong case, recognized in other sections of the Wallace program, for measures that increase the resilience, adaptability, and staying power of farm credit and marketing organizations. But such measures defeat their own purpose when they seek to isolate the agricultural economy from the long-run influences that determine the allocation of productive resources. American policy would have been more beneficial had it stuck to its announced aim of agricultural *adjustment,* without seeking to counteract the phenomena that indicate the necessity and the scope of the adjustment.

American policy, like that of Britain and other countries, is rightly concerned to preserve agriculture as a way of life, and not merely for economic reasons. With this aim liberalism has a profound sympathy; but liberalism does not consider the aim well served by severance from economic realities and permanent dependence on state action. State action, based on justice, is in order to relieve agriculture of special disabilities insofar as it can do so. In Britain these mainly arise from landlordism; and the claims of landlords are therefore subject to special scrutiny and, if necessary, correction. The Liberal Party sponsors the principle of compulsory sale of land for public use or redistribution. But there are now very few landlords who "grow rich as it were in their sleep," very few who enjoy a nonfunctional return; and much land passes into state ownership by that grisly method of confiscation called death duties. The Party also sponsors agricultural subsidies as an emergency measure for the postwar period; it opposes the alternative method of tariff protection because it still urges a return to unfettered international trade; and its permanent policy aims at the restoration of agriculture, with a minimum wage law, as an efficient self-supporting industry—a not unreasonable aim in view of the strength of the English agricultural tradition and the efficiency of British farming.

No permanent system of agriculture can be built on a basis of coercion and subsidy; and a liberal policy for the United States would seek to get rid of these features while conditions are favorable. The present Congressional commitment to maintain artificial prices for two years after the war is likely to prove a boomerang. It can only enhance the difficulty of adjustment to a smaller share of a shrunken world market, and it stands in the way of an expansion of the home market and the development of new uses for agricultural products. On the other hand, the assistance given to the education and organization of farmers deserves continued public support insofar as it leads to really constructive action; and the work of the Farm Security Administration may well be continued, and possibly extended, through many years to come. In this field also a well-planned policy of economic decentralization would be of lasting benefit.

§ 6

A THIRD type of special case concerns those industries which exploit irreplaceable natural resources. This covers not only the minerals, but also those branches of genetic production in which the replenishment period is longer than that covered by ordinary commercial discounting. The maintenance not only of the power and fecundity, but of the beauty of the national heritage, is a cardinal responsibility of government. To say that the land belongs to the people is not to say that the land belongs to the state; but the concept of the people includes the future generations, and the community, acting through its responsible agencies, is bound to defend their interest from spoliation in the course of ordinary short-run operations. A state that so lavishly burdens them with debt has a moral duty to preserve and enhance for its future citizens their natural assets.

The field of conservation is therefore the one field in which state action not only may, but on occasion must, override legitimate private enterprise, including the counterassertion of private property right. An alert and intelligent government will not as a rule need to resort to coercion; but the right is indubitably there for use when needed.

In the care and development of natural resources the American Federal Government, well supported by some of the States, has done work of a scope and excellence far greater than is generally realized. Forests and fish hatcheries are less dramatic than bombing planes, and the destruction of a European city excites the adolescents more than the harnessing of a great river. The future will show which was the more fruitful enterprise. On the other hand, the record of the coal industry this past thirty years, in both Britain and America, tells a tragic tale of failure of both courage and foresight; nor is this the only case. While one watches with a certain apprehension the advancement of American economic policy in Latin America, Liberia, North Africa, Arabia, Persia, and the Far East, one wonders whether a more courageous initiative in the home territory might not also be a good investment: especially as it would not ordinarily be saddled with those expenses of military and naval expeditions which are properly chargeable against economic gains secured abroad.

§ 7

ASSOCIATED with the conception of the state as entrepreneur is the assertion that it is the duty of the state to provide "full employment." [5] The idea is neither new nor good. As Dr. Wriston very well puts it, "Full employment by the intervention of political power is based upon defeatist assumptions about our economy." He further points out the vagueness of the goal. The figure of "60,000,000 jobs" has been mentioned by prominent politicians; any careful examination shows that this is a gross overestimate under any circumstances. The overestimate, like the insistence, does indeed reflect that distrust or dislike of free enterprise which has characterized so many utterances of the New Deal. Lord Keynes, writing in 1940, gave the show away: "It is, it seems, politically impossible for a capitalist democracy to organize expenditure on the scale necessary to make the grand experiment which

5. For an excellent discussion see Wriston, H. M., *Challenge to Freedom*, chap. xi.

would prove my case—except in war conditions." [6] So, despite all the expenditure that the American Government has "organized" since 1932, its spokesmen now appeal to the war economy as a model demonstration.

But it is not the model of a free society. This becomes startlingly evident when one reflects that the ideal of "full employment" contains a hidden stipulation; it means more than it says. If full employment means merely that every willing worker should find a job, while there is no downward limit on earnings, then a slave economy could take care of it. Full employment, in every current proposal, actually means employment at a predetermined standard of real wages. And when the double stipulation is applied, the degree of constraint becomes apparent.

The primary object of economic activity is the production of goods and services, not the distribution of "purchasing power" nor the "creation" of employment; both these are secondary and consequential to the main function, and if they are made primary, free enterprise breaks down. The constant adjustments of a voluntary economy rest on a far more elaborate and sensitive organization than that of any conceivable centralized system; and while they entail from time to time disturbing (though not unmanageable) alterations in the quantity and location of the factors of production, those changes are far less onerous than the manifold and clumsy coercions on which a centralized system must depend.

The government of a voluntary system will therefore be guided by two leading principles: it will endeavor to see that its own demands impose as little restraint and embarrassment as possible on productive enterprise; and it will provide only such relief to both capital and labor as is necessary to render the transitions relatively innocuous. If this sounds very conservative by present-day standards, it must be noted that opponents of the voluntary sytem are in the habit of criticizing it as if there had been no rampant nationalism, no aggressive imperialism, no piling up of political debt, no forced deflation, no competitive currency depreciation, and no World War I.

Those who would saddle the state with responsibility for maintaining "full employment" suffer from a double fear: they are afraid of what may happen if the voluntary system fails, and they are afraid to give it full opportunity to succeed. If the American

6. Quoted by Wriston, *ibid.*, p. 148.

Government wishes to try a bold postwar experiment, let it cut its own expenditures; slash taxes that bear hardest on business, especially small business; and follow that up, as backlog demand declines, by remitting the bulk of the direct taxes on consumption. The risks and costs would be no greater than those attendant on an infinitude of deficit financing; and the assurance that the Administration genuinely believed in the recuperative power of American enterprise would itself be no small contribution.

No similar suggestion can be tendered to those countries whose assets have been so largely destroyed. For them the task of recovery and reconstruction is so great that in many fields a total mobilization of effort will be necessary. But they too will be aided by a speedy American readjustment; for the misfortune of one affects all, and the recovery of one may inspire hope where hope is sorely needed. It must not, however, be a false hope. The costs of war cannot be evaded. To recover even the prewar standard of living will be a great achievement. To promise, as a prominent banker did recently,[7] a 40 per cent rise in the standard of living after the war savors of the irresponsible.

§ 8

FINALLY, among popular modern conceptions, we must consider that of the state as the source of economic benefits: the so-called "welfare state," offering cradle-to-grave security. The phrase is an apt one; for to be born is risky, and there is no security comparable to that of the grave.

This emphasis on security, in domestic as well as international affairs, is the mask of terror. Everywhere, as they recall the recent past or contemplate the future, men are afraid: afraid of themselves, of their own powers and passions; afraid of the future, afraid of the unknown. This root of fear, we have repeatedly suggested, lies at a deeper level than social and economic reforms can reach; it is the nemesis of materialism,[8] and can be exorcised only by a spiritual revolution. Of this we shall not further speak, though all other comment presupposes the thesis.

In the welfare state it is generally assumed that production and

7. Beardsley Ruml, as reported in *The New York Times*, February 21, 1945.

8. The writer called attention to it many years ago in certain studies of modern literature; see especially "The Genealogy of the Superman," *Texas Review*, July 1924, and "Leonid Andreyev," *American Review*, March–April, 1925.

distribution will remain for the most part voluntary; but that the state will not only ensure that everybody is employed, but will use its compulsory power to secure that everybody is covered by certain insurances and benefits. The scheme adopted by the British Government on the basis of Sir William Beveridge's 1942 report applies to all persons regardless of rank or income, and provides maternity benefits, family allowances after the first child, sickness, unemployment, and invalidity benefits, retirement (old age) pensions, death grants, pensions and benefits for widows and orphans. From 54 to 64 per cent of the whole cost of the service is to come from taxation; of the insurance features alone, from 31 to 50 per cent. The cost will be very high; and with the increasing age composition of the population during the next thirty years, it will steadily grow higher. The aim is to establish for everyone, as of right, a minimum subsistence level under all circumstances.

The popularity of the scheme lies undoubtedly in its promise of a degree of security to millions of persons that they would not otherwise be able to count on; but inasmuch as the scheme does not put the state into business nor provide any new sources of income, it is evident that it will not provide them with something for nothing. The only extra resource the state has at its disposal is the power to coerce through taxation and compulsory contribution; though we might include the ways by which a state can get itself into or out of debt that are not available to ordinary businessmen. Undoubtedly, however, the mass of the people do expect to receive more than they pay in. That cannot be true of the entire community; but since the number who expect to be mulcted is far smaller than the number who expect to win, popular support is assured.

If, one would suppose, the ordinary worker in private employment cannot earn enough to provide, with reasonable care and foresight, for the ordinary contingencies of life—including marriage and the raising of children, occasional sickness and misfortune, and provision for old age—then there is something wrong with the level of wages, or the conventional way of living, or both. If we assume that minimum wage laws plus collective bargaining plus collective insurance against abnormal unemployment have achieved a fair standard of earnings, then our working community divides into three classes: those who can and do make voluntary provision; those who can and do not; and a smaller group who for

one reason or another cannot. In this view the case for all-round coercion would appear to be weaker; and it would also appear probable that an all-inclusive scheme would exert a depressing effect
upon real wages.

Some doubt may also be felt about divorcing economic security
from economic function. While no complete occupational stabilization is possible or desirable, the sense of responsibility of both
firm and industry for the economic status of their own working
forces is surely to be encouraged. State responsibility does not
necessarily weaken it, but it tends to do so. And in the same way,
the employees' interest is increasingly concentrated on the state
as the source of benefits. That is in fact one of the principal reasons why collectivists and conservatives have usually been more
cordial toward state paternalism than have liberals; the "strong
state" has not hitherto been a liberal ideal, and a coöperative commonwealth is not necessarily monistic and state centered.

§ 9

The British Liberal Party has however—not without dissentient
voices—decided to go all the way with Sir William Beveridge. A
delegate [9] to the 1945 party conference wondered whether Sir
William had joined the party or the party had joined Sir William;
it will be of great interest to see how far he will take it. In his
"second report" [10] the state emerges in full uniform as commander
in chief. The liberty of the individual to own means of production
and make independent decisions about output and wages, even
the liberty of corporations and trade-unions to make such decisions, is put in jeopardy: an all-wise state with its "Department
of Control" knows better, and dictates all major strategy. Everything is planned, and all activity is *gleichgeschaltet* (have the intellectuals forgotten that word?).

Full employment becomes the permanent aim of an active and
expanding policy of state management. Every officer knows how
much more difficult it is to keep the men fully occupied in peace
than in war, and the policy therefore calls for careful elaboration.
Yet the definition of full employment remains curiously vague. It
is not clear, for example, whether it includes the provision of jobs

9. Reported by George Murray in *Transatlantic Daily Mail*, February 14, 1945.
10. Beveridge, W. H., *Full Employment in a Free Society* (1944).

for that large number of married women and mothers who will always seek work at good money wages in preference to staying at home and having less to spend. The question of hours of work is practically ignored. The older liberalism accepted the view that the primary benefit of increased productivity under mechanization should be increased leisure; many liberals looked forward to the six-hour day for factory employment—even if it meant some increase in per capita physical cost—and desired increasing facilities for spontaneous activity, including access to land. While these ideals are not excluded by the terms of the report, they are certainly not emphasized and the prospect of full employment looks a little grim.

Underlying the Beveridge scheme is the patent assumption that a voluntary economy will never again provide full employment, but will fall short of it in such degree and with such frequency that the state must assume permanent control of all major phases of economic activity. This assumption is made more plausible by the rigidity of the employment datum that is postulated. It also gains plausibility by what, to the writer, is a gross underestimate of the warping of the entire free economy by the first World War, the nature of the political and economic settlements, the reactions to which they gave rise, and the wave of rearmament that followed.

The argument accepts without reservation the Keynesian thesis that the spending of money, not the production of goods, is the mainspring of the entire economic system. It rejects the traditional liberal thesis that the voluntary production of goods in such kinds and quantities as their exchange value determines will of itself provide adequate purchasing power. So we are told that "it must be a function of the State in future to ensure adequate total outlay" (par. 31). This goes far beyond a policy of merely supplementary state expenditure in depression periods. Sir William sharply criticizes the present government proposals for not going beyond this policy (Postscript, p. 262). His scheme envisages state expenditure on a scale hitherto undreamed of: "Under the conditions envisaged in this Report, probably not more than 25 per cent of the total national investment will be accounted for by private manufacturing industry" (par. 241).

It is natural in this prognosis, as in its American counterpart, that far more attention is concentrated on the amount of state expenditure than on the goods and services which that expenditure is designed to produce. In general, of course, they will be such as the officers in charge deem desirable for the good of society; and the intentions, so far as they are specific, are excellent. There is however a marked disposition to minimize the differences that result from state expenditure on goods that do not enter into the standard of living—the requirements of military and imperialist strategy—and those that do. "Adequate total outlay" is the main thing.

But in order to calculate and control the amount of both current and investment expenditure that the state will need to make, it is necessary that the state assume complete supervision and direction of the amount that voluntary enterprise may contemplate. "Full employment at the rising standards of life made possible by technical progress means that the outlay is wisely directed." Obviously it is the state, not the consumers or the voluntary risk bearers, that possesses this wisdom. "The State cannot escape ultimate responsibility for the general direction of outlay by reference to social priorities, however much it may be guided in its direction by the preferences expressed by citizens, in buying as well as in voting. The State cannot undertake the responsibility for full employment without full powers" (par. 264). Those powers have to be specific as well as inclusive. They comprise therefore not only power over the location of industry, but a veto power over projects advanced by private enterprise. They also comprise price control of "all goods or services which enter heavily into the cost of living of the average citizen." Liberal economists will note with particular interest that "the need for a control of prices . . . is also great with regard to all essential goods which are temporarily in scarce supply" (par. 292). That is the measure of reliance now placed on the operations of a free market; but since the state is to have control of all capital outlay, it is what one must expect. Consumers and voluntary risk bearers now come last, not first.

Sir William argues with considerable force not only that consumers do not always spend wisely, but that they do not have the chance to spend wisely. "In a free market economy under pressure of salesmanship the Negroes of the Southern States of America have, to a large extent, obtained automobiles and radios and have not obtained good housing, sanitation and medical service" (par. 259). We are all aware of that; and the point is well taken. But unfortunately, the case is generalized. "The additional citizens' outlay might not be directed to those forms of consumption which were socially most desirable" (*loc cit.*). The state knows best. Thus, like his American supporters, Sir William deserts the humane empiricism of the Aristotelian tradition for the Platonic wisdom of the philosopher-king; forgetting that the latter exists only in literature. Thus the mistakes and stupidities attending the exercise of freedom are made a general ground for the curtailment of freedom; and liberty ceases to be the "highest political end."

It is inevitable in this philosophy that all the customary institutions and activities of a free economy exist on sufferance. Beyond a very narrow range, the sacred right of free men to make fools of themselves and suffer the consequences of their folly is taken off their shoulders. Collective bargaining by sectional trade-unions is allowed to survive on the assumption that the "central organizations of labor" will hold the demands within a general pattern. But private initiative and the role of venture capital in creating, owning, and managing economic enterprise hang by a very slender thread. Sir William pays homage to the recognized political liberties; but his list "does not include liberty of a private citizen to own means of production and to employ other citizens in operating them at a wage. Whether private ownership of means of production to be operated by others is a good economic device or not, it must be judged as a device" (par. 17). The generality of the description is inevitable, but noteworthy: does it cover a farm, a tannery, a quarry, a plantation, a coal mine? While the rule may be general, its execution would surely have to be particular. Owners in practice would hold on condition of good behavior, as judged from the standpoint of full employment; and the right of bequest would be even more conditional.

The administrative machinery by which the full employment policy is to be maintained is, of course, both more ubiquitous and more authoritative (one must not say authoritarian) than any that now exists; and its actions would seem to lie outside the scope of detailed parliamentary accountability. The "social conscience" in approving the end would be committed to approving the means. And the means depend on state expenditure additional to all other expenditure, public plus private, and covered by loans. The author commits himself to the unlimited deficit financing policy advocated by the American economists Hansen, Harris, and their school. A "cheap money" policy, he says, is "integral" (par. 199); the problem of determining the ratio between tax revenue and current expenditure must be approached "not from the angle of public finance, but from the angle of social policy" (par. 200); taxation is to be regarded "as a means of reducing private expenditure on consumption and thereby freeing real resources for other uses" (*ibid.*). Obviously the taxing authority will decide the other uses. There may be occasions on which budgetary balancing is a legitimate aim; but it is never to be a primary aim.

This freedom of the administration from financial accountability is to be achieved—as it has been in the United States—on the principle that "the State in matters of finance is in a different position from any private citizen or association of private citizens; it is able to control money in place of being controlled by it" (par. 198). This means that the state is able to carry on indefinitely a borrowing-spending program that would break any corporation in no time at all: but only the state. (Sir William is not unaware that too stringent a taxing policy might lose votes.) What a wonderful virtue is there! A citizen unversed in this gospel might ask whether the interminable loans would always be forthcoming. The answer is that, in contrast to previous declarations of Liberal Party policy in Britain and of orthodox finance in America, the state is to take over the central bank of issue, which will "become in peace as it is in war an agency of the State, to give effect to the national policy, and with the Governor of the Bank formally appointed by the Government" (par. 242).

On the above lines, Sir William is able to argue, as Professor Seymour Harris has done, that a further, and almost unprecedented [11] expansion of public debt is not only sound, but supportable without increase of the tax burden; since the expanding tax base provided by the expanding expenditure will take care of the expanding interest and sinking-fund charges, and these are all that need be seriously considered. If there are secondary effects adverse to the provision or maintenance of employment by private enterprise, the state is fully equipped to counteract them by an expansion of its activities. There is no stop this side of paradise; for the inflationary spiral is constantly held in check by an ex-

11. Almost, but not quite: the experience of Germany is highly relevant. Cf. Flynn, J., *As We Go Marching*.

pansion of state control over private investment, prices, and, if necessary, wages and consumption.

This is the pattern of the future that the British Liberal Party, at its 1945 conference, saw fit to adopt. Obviously, it has popular appeal. The god of religion never promised such ease and security as the god of materialism. Perhaps he had other ends in view; perhaps he demanded too much. Sir William Beveridge, addressing the conference in behalf of his program, represented liberty as "release from economic servitude." That was one way of putting it. Another way is suggested by the titles of two significant works by European authors: Erich Fromm's *Escape from Freedom* and F. A. Hayek's *Road to Serfdom*.

There were dissident voices at the Liberal Party conference; notably that of the staunch exponent of Anglo-American friendship and freedom of trade, F. W. Hirst. But perhaps the most eloquent protest came from America. It is worth preserving, as a salute to those whom Sir William called "bow-and-arrow liberals":

Is this really the face of the brave new world that the planners have in mind? Is this the free society of the future, with its swarm of functionaries who will supervise every economic intention on the part of enterprise and every move on the part of labor? Where is that traditional England, which, under the lead of its bold and speculating business men, smashed the closed ring of the earlier authoritarian system —that of mercantilism—and created a climate of freedom in economic and political affairs? In the process England left the whole Western world these twin heritages: a vision of material abundance and social welfare, and the noble defenses of human freedom to be found in the utterances of Milton, Locke and Smith. America fulfilled that promise through its own American Revolution. It would be a tragedy if England, today, turned her back on her own great past.[12]

12. Louis Hacker in *The New York Times Book Review*, February 18, 1945.

XV

Echo of an Old Song

§ 1

THE liberal tradition is a call to adventure: the adventure of growing up, becoming autonomous, living spontaneously. There are times when men do not want to hear it; when they are too tired, too hopeless, too frightened to respond. Then they cry for security, think of the state as mother and father, of the stranger as the enemy, of the universe as indifferent or hostile. The universe is stern; its laws are the instruments of order and harmony; all that makes for discord is doomed. That was Plato's warning.[1] Men cannot always discriminate. Even under the best of mental and spiritual disciplines, they fail and blunder; and every error is punished. But the universe is alive: it is on the side of life. Men are required to take their beating, get on their feet again, lift up their heads and resume the adventure:

> Allen Gewalten
> Zum Trutz sich erhalten,
> Nimmer sich beugen,
> Kräftig sich zeigen,
> Rufet die Arme
> Der Götter herbei.[2]

Surely the poet was speaking to all of us.

Goethe's man, like Aristotle's, would make trouble in the Platonic republic. Not that he is a troublemaker, nor that he rejects the ideal of the good life; but he must fashion it for himself, for that is part of the goodness—the "working of the soul in the way of excellence." He asserts the right to learn by experience (even by bitter experience), not merely by precept. But in so learning and so working, he discovers that it is himself he must be working on.

1. Cf. p. 45, *supra*.
2. Take fate as a challenge: don't cringe, show your strength: that's the way to appeal to the gods.

The ideal must form in him before it can form outside him. The new world he dreams of may lie beyond the plane of his physical being; but at least, says Paul, he can attain the new manhood that it is to house.

On the Greek planetary consciousness that Christian vision imposed a new dimension. The kingdom of heaven, of harmony, had been thought of as belonging, at least in principle, to the realm of the actual; as indeed, in one aspect, it does. But since so little sign or hope of it appeared there, early Christian thought, like much modern Protestantism, despaired of the connection; and the kingdom became the eschatological target that ended the flight of the arrow (as it still is for several sects). But it was not so certain that the arrow wanted to be stopped dead, even in the bull's-eye. If we knew that Gabriel was going to blow next Easter, some of us might take a rest—but not the police: for what would society be like in the meantime? Good people as well as bad would be praying him to wait a little longer. If only inventiveness would dry up, and birth and death rates stay just as at present, some part of the human problem would be solved; we could more surely devise a pattern of comfort, and plan a scientific euthanasia against the coming ice age. But we should not have to wait for the ice age: our society would collapse from within.

So, in another metamorphosis, the kingdom of heaven became a sort of asymptote, set over the earth-bound root of mortality; and life the locus of the curve between. Much better now could men explain that state of tension which is consciousness and volition: the "borderline creature," as Evelyn Underhill calls him, would naturally feel the double pull. But if it is a pull upward on the root, it is also a pull downward on the ideal; thus full personality, not brain alone, becomes the vehicle of creativity in the time process. For only in personality is the pattern apprehended. There only, since any part of the curve implies the whole, is macrocosm in microcosm, eternity in every moment. Thence only arises the thrust of eternal becoming. Not therefore in the simple resolution of materialism (where we are from) nor in the simple resolution of mysticism (whither we are bound) does our destiny permit us to dwell in peace. The way of life is open ended; for we are the process, personality is actuality, and love the hidden name that forms our world.

§ 2

BUT we do not proceed in a vacuum. Intelligence confronts inertia, becoming beats on formlessness: "the Boyg conquers but does not fight." Every creative intention lances as it were a viscous ether, that presses every achievement in upon itself and makes for closedness, finiteness, fixity—not without useful effect. Every effort has its exhaustion point: the bounds of reason, the acme of generosity, the limit of forgiveness. But the limit seldom appears as the limit of effort, it appears as the limit of possibility; and every achievement is invested by the mirage of perfection. As the artist's effort is completed, how good the picture looks! But the chances are that never again will it look as good as it does at that moment. A week or two later the verdict will be: good so far—but thus and thus it might be better. Once in a great while something will transpire that lies completely on the line; such work, enduring through the years, has something of the miraculous about it, conveying not so much pleasure as a mysterious healing and reassurance, like the beauty of nature.

But it is not merely in contemplation, but in action that we live; and the results of our action may never remain, if ever they were, perfect. Atlantis is drowned, we are thrust out of the garden, the golden age was always a long time ago. Systems of thought, systems of science, systems of society, in so far as they become closed become obsolete. Either we preserve their open-endedness, or what we call the force of circumstances will tear them open—and we ourselves shall be its instruments. That is the recurrent tragedy of history. Surely we must defend our institutions, our values, our security, our interests, our heritage. Yes indeed; but in defending them against challenge we are too easily tricked into defending them against change. The role of liberalism is to forestall the catastrophic phase of change.

§ 3

WHAT Bacon wrote of death is true of destiny. "Men fear death as children fear to go in the dark, and as that natural fear in children is increased with tales, so is the other." But what an effort of faith and imagination it takes to conceive of social change in optimistic terms! Of course, the apostles of "progress" could be optimistic: more science, more power, more travel, more bathtubs, more contraceptives, more medicines, more "education." But most of that might prove to be involution rather than evolution; as one meets it in the popular literature it implies the extension rather than the modification of the current set of values. Catholics and Chinese, the Latins and the Irish, all men everywhere, are to take it and like it—since it appears they are going to get it anyway. A real modification of the set of values demands far more imagination. There are a couple of rarely printed letters of Macaulay written in 1857–58 to H. S. Randall, the biographer of Jefferson,[3] in which Macaulay demonstrates the folly and futility of the Jeffersonian ideal. "I have long been convinced," says Macaulay, "that institutions purely democratic must, sooner or later, destroy liberty or civilization, or both." France in 1848 set up a pure democracy, and there was every reason to expect a general collapse of society. "Happily, the danger was averted; and now there is a despotism. . . . Liberty is gone, but civilization has been saved." Under the American Constitution, says he, it is only a matter of time for collapse to be inevitable; for "your government will never be able to restrain a distressed and discontented majority." Adversity will give the demagogue ultimate victory over the statesman, and either civilization or liberty must perish.

Either some Caesar or Napoleon will seize the reins of government with a strong hand, or your Republic will be as fearfully plundered and laid waste by barbarians in the 20th Century as the Roman Empire was in the fifth, with this difference, that the Huns and Vandals who ravaged the Roman Empire came from without, and that your Huns and Vandals will have been engendered within your own country by your own institutions. Thinking thus, of course I cannot reckon Jefferson among the benefactors of mankind.

Macaulay's case is well argued. The English nineteenth century is studded with similar forebodings, both Whig and Tory, as to every extension of the franchise. And the warnings still have their relevance, the danger is still there. So what? The one thing we cannot do is turn our backs on it. If we accept it and wrestle with it, such a triumph is possible as only cranks and visionaries dreamed

3. See Beck, J. M., *The Constitution*, Appendix IV.